Endorsements:

'Chris' book melds both the supernatural gift of knowledge and the natural gift of genealogical research. It's a missing link in terms of a "book not yet written." We all have ancestors, and not without trauma inherited from them. This could minister healing to a lot of people as they focus more sharply on those past wounds. The church is often fine with supernatural revelation, but would disparage the related research as lesser--and the world has the same prejudice back in the opposite direction. This approach is not simply descriptive, but prescriptive as well, in combining both genealogy and healing prayer. This is a message that's waiting to be heard.'
Rev. Gordon Dalbey, author of *Sons of the Father: Healing the Father-Wound in Men Today* and *Healing the Masculine Soul*.

'I have known Chris Eve for a number of years and he is a man who will have studied this subject in depth. His findings will be well worth considering.'
Ruth Hawkey, author of *Freedom from Generational Sin*, *Generational and Family Blessings*, and *Healing the Human Spirit*. Former Director of Ellel Glyndley Manor, UK.

'John Bunyan writes, 'So I saw in my dream that just as Christian came up with the Cross, his burden loosed from off his shoulders, and fell from off his back, and began to tumble, and so continued to do till it came to the mouth of the sepulchre, where it fell in, and I saw it no more.' It is interesting that Bunyan allowed his pilgrim to struggle through the slough of despond and to be led astray by Mr Worldly Wiseman before he comes into freedom from his burden at the Cross. Many Christians find that they have more than one burden on their back and need help to bring each to the Cross.

This book explores issues upon which sincere believers may differ and upon which I do not feel qualified to comment. However,

I would recommend it as a very useful tool for those who are already engaged in Christian counselling particularly regarding generational issues, and it is a useful resource for those who are seeking to deepen their understanding of the interaction between genealogical research and Christian healing ministry.

Chris Eve who has considerable training and experience in this field, has compiled his book in such a way that each chapter is complete in itself, and each chapter supplies many useful contact websites to aid in researching the family tree.'

Rev. Norman Moss B.A., B.D.(Lond). Norman & Margaret Moss were pastors in London, spending 9 years in Chiswick and 31 years in Wimbledon. They led their church into renewal in the early 1970s and in 1994 the church experienced a further powerful move of the Holy Spirit resulting in hundreds being strengthened and blessed in their faith.

Since then, Norman and his wife Margaret have been involved in extensive ministry within the U.K. and overseas. They have served together as international coordinators for Partners in Harvest churches in the UK & Europe for 24 years. They are founding members of 'Harvest Alliance U.K.' and supply weekly devotionals for the VoV website. Amongst other writings, Margaret was a contributor to the Dictionary of Christian Ethics and Pastoral Theology, IVP, and Norman has published several children's books.

'We all have known and unknown ancestors; therefore, we hold the potential for involuntary generational inheritances, both good and bad. Eve pairs genealogical expertise with inner healing experience. He guides you through a systematic, biblical strategy to identify and resolve issues caused by ancestral sins, curses, and soul ties. His unique approach introduces topics to consider and many unexpected resources for personal research. Along the way, Eve includes relevant Scriptures, practical prayers, and points to others who could help you on your journey to wholeness.'

Quinn Schipper, Author of *Trading Faces* and *The Language of Forgiveness*.

'In his interesting and useful book, 'Healing Ancestral Wounds,' Christopher Eve provides a comprehensive analysis of the validity of the connection between research into, and redeeming of sin, in ones' family history.

He carefully shows, with foundational evidence, the devastating effect that ancestral sin can pass on to future generations.

Anyone who knows Chris personally will personally admire the beautiful way that he combines his Christian experience with his thorough knowledge of genealogical matters, in order to give a complete picture of intergenerational effect of inherited sins of the past generation.

I like the way that he includes appropriate and meaningful prayer models to end each chapter in the book. It is worth pointing out that ancestral problems highlighted in the chapters are listed, and appropriate prayers are chosen, which are comprehensively designed to effectively deal with these problems. In this way the reader is encouraged to exercise their faith and be enabled to experience personal transformation through application in their own life.

I also commend him highly for beginning every chapter with a text from Scripture. I believe that the Word of God cannot be argued against. To this end I would say. "Praise the Lord!"'

Rev. Canon Dr. Herrick Daniel, author of *Hundred Mile Prayer Walk*, Professor of Theology, former Principal of St Barnabas Christian Foundation College and former vicar of St Barnabas Church, Blackburn, UK.

'Chris' book is a very well-done piece of work. It is clear he has done a lot of research and has put a lot of effort into his writing. This has produced a balanced and understandable piece of work. I feel the outcome will appeal to many readers.'

Pastor John Clayton, Gateway Church, Morecambe, UK.

'Christopher Eve is a complete reflection of what he has written in this book! A man on a journey with Jesus, with so much passion to gain knowledge and to serve. This book is a well-researched study about family and generational history with a significant amount of healing solutions. Chris has offered and expounded on detailed, strategic, spiritual, and human approaches to how deliverance can be achieved; from mental illnesses, anxiety, depression etc, and how this healing process can be initiated and sustained. Finally in his book, Chris does justice to how he explains that the believer's conviction of Jesus' death on the Cross and His resurrection has offered the complete deliverance from all curses; *for He became a curse for the believer to be free.* Pick a copy of this book and change your life.'
Rev. Dr Ayodele Afuye DMin, MSc, BA (Hon), Dip.Th. Senior Pastor, The Dynasty Church, Lancaster, UK.

'Chris has bequeathed to us a vital resource that should gain traction with those involved in the healing and deliverance ministry. Using the lens of genealogy, he has offered us some vital clues and insights on how to research, unearth, and pray into generational issues with greater knowledge and understanding as we journey towards healing and wholeness in Christ. This book is an essential source of material and a store of knowledge for pastors, prayer ministers, leaders, and laypeople. It will help us connect the dots between our family lineage, spiritual heritage, and faith. It will aid our discernment with critical insights that will enable us to find through prayer ministry and support spiritual breakthroughs to enter into the glorious freedom of the children of God purchased by the sacrificial death and resurrection of our Lord Jesus Christ.'
Revd. Peter A. Brown, Methodist Minister.

Healing Ancestral Wounds

Researching and Redeeming Family History

By Chris Eve

© 2023 Christopher R.T. Eve

Printed by Amazon, 2023

Christopher Eve has asserted his right under the Copyright, Designs and Patents Act, 1988, to be identified as the author of this work. All rights reserved. No part of this publication may be reproduced, stored in a retrieval system or transmitted in any form or by any means – for example, electronic, photocopy, recording – without the without the prior written permission of the publisher. The only exception is brief quotations in printed reviews.

All Scripture quotations, unless otherwise indicated, are taken from the Holy Bible, New International Version®, NIV®. Copyright ©1973, 1978, 1984, 2011 by Biblica, Inc.™ Used by permission of Zondervan. All rights reserved worldwide. www.zondervan.com The "NIV" and "New International Version" are trademarks registered in the United States Patent and Trademark Office by Biblica, Inc.™

Scripture quotations labelled BSB are from the Berean Standard Bible. Copyright © 2016, 2020 by Bible Hub and Berean.Bible. Used by permission. All rights reserved.

Scripture quotations are from the ESV® Bible (The Holy Bible, English Standard Version®), © 2001 by Crossway, a publishing ministry of Good News Publishers. Used by permission. All rights reserved. The ESV text may not be quoted in any publication made available to the public by a Creative Commons license. The ESV may not be translated in whole or in part into any other language.

Scripture quotation labelled ESV® Bible is from the *ESV Archaeology Study Bible*, is from the Holy Bible, English Standard Version®. Copyright © 2017 by Crossway Bibles, a publishing ministry of Good News Publishers. Used by permission. All rights reserved.

Scripture quotations labelled KJV are from the King James Version of the Bible by Bible Hub.

Scripture quotations taken from the (NASB®) New American Standard Bible®, Copyright © 1960, 1971, 1977, 1995, 2020 by The Lockman Foundation. Used by permission. All rights reserved. lockman.org

Scripture taken from the New King James Version®. Copyright © 1982 by Thomas Nelson. Used by permission. All rights reserved.

Scripture quotations marked (NLT) are taken from the *Holy Bible*, New Living Translation, copyright ©1996, 2004, 2015 by Tyndale House Foundation. Used by permission of Tyndale House Publishers, Carol Stream, Illinois 60188. All rights reserved.

[Scripture quotations are from] New Revised Standard Version Bible, copyright © 1989 National Council of the Churches of Christ in the United States of America. Used by permission. All rights reserved worldwide.

[Scripture quotations are from] Revised Standard Version of the Bible, copyright © 1946, 1952, and 1971 National Council of the Churches of Christ in the United States of America. Used by permission. All rights reserved worldwide.

The publisher has endeavoured to ensure that the URLs for external websites mentioned in this book were correct and live as at press production. Thus the included citations are purely for emphasis as deemed helpful to the author's point. The publisher, however, is not responsible for the entire content of these websites and cannot guarantee that they will remain live or that their content is or will remain appropriate.

ISBN: 979-8-8695498-5-3

Book cover design by Vessels of Virtues Publishers and printed by Amazon.

Published by Amazon.com.

Dedication and Acknowledgements

This book is dedicated to Rev. Norman Moss, a retired Baptist pastor who first led me to a living faith in Jesus at Wimbledon Baptist Church, at 9.30pm, 16 June, 1986 (give or take a few minutes!). I also dedicate this book to Rev. Gordon Dalbey, of Santa Barbara, California, my mentor for the last 30 years, since about 1993, whose loyalty and friendship I am privileged to enjoy, and whose books have helped to transform my life for the better. Without the input of these two men, this book would never have been written, and indeed, I would not have been here to write it.

I would also like to pay tribute to numerous others, whose influence, both personal and institutional, have contributed, even distantly, to this project. My parents (now deceased), my sister, Theresa, cousin Tamsin, and Gill Edwards.

To Ellel Ministries, (Pierrepont and the Grange) and to Ruth Hawkey, former director of Glyndley Manor, whose book, *Freedom from Generational Sin* inspired and helped me in the concept for this book. Thanks also to Victor Aramanda for ideas gleaned from his book, *9 Easy Steps to Write and Publish Your Book*, on how to publish and for subsequent help in publishing my book.

My grateful thanks go to Quinn Schipper for permission to quote from his book, *Trading Faces* and for his endorsement. Similarly, and with grateful thanks again to Rev. Gordon Dalbey, and Rev. Norman Moss, for their endorsements for this book. I would also like to thank Rev. Canon Dr Herrick Daniel, Ruth Hawkey, Pastor John Clayton, Rev. Dr Ayodele Afuye, and Revd. Peter Brown for their endorsements. To John Western and Craig Robertson for their proofreading skills and time taken to do so. To Steve Bradshaw and to the graphics team at Vessels of Virtues Ministries and the books publishing unit, for completing the design of the book cover.

The key Christian books which have helped me consider the design approach to this book have been:

Freedom from Generational Sin by Ruth Hawkey
Healing the Masculine Soul by Gordon Dalbey
Healing your Past, Releasing your Future by Frank & Catherine Fabiano
Healing the Family Tree by Dr Kenneth McAll

Grateful thanks to Mark and Mary Fleeson of the Lindisfarne Scriptorium on Holy Island, Northumberland, for permission to photograph a print of theirs I bought some while back, entitled, *Spirit of God*. This is incorporated faintly into the front cover design of my book, underneath the title.

Also, grateful thanks to Harriet Fielding of Pen & Sword Books Ltd for permission to include an image of part of the cover of one of their publications, *Tracing Your Army Ancestors: A Guide for Family Historians* (2nd ed), by Simon Fowler, on to the cover of my book. To the Institute of Heraldic and Genealogical Studies (IHGS) and Les Mitchinson, my former tutor for guiding me through much of the correspondence course in genealogy.

To Rev. Canon Dr Herrick Daniel, chairman of the Lancashire Prayer Conference (LPC), Rev. Peter and Carole Brown, formerly pastor of Brookhouse Methodist Church, Jill Southern, formerly director of Ellel Pierrepont, Ian Coates, formerly director of Ellel Grange, Mary Munro, and Ian and Penny MacDonald, Dr Andrew and Mrs Sye Wright, also formerly of Ellel Grange, Rev. Craig Abbot of Ellel St John's, Galgate, and Dr Mike Bullock. To Jim Hutchinson, Ruth Hawkey, Iris Atkinson and other members of Brookhouse Community Church home group, Rev. Dr and Mrs Ayodele Afuye, senior pastors of the Dynasty Church, Lancaster, and John and Carole Clayton, pastors of Gateway Church, Morecambe.

To my good friends, Alex and Anna Bayman, and Dr Wayne Campbell, Capt Doug Evans (deceased), Annette Lassey, Flt Lt Dick King, RAF (Retd), Lt Col Keith Eve, RA (Retd) (deceased), Michelle Eve, Julienne Fomin, David and Sheila Betts, Jonathan Maher, Pat Jarratt and Ted and Claire Richardson. To Rev. John Robson, LVO, former Chaplain of the Queen's Chapel of the Savoy, London (1989-

2002) and a former chaplain to Her late Majesty, Queen Elizabeth II. To Roy Burrell, Tim and Val Page (the latter deceased), Greg Norden, Bernard Shaw (deceased), Rebecca Shaw, Paul and Angie Clark, Revd Steve Karma, Betty Cook (deceased), Graham Dye, Ann Colenutt, Jeff Tye (deceased) and his wife Margaret, and to Ray Dadswell of Eastbourne. To the folks at Gateway Church.

To Richard Rhydderch, formerly of Guildford, recently deceased. And lastly to my darling wife, Vanessa, who I look forward to one day being reunited with in the presence of Jesus. All these men and women have made their loving pastoral mark on my life and/or been my friends, indirectly shaping this book, for which I am truly grateful. And to anyone else I have forgotten; I offer my sincere apologies.

Contents

Endorsements

Dedication & Acknowledgements

Contents

Preface: A Personal Testimony and Encouragement   xiii

Introduction   xxiv

Chapter 1   What is Generational Sin?   1

Genealogical Evidence for: -

Chapter 2	Generational Sexual Sin	22
Chapter 3	Rejection and Abandonment Issues	43
Chapter 4	Educational Background	64
Chapter 5	Occupational Background	80
Chapter 6	War Trauma	105
Chapter 7	Generational Poverty and Wealth	130
Chapter 8	Criminal Ancestry	163
Chapter 9	Mental Illness in the Family Line	185
Chapter 10	Religious Affiliations	203
Chapter 11	Generational Idolatry	242
Chapter 12	Generational Freemasonry	255
Conclusion		269

Appendices	**271**
Appendix A – The 10 Commandments	**271**
Appendix B – Baptism in the Holy Spirit	**273**
Appendix C – Seize Quartiers	**276**
Appendix D – Renunciation of Generational Curses	**277**
Appendix E – Abbreviations	**279**
Appendix F – Further Help	**281**
Select Bibliography, Organisations & Websites	**285**
Endnotes	**294**
About the Author	

Preface

A Personal Testimony and Encouragement

Back in December 2015, during the height of 'Storm Desmond', when much of the country was being lashed by torrential rain and pounded by strong winds, I was trying to stay warm and dry near Lancaster. The city centre was flooded, when the storm, combined with an unusually high spring tide, burst the banks of the River Lune, sending millions of gallons of dirty water into the low-lying areas of the city centre. Some businesses were up to 9 feet deep in water and out of action for months. Lancaster virtually closed down for days because of the power outage.

In the midst of this extraordinary weather, God revealed the outline of a book He wanted me to write: combining my training and experience of the Christian healing ministry with my growing knowledge and experience in genealogy. I had no ambition to write this book, rather it came as an assignment from the Lord. For some years, since writing a self-published biography of my father in 2005, I had sensed the Lord saying to me, that one day, I would be writing a Christian book. I had no real idea what that book would be about. Now, at the height of 'Storm Desmond,' God revealed it to me.

It made me think of Shakespeare's play, *'King Lear,'* (studied for A-Level English many years before), where the aged and deposed king, out in a terrible storm, shouts out in his distress: *"Blow, winds, and crack your cheeks!,"* before soon after, coming to his senses with a knowledge of the truth of his situation.

The Christian healing ministry is close to my heart and I have been involved with it since the early days of my conversion in June 1986, having been both led to the Lord and introduced to deliverance ministry by Rev. Norman Moss, formerly the minister at Wimbledon Baptist Church. In 1990, I came across the work of Rev. Gordon Dalbey of Santa Barbara, California, whose books specialise in the healing ministry for men. We have known each other since

1993 and he has been my mentor and confidant for the last 30 years. For many years, I have been his book distributor for the UK.

For fourteen years, I was involved with Ellel Ministries, whose headquarters base is near Lancaster and for seven and a half of those years, after training by them, I worked in a variety of capacities at Ellel Grange. This is a non-denominational Christian healing ministry with an evangelical charismatic emphasis. Over this time, the Lord brought me much healing from past wounds, and gradually I was trained to help and pray for others. My book collection on the healing ministry is large!

Now, as a genealogist since 2013, I help clients trace their ancestors and have been training with the Institute of Heraldic and Genealogical Studies (IHGS) based in Canterbury. Family history has been a particular interest of mine for decades, since about the mid- to-late 1980s. Coming from a background of parental divorce, I knew very little about my family and felt rootless. This provided the impetus to find out who and where my ancestors were from. In doing so, I learnt both the good and some not-so-good aspects of my family; the blessings and the curses, so to speak. As I absorbed and processed this information, it helped shape my identity and provided some clues as to God's purpose and direction for me.

Some years ago, I asked God to confirm the rightness in pursuing genealogy as a new career. Shortly afterwards, I was talking to a former neighbour in the Sussex town of Eastbourne, about genealogy. This neighbour was 92 years old at the time, an Army veteran of Dunkirk and a retired policeman. To my amazement, he told me that he had once known a genealogist named Humphery-Smith. They had played cricket together as teenagers in the 1930s, in another Sussex town called Midhurst (I think). This was none other than Cecil Humphery-Smith, the founder of the IHGS, the very institution through which I was studying genealogy! There is no word for 'coincidence' in Hebrew, I'm told. At moments like this, you can but thank God and worship Him in awe and wonder.

PREFACE

It is a well-known fact both in the Christian healing ministry and in common sense knowledge, that damage in the family line, can and does affect the children and later generations. The 'sins of the fathers visit to the third and fourth generation,' as the Bible declares (Deuteronomy 5:9, Exodus 20:5, Exodus 34:7, Number 14:18, and Isaiah 14:21). However, in Jesus, the curse of sin is broken and we can all be set free from the effects of the sins of our ancestors (Jeremiah 31:29-34) and from our own sins.

But how do we know what the sins of our ancestors were? Most of us will know or remember what our parents' issues and sins were and how they affected us. Think of an alcoholic father or verbally abusive mother, for instance. We will also remember their good points and how they loved us. Many of us will remember our grandparents fondly, how they doted on and loved us. However, we also may remember some of their faults. Do we carry any similar faults or sins from our parents or grandparents? Hardly any of us will have known our great-grandparents, though some of us may have heard stories from our parents or even our grandparents about them.

Fortunately, my paternal grandmother, Alice Emily Eve, née Rigden (1900-1999), (in her early 90s at the time), once told me a story about a time over 100 years ago now, when she and her sister Gladys, had been visiting their paternal grandparents in Dover, during the summer of 1917. Her grandfather, Daniel Thomas Rigden, (1847-1919), was a retired Trinity House pilot, who used to guide the ships up and down the Thames Estuary, between Dover and the Pool of London. She said he was a very dignified but jolly man who looked just like King Edward VII. (Photos of him bear that out!). On that or a similar visit, Grannie went on to describe how, out of a clear sky, she and her sister heard the sound of aeroplane engines. German Gotha bombers were dropping bombs on the town, which fell quite near to where they were walking, causing them to run for cover.

But beyond personal recollections, or maybe even from a

book, how do we know what our forebears were like or what they did? That is where genealogy can come in and unravel the lost past of family history – even history which is dark, that perhaps we don't know, or would rather forget about. But in Jesus, we need not fear that the power of the past will negatively affect us anymore. We can all be set free from the effects of the sins and iniquities of our ancestors and live as Jesus meant us to live – with a new identity, free to love and be loved, and free to serve Him, as we were created to.

But it is good to remember that the discovery of our past will also bring blessings, as we find out about unknown ancestors, their achievements, and the places they came from. From my own experience and that of my clients,' this new-found knowledge brings a real sense of identity and belonging.

Déjà-vu experiences are not that uncommon. I remember one in particular, when travelling slowly on a train from London to the Port of Dover, in about 1984 or '86. I was a youthful 20-something (recently finished?) student on summer holiday, starting a great 'Inter-Rail' adventure with my dear friend, Richard, heading first for Calais, and then Rome, via Milan. As the train clanked slowly and noisily along the backs of old Victorian houses, approaching the port of Dover, I suddenly exclaimed, *"I know this place!"* sensing that part of me 'belonged' there! But I had never been to Dover before! It was only several years later, in the early days of my interest in family history, that I discovered through the death certificates of my great-great grandparents, Daniel and Emily Rigden, née Kemp (1849-1923), that they had lived in that same part of Dover! And this was *before* I knew anything about them or where they lived and *before* my grandmother had told me her story about them! It's on occasions like these that you can only take your shoes off, as it were, in awe and wonder. God was surely trying to tell me something.

PREFACE

Four Key Prayer Experiences

A key event in the development of my thoughts about generational sin came in the mid-1990s. Over a period of time, I had sensed something like a noose around my neck and a desire to take my life. The former was especially noticeable during times of ministry in church, when I also experienced a shortness of breath, as I sought prayer for freedom from this unpleasant sensation. But the prayers were not working.

Shortly afterwards, I was visiting St Catherine's House, in the Aldwych, London, again, which at that time before the age of the internet housed the nation's birth, marriage and death indexes. I was now back to my 16 great-great grandparents who were dying off at the end of the 19th century and into the early part of the 20th century. However, one couples' death certificates could not be found during this period. I had the marriage certificate for William Edward Eve (1815-1870) and Eliza Steele (1829-1868), dated 14th April 1855, but not their death certificates. So, I extended my search backwards in time and kept going. Then at last, I found the index record for William Edward Eve in the April quarter of 1870 and so ordered his certificate. This arrived a couple of weeks later, but I was unprepared for its contents: *'Suicide by hanging'* on 28th April 1870, at home in Peckham, Surrey, (now South London). He was 55 years old and had been a 'heraldic artist'. It was a shocking discovery. There was no family legend about this occurrence and my assumption is that ensuing family shame caused it to be hushed up. Certainly nothing had been told me of his existence.

From this information, I was able to locate two South London newspaper articles, held in the British Newspaper Library (then in Colindale, North London), recording the inquest into the death, giving the circumstances. William Eve had become depressed since the death of his wife, Eliza in childbirth, two years previously (in 1868) and then suffered financially from loss of earnings because of a recession. Friends had remonstrated with him not to harm himself, but he was eventually found hanging by the neck in an upstairs bedroom, by his 12-year-old son, Richard (1857-1921), (my great-grandfather), who had just come home for breakfast after an early morning job of work. Richard was left an orphan, but subsequently brought up by an aunt and uncle.

Armed with this knowledge, I sought specific prayer at church and prayed into it myself, breaking in the spirit, the 'noose around my neck' and the spirit of suicide, having forgiven my ancestor for killing himself. I was never again troubled by the sense of a noose around my neck.

In 1995, while this was going on, I came across the book, *Inheritance: A Psychological History of the Royal Family* by the psychiatrist, Dennis Friedman.[1] This book further confirmed to me the possibility of generational transmission of personal brokenness. For instance, he wrote:

> We are,..., driven to repeat the childhood patterns which our parents acted out with their parents, and their parents with our great-grandparents.[2]

The **second** significant prayer event came during a ministry time at Ellel Pierrepont near Farnham, in about 2005, when two men prayed for me to be set free from the memory of a trauma from a near gliding accident, I had had in 1980, and the generational effects of my father's flying traumas. Denis Eve (1924-1999), had been a career pilot, firstly trained as a bomber pilot in the RAF in WW2 and later working as a civilian airline pilot. In 35 years of flying, he had a number of hairy episodes, as attested by what he told me, and from his diary entries, log books and official correspondence. As the team prayed, I went into a sort of re-enactment of the sense of being in a centrifugal spin. It reminded me of Dad's description of an evasive manoeuvre called, *"corkscrews left and right,"* he practiced in his Wellington bomber, when avoiding simulated fighter affiliation attacks by Spitfires in the Middle East. It was a very unexpected and disturbing experience! A profound deliverance occurred which took

PREFACE

a considerable amount of time and prayer before peace and freedom were achieved.

A **third** and similar experience to the previous one, was of gradually being set free from generational trauma caused by my paternal grandfather's WW1 Army experiences. William Francis Eve (1894-1981), had served in the trenches between 1914-16 as a rifleman in the 1/16 Battalion, Queen's Westminster Rifles, at Ypres, and then as a 2nd Lieutenant and battalion signals officer, with the 3/6 Battalion, City of London Regiment, on the Somme. Although he never spoke to me of his experiences, his secretly-kept trench diary covering the period from November 1914 to October 1915, only found in my grandmother's bureau in 1993, some 12 years after he died, is full of the horrors of war. It, and other WWI memorabilia are now in the possession of the National Army Museum (NAM) in Chelsea, London. My protracted deliverance and inner healing experiences brought home the reality of the lasting effects of generational trauma.

Research into official military records at the Public Record Office at Kew (later renamed The National Archives (TNA)), helped me piece together and understand the significance of both my father's and grandfather's experiences, which they'd long ago noted down and kept in surviving diaries, photos, records and memorabilia.

A **fourth** and final personal example is that of the damaging effects of Freemasonry involvement. Neither I nor my parents were Freemasons. So how could I be affected by the curses of Freemasonry? By simply inheriting the effects from my grandfathers and other, more distant ancestors. I discovered through items that my family left behind, that both my grandfathers had been Freemasons. My paternal grandfather's 'jewel' (a medal) was found, on clearing out my father's house after he died. In researching the life of my maternal grandfather, I came across an article which mentioned his involvement in Freemasonry. Knowing of its dangers and of generational inheritance, (taught me by Ellel Ministries), I sought prayer in 2001 and found that I now had a sense of the presence of and freedom to move in the Holy Spirit's anointing.

It was some years later, under pressure from public opinion, that Freemasons' Hall in London published their historic membership records online, dating from the 1750s, up to 1921. Because of the need for compliance with the Data Protection Act, no membership records are available (as yet) to the public for the years after 1921. Armed with this piece of news, I was then able to systematically enter the names of known ancestors from my expanding family tree, on to their online search facility, to see if any more of them had been Freemasons. To my dismay, six more of my ancestors' names were found. This meant more prayers were needed!

Fortunately, I was able to enrol on a course entitled, 'Freedom from Freemasonry' in January 2018, which is run by Gilgal House and held regularly at Stony Stratford Community Church, near Milton Keynes. During this course and later, by praying through a specialist Christian healing book on the subject, entitled, *Freemasonry: Death in the Family* by Yvonne Kitchen, I was able to be set free from these generational influences. It is interesting to recall how at certain points during the prayer times, I found myself manifesting in various ways, as the power of the Freemasonry curses were systematically broken off me. I felt freer still.

So, the thesis of my book is that apart from stories relayed by living relatives, which can give an indication of blessings, curses or sins coming down the family line, research into official genealogical records can reveal yet further information. These can then form the basis of knowledgeable and well-informed prayers to set the captive free from his or her generational issues. So, sometimes it is important to look back, in order to go forwards. Well-aimed prayers will be like a well-aimed arrow hitting the target. In fact, the word, 'sin' is an old Norman-French archery term for 'missing the mark.' (It just so happens that this symbolism is used by No. 10 Squadron, RAF (whose Association I enjoy a membership of), in its badge and Latin motto, *Rem Acu Tangere*. This loosely translates as, 'To hit the mark.').

PREFACE

Think of this scripture, where the words 'rock' and 'quarry' allude to the personal ancestry from which we all originate. (Words placed in **bold** by me):

> Listen to me, you that pursue righteousness,
> you that seek the Lord.
> **Look to the rock from which you were hewn,**
> **and to the quarry from which you were dug.**
> Look to Abraham your father
> And to Sarah who bore you;
> For he was but one when I called him,
> But I blessed him and made him many.
> For the Lord will comfort Zion;
> He will comfort all her waste places,
> and will make her wilderness like Eden,
> her desert like the garden if the Lord;
> joy and gladness will be found in her,
> thanksgiving and the voice of song.
> (Isaiah 51:1-3, NASB)

Consider also the following scriptures which give a precedent for confessing the sins and iniquities of ancestors:

> **If they confess** their iniquity **and the iniquity of their forefathers**, in their unfaithfulness which they committed against Me, and also in their acting with hostility against Me ... so that they **make amends** for their iniquity, then I will remember My covenant with [Jacob, Isaac, and Abraham]...   (Leviticus 26:40-42, NASB)

> Please let Your ear be attentive and Your eyes open, that You may hear the prayer of Your servant which I pray before You now, day and night, for the children of Israel Your servants, and **confess the sins of the children of Israel which we have sinned against You. Both my father's house and I have sinned.** (Nehemiah 1:6, NASB)

> The descendants of Israel separated themselves from all foreigners, and stood and **confessed their sins and the iniquities of their fathers.**   (Nehemiah 9:2, NASB)

It is both wonderful and essential to have the gifts of discernment and words of knowledge when praying into various areas of personal dysfunction, as well as the gifts of healing and deliverance. However, these can and should be supplemented with targeted knowledge to aid the effectiveness of counsel and prayers. Personally, I think it is a mistake to just rely on the supernatural gifts, without benefiting from the information available through genealogical research. God can use both methods to reveal past events. It is said that the ancient Israelites kept their genealogical records in the Temple in Jerusalem. These, unfortunately were destroyed when the Temple itself was destroyed by the Romans in AD 70. Had Jesus been born after this date, it would not have been possible to prove his lineage from these records!

The church can be good at seeking supernatural knowledge to answer questions about personal brokenness, but sometimes disparages the natural task of related research into family history. Likewise, the world has the same prejudice back in the opposite direction, shunning belief in the miraculous. Hebraic thinking knows no such division between the sacred and secular.

As with my own experience of the noose around the neck back in the 1990s, it was not until I had stumbled across the cause of death of my great-great-grandfather and prayed / had targeted prayer into the issue, that I was finally set free from that curse.

Sometimes, personal problems just don't go away, whatever prayers are said. Repeated cycles of sin, repentance, forgiveness and sin again, or family patterns of curses and illnesses running down the family line, can defy all attempts to get free. The sufferer can lose heart when they are blamed for not having enough faith, for being weak, for not believing for their healing, or experience all manner of rejections, leaving them discouraged and defeated. Christians are sometimes encouraged not to dwell on the past, leaving them with few options other than to pretend that all is well and wear a fake smile to church. Some even give up on God, blaming Him for His apparent powerlessness. All along, the root

PREFACE

cause may simply be an unbroken generational curse or iniquity, which, with a little time and effort, can be revealed and dealt with through research and prayer.

This book is therefore a simple exposition of the various types of generational sin or iniquity, together with a description of what genealogical resources are available for research, to prove or disprove the presence of such issues. Rather than being purely diagnostic and descriptive, what follows is also prescriptive. In each chapter there is a guide for inner healing prayers and deliverance from each issue, offering hope and freedom for the sufferer. This is not an exhaustive manual, rather a fairly basic guide linking the healing ministry, particularly with regards generational sin and iniquity, and how it relates to and can be enhanced by a knowledge and use of the increasingly popular subject of genealogy.

Any factual errors or omissions discovered by more qualified and experienced persons than I, are my own, for which I apologise in advance.

May those who are helped by this book identify with the prophet Isaiah, when he wrote:

> Sing for joy, O heavens, and exult, O earth;
> break forth, O mountains, into singing!
> For the Lord has comforted his people,
> and will have compassion on his suffering ones.
> Isaiah 49:13, (NRSV)

Chris Eve, Lancaster, Summer 2023

Introduction

This book is aimed at Christians who know the Lord Jesus Christ as their personal saviour, have repented of their sins, sought and received forgiveness, are open to the filling and workings of the Holy Spirit in their lives, and are working to make Him Lord of their lives too. It also assumes that the reader has become aware that they have personal issues (who doesn't?!) with which they are struggling and for which ordinary prayers and willpower are not resolving. Some of these issues may be being caused by unresolved generational baggage that the reader may or may not be aware. This book aims to shine a light of revelation on what sort of issues can be caused by the sins of our ancestors, and how to discover what actual sins were committed by them. By delving into British historical records, evidence for these ancient sins can be revealed, and once done so, it is then explained how to pray into what is found. It is anticipated these prayers will bring release and freedom from the effects of our ancestors' sins.

As a practicing genealogist and former prayer minister who was trained by and worked for an international Christian healing ministry, I believe I am well placed to be able to combine these two subjects. This interdisciplinary approach is a phenomenon which is becoming more common across other academic fields of study. The combined study of archaeology and genetics, properly named 'archaeogenetics,' is one such area, offering exciting possibilities for the extension of genealogical research into the deep past.

The most well-known example of this was the discovery of the mortal remains of King Richard III (1452-1485) in a social services car park in Leicester, England, in 2012. DNA analysis of his battle-scarred bones and DNA samples taken from two of his living descendants ascertained via genealogical research, confirmed the linkages. Additional scientific testing concluded that there was a 99.999 % probability that the skeleton was indeed that of the long-lost King. He was subsequently reburied with due pomp and

INTRODUCTION

Christian ceremony - as befits an English king – in Leicester Cathedral in 2015.

I have divided up the chapters in this book according to the sins as defined by God in His 10 Commandments, as recorded by Moses, and then linked them to topics in genealogical research. Different archive repositories, genealogical websites and books are listed, as well as what information of relevance to the discovery of ancestral sins can be found in the record sources. It is one thing to describe what constitutes generational sin and iniquity and where such records are located, but quite another to explain how the struggling Christian can get free of his or her generational baggage, once proof of it has been found. It is no good going to the doctors and them just diagnosing the problem, but not prescribing any medication, therapy or surgery! So, I have been at pains to include and take the reader through the various prayers and declarations which will aid in his / her recovery. These should help in finding the sought-after freedom.

Each chapter's later sections have these relevant prayers and declarations tailored to the particular issues it discusses. Although repetitive, I felt it best to include these prayers at each chapter's end, thus continuing the flow of reading and emotional / spiritual processing, rather than break that flow and concentration up. This saves having to move around the book, and potentially confusing the reader or losing out on a relevant prayer. So, each chapter is intended to be a complete, stand-alone unit, whole unto itself, allowing the reader to focus on any chapter they choose. May you be blessed in your reading and prayers!

Having said that, where there is an overlap in genealogical topics across chapters, I have directed the reader to the material where it is at its fullest in that particular chapter. This occurs, for example, with military records, as they relate both to war trauma and occupations.

This book focuses primarily on the type of English historical records and their location within various archives, as my experience is almost entirely with English records, though some Welsh, Scottish and Irish records and archives are included. It will appeal both to British Christians and those who have British ancestry, whether they live in the USA, Canada, Australia, New Zealand, South Africa, Gibraltar, or indeed, any other part of the world.

I have also concentrated on those primary records dating from the mid-17th century onwards (known to historians as the early modern period), rather than earlier, medieval sources, as this project concerns itself with the sins of the ancestors going back no more than ten generations. I will show that (from 2023, when this book was released), ten generations takes us back no earlier than the 1640's - the time of the English Civil War. For those unfamiliar with British historical records, it may be of interest to know that written sources for British history of relevance to genealogists go back in some instances to the Norman conquest of the 11th century, or even further back in time. Indeed, some of our historical records describe events occurring in the early years of the Roman occupation after AD 43 - some 2000 years ago! Compared to many other countries' records, we are blessed beyond measure!

Chapter 1

Defining Generational Sin and Iniquity, Defining Genealogy

You shall not bow down to them or worship them; for I, the LORD your God, am a jealous God, visiting the iniquity of the fathers on their children to the third and fourth generations of those who hate Me, but showing loving devotion to a thousand generations of those who love Me and keep My commandments.

Exodus 20:5-6, (BSB)

What is Generational Sin?

Ruth Hawkey in her book, *Freedom from Generational Sin,*[1] gives the following as modern examples of generational sin: sexual sin, alcohol and adultery, dishonouring parents, murder, rage and anger, stealing, idolatry and familiar spirits. These can come from curses passing down the family line, caused by previous ancestors' sins. Catherine and Frank Fabiano define generational curses as:

> Generational curses and bondages are strongholds of the enemy in us that we inherit from our forefathers. Just as we inherit physical characteristics from our ancestors, so too we receive a spiritual inheritance of blessings and curses. For the blessings, we can be truly thankful. The curses need to be broken.[2]

Ruth Hawkey outlines the biblical evidence for generational iniquity, focusing on sexual sin, dishonouring and deception, murder and idolatry in the family line. She then goes on to explain how to find out what sins occurred within the family line by observing and asking relatives sensitively and then recording this information on a simple family tree chart, to see what patterns emerge. However, it is worth adding that generational iniquity can pass down lines of adoption, not just natural birth.

Generational sin is revealed in a family weakness being passed down from fathers and mothers to their children (and adopted children) and then to their grandchildren and so on. Parents are supposed to keep their children safe, partly by setting an example and partly by love and nurture, good teaching and firm boundaries. A weakness in the lives of the parents can be likened to them holding a leaking umbrella over their children's heads on a rainy day. The water will only come through the umbrella at the point of its tear and wet the children in approximately the same places that the parents got wet.

For instance, over the issue of forgiveness, Rev Patricia Smith writes:

> I have had people come to me filled with a desire for revenge that had been passed down, generation to generation, by forebears who had never forgiven a wrong done to them. The people who come to me don't even know why inner feelings of bitterness and anger have such a strong hold on them.[3]

Regarding the importance of forgiveness, she continues:

> *Let me emphasize*, in order for this reconciliation to be complete it is necessary for the supplicant, as a representative of the family being healed, to extend forgiveness to the ancestor. The family as a whole has been deeply hurt by the actions of this ancestor. This hurt needs to be acknowledged and the problem worked through to forgiveness, if the family line is to receive true healing and release from the bondage that their ancestor's sin has put them in.[4]

Dr David Wells in his succinct booklet, *Praying for the Family Tree*, writes:

> ...our experience is that many current mental, and some physical diseases may stem from past family trauma, such as suicide, abortion, miscarriage, murder, curses, occult involvement, or war dead.[5]

Another clinician, Mark Wolynn, though trained as a secular psychotherapist, specialising in neuroscience and post-traumatic stress disorder (PTSD), has this to say:

> What I've learned from my own experience, training, and clinical practice is that the answer [to our pain] may not lie within our own story as much as in the stories of our parents, grandparents, and even our great-grandparents. The latest scientific research, now making headlines, also tells us that the effects of trauma can pass from one generation to the next. This "bequest" is what's known as inherited family trauma, and emerging evidence suggests that it is a very real phenomenon.[6]

He also writes:

> Along the way [of our search], we're likely to meet family members both known and unknown. Some have been dead for years. Some aren't even related, but their suffering and cruelty may have altered the course of our family's destiny. We might even uncover a secret or two hidden in stories that have long been laid to rest. But regardless of where this exploration takes us, my experience suggests that we'll arrive at a new place in our lives, with a greater sense of freedom in our bodies and an ability to be more at peace with ourselves.[7]

Pastor Henry Wright (1944-2019), founder, former president and CEO of the non-profit organisation, Be In Health, dedicated to understanding and treating the spiritual roots of disease, wrote in, *A More Excellent Way*:

> ...the enemy does not have to afflict your life just because he wants to. There must be open doors, historically, both in your family tree and in your personal life, in which you have wandered outside the parameters of God's knowledge, His provision and His covenant.[8]

Differences Between Generational Sin, Transgression & Iniquity

I owe a debt of gratitude to Robert Morrissette for

explaining the differences in the Bible between generational sins, transgressions and iniquities. Used interchangeably in English translations of the Bible, without truly reflecting their Hebrew meanings, they have led to confusion as to what is meant. In brief table form, Morrissette [9] explains that: -

English	Hebrew	Meaning
Sin	*chatta' ah*	"To miss" [the mark]
Transgression (or trespass / rebellion)	*pesha*	"To break away" or "revolt"
Iniquity	*avon*	"Perversity" [i.e., an evil inclination]

A sin is obviously something done which is wrong. An iniquity is a sin indulged, whilst a transgression refers to the rebellious manner in which a sin is committed. An iniquity develops when a sin is not resisted, but repeated many times to become an 'acceptable' habit and a stronghold. So, it can be much more serious than a single sin and therefore has more power to influence succeeding generations. A 'worker of iniquity,' one who is committed to getting better at sinning, is translated as *aven* in Hebrew. Iniquities can be defined as personal, communal or generational. Morrissette succinctly defines generational iniquities as,

> ...those we have inherited from our ancestors and which we pass on to our descendants.[10]

This is exactly what scripture says in Lamentations 5:7: –

> Our ancestors have sinned, they are no more, and we bear their iniquities.

Morrissette writes,

> Generational iniquities produce negative tendencies in family lines that influence subsequent generations to behave in manners similar to one's ancestors.[11]

He further describes generational iniquities as being,

> an unseen, felt, motivating force, coming from outside of you, whereas, unresolved issues from your past tend to feel like an influence coming from within you.[12]

However,

> while becoming a Christian saves us from eternal death, it doesn't stop the reaping of what we and our ancestors have sowed.[13]

To quote Pastor Henry Wright:

> Isaiah 59:1-2 says that our sins can separate us from our God. Not only can our sins separate us from our God, but also the consequence of our ancestors' sins transfer into us. We have evidence of this through genetically inherited disease.
>
> Not only do we have genetically inherited disease, but the psychiatric industry over the years has determined that certain non-genetic factors such as disposition, personality quirks and idiosyncrasies can also be passed down through family trees without a genetic component being seen or known. These are iniquities.[14]

Morrissette rightly makes the point that we still have the responsibility to resist the influence of generational iniquity and sow good character and blessings into the family line.[15]

Blessings and Curses

The key scriptures for these blessings for obedience or consequent resulting curses for sin and disobedience, are found in Exodus 20 and Deuteronomy 5:6-21, where God gave the 10 commandments through Moses to His people, the Israelites and to all people, through Jesus. Abbreviated, they read:

1. *You shall have no other gods before Me.*
2. *You shall not make for yourself an idol.*
3. *You shall not take the name of the Lord your God in vain.*
4. *Remember the Sabbath day to keep it holy.*

5. *Honour your father and your mother.*
6. *You shall not murder.*
7. *You shall not commit adultery.*
8. *You shall not steal.*
9. *You shall not bear false witness against your neighbour.*
10. *You shall not covet.*

Critically (and it bears repeating), God speaks both a warning for disobedience and a blessing for obedience in the keeping of the commandments:

> "...for I the Lord your God am a jealous God, punishing the children for the iniquity of parents, to the third and the fourth generation of those who reject me, but showing steadfast love to the thousandth generation of those who love me and keep my commandments." Exodus 20:5-6, (NRSV)

Marilyn Hickey, in her book, *Break the Generation Curse*, supports the reality of this scripture:

> The scripture [Exodus 20:5] says that every man shall answer for his own sin. They will be accountable to God for their sins, but that weakness in an area of their lives – physically, mentally, emotionally – is transmitted to the next generation, or maybe the generation after that.[16]

And says:

> So, the Bible says that some negative hereditary things are curses. Curses always start with sin, for "... the curse causeless shall not come" (Proverbs 26:2).[17]

These scriptures are given balance by Jeremiah 32:18:

> You show steadfast love to the thousandth generation, but repay the guilt of parents into the laps of their children after them, O great and mighty God whose name is the Lord of hosts, great in counsel and mighty in deed, whose eyes are open to all the ways of mortals, rewarding all according to their ways and according to the fruit of their doings.

DEFINING GENERATIONAL SIN & GENEALOGY

Jesus reiterated the importance of the law in Matthew 5:17-19, Mark 10:17-19 and John 14:15:

> "If you love me, keep my commandments."

The apostle John later wrote,

> For this is the love of God, that we keep His commandments. And His commandments are not burdensome.   1 John 5:3, (ESV)

The apostle Paul also confirmed this:

> Therefore, the law is holy, and the commandment holy and just and good.   Romans 7:12, (NKJV)

Just in case there is any doubt in this modern age, the book of Hebrews includes:

> Jesus Christ is the same yesterday, today, and forever.
> Hebrews 13:8, (NLT)

Lastly, in the book of Revelation, Jesus, speaking through the apostle John, some 60 years after His death and resurrection, explains that faithful members of the church are,

> ...those who keep the commandments of God and the testimony of Jesus.   **Revelation 12:17, (BSB)**

In some of the final verses of Revelation is the admonition:

> Blessed are those who do His commandments, that they may have the right to the tree of life, and may enter through the gates into the city.   Revelation 22:14, (NKJV)

There are numerous other New Testament scriptures which reveal the importance of keeping every single one of the ten commandments. A brief internet search proves this. So, it is pretty clear that God intends for us, with His help, to keep the 10 commandments. To reject them is to cause problems for ourselves and our descendants, in the way of inherited curses and difficulties.

Realising what sins and iniquities we and our forebears have committed, we are shown in scripture what to do next:

> We **acknowledge** our wickedness, O LORD, the iniquity of our ancestors, for we have sinned against you.
> Jeremiah 14:20-21, (NRSV)

> I said, "O LORD God of heaven, the great and awesome God who keeps covenant and steadfast love with those who love him and keep his commandments, let Your ear be attentive and Your eyes open, that You may hear the prayer of Your servant which I pray before You now, day and night, for the children of Israel Your servants, and **confess** the sins of the children of Israel which we have sinned against You. **Both my father's house and I have sinned.**" Nehemiah 1:5-6, (NKJV)
> (See also: Nehemiah 9:2 & Daniel 9:16)

We are to acknowledge these sins, confess them and where we have sinned, to repent and turn away from them. This is the beginning of the route to freedom. However, often we do not know what sins our ancestors committed. They may have died long before we were born. In these cases, we can still find out a great deal, by researching our ancestors' lives. Modern family history internet sites which give access to old records can help us immeasurably.

What is Genealogy and How is it Relevant to Generational Sin and Healing?

Otto Bixler writes,

> ...you may have realised that you lack information about some aspects of your spiritual inheritance. This ignorance may be keeping you from enjoying God's blessings for your life and from walking in his plans and purposes.[18]

Genealogy is more than just discovering the most basic information about our ancestors, such as birth, marriage and death dates. The study of family history helps put flesh on those bare bones, by finding the forgotten stories and details of these long-gone people. Inevitably, we may discover failings, shortcomings and skeletons in the cupboard, but there will also be things about our ancestors which can make us feel proud of them. Apart from achievements, we may see aptitudes and skills we've inherited from them, or areas of the country they came from, which we have instinctively felt a sense of connection to. These 'aha' moments are precious.

However, when, rather than if we find those things that cause us embarrassment or shock, then as Christians, we need not fear, for God has provided an answer in the cross and the gift of healing, to overcome any negative effects of generational sin.

This is all part of, 'work[ing] out your own salvation with fear and trembling.' (Philippians 2:12, (ESV)), post conversion and new birth. We may be free before Christ positionally, but not yet in experience. As scripture explains, we have been saved (Romans 8:15), (2 Corinthians 5:17), we are being saved (Romans 8:23) and we will be saved (Ephesians 1:5). Jesus will guide us as we seek Him to become free in difficult areas of our lives.

Does Scripture Warn Against Genealogy?

There may be those who are concerned about the relevance of genealogy to their Christian walk and who might be thinking of another New Testament scripture; 1 Timothy 1:3-7, (and Titus 3:9) which warns people against getting involved with endless genealogy, because it 'promotes [fruitless] speculation.'

> As I urged you when I was going to Macedonia, remain at Ephesus so that you may charge certain persons not to teach any different doctrine, nor to devote themselves to myths and endless genealogies, which promote speculations rather than the stewardship from God that is by faith. The aim of our charge is love that issues from a pure heart and a good conscience and a sincere faith. Certain persons, by swerving from these, have wandered away into vain discussion, desiring to be teachers of the law, without understanding either what they are saying or the

things about which they make confident assertions.
1 Timothy 1:3-7, (ESV)

However, this scripture was probably aimed by Paul at those who were more concerned to prove some lineal descent from a priestly line in order to give themselves some sort of kudos amongst their fellow Christians. The notes section in the *ESV Archaeology Study Bible* reads:

> The specifics of these false teachings in Ephesus are uncertain. The linkage of myths and genealogies suggests speculations on the OT, perhaps attempts to link local Jewish and Greek church members' family lines to biblically attested families or genealogies. This could lead to the establishment of an exclusive "inner circle" of members, who felt superior to regular "unconnected" members. [19]

We all need to guard against finding 'important' ancestors in our family line which, once found, can puff us up with the wrong sort of pride! The bountiful scriptures referring to genealogies in the Old Testament were very often included to prove legal rights of inheritance to property and land, and to entitlement to train and serve as Levitical priests.

How do You go About Doing Genealogy?

The basic rule of thumb is to start with what you know and work backwards. So, start by asking parents and grandparents, siblings, cousins, aunts and uncles about your family. When interviewing family members, it is best to start with the eldest members first, while they are still around! While the elderly may suffer from short-term memory loss, usually they will have good memories of people and events from long ago. Your grandparents may remember stories their grandparents told them about their youth. This could give you a five-generation family tree straight away, covering about 150 years!

In terms of the spiritual / emotional impact of genealogy, ask your family and make a note of what your ancestors were like. Were they happy / sad, loving / unloving, kind / cruel, peaceful / angry? What did they do for work? Had they seen military service? Were they poor / middling / rich? Were they Christians or not? Were they honest? Did they fall fowl of the law? Did they have any addictions to alcohol or other substances? Were they happily married or otherwise? Did they have more than one wife / husband? Is there a history of accidents or other trauma in the family line? Were there any Freemasons in the family?

Write this information down and start to construct a family tree, known as a 'drop-line pedigree chart' or 'Seize Quartiers,' starting with yourself and working backwards. (See chart on next page). Start with just direct ancestors first and perhaps later on, construct a chart showing siblings as well. See chart below. Husbands / fathers should always be written on the left side in a pedigree chart and wives / mothers on the right side.

Dr David Wells writes:

> As a way of ordering the fact we now have, and to build up a picture of the family's spiritual inheritance and needs for healing, we find that it is often very helpful at this stage to draw out a family tree on a large sheet of paper.[20]

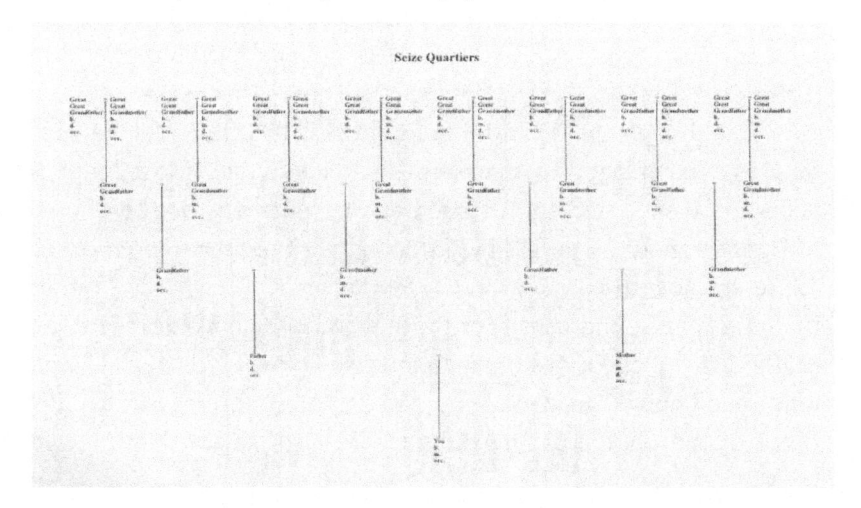

Figure 1. 'Seize Quartiers' for constructing a drop-line pedigree chart

Next, turn to the records. For the purposes of this book, I will only consider English and some Welsh, Scottish and Irish records. However, people from America, Canada, Australia, New Zealand, South Africa and elsewhere, with British ancestry, will find research pointers in this book useful. This is just a fairly basic guide, and does not aim to go into details of all the types of records available or all the useful websites one can use.

First of all, find out and order copies of birth, marriage and death certificates from the General Register Office (GRO). These will take you back to 1837, when civil registration began. You can find the references for these free from www.freebmd.org.uk and from subscription websites such as www.ancestry.co.uk and www.findmypast.co.uk, but you'll need to pay for the actual certificates. These should be ordered and paid for from the GRO direct at: www.gro.gov.uk.

Your ancestors can be found on the national censuses, (using Ancestry.co.uk or Findmypast.co.uk), taken every ten years, starting in 1841, up to 1921 at present. Because of the 100-year data protection restriction, the censuses are only currently available for public viewing up to 1921. It would be best to start with the 1921 census and work backwards, extracting such information as names, relationships, ages, address, occupations and birthplaces. The further back you go, the less detailed the censuses become.

Although they still do, before 1837, the church alone kept records of birth, baptism, marriage, death and burial. Most people's ancestors were 'hatched, matched and despatched' via the Church of England and their details recorded in parish registers and records. These are now usually kept in County Record Offices (CROs), rather than the specific churches. For those who were nonconformists, i.e. Methodist, Baptist, Congregationalist, Presbyterian, United Reformed Church, Quaker and Roman Catholic, their records parallel those of the Church of England and are also usually deposited in CROs.

The further one goes back, the more difficult it will be to

read old handwriting and the more careful you will have to be in recording information accurately. Don't make unproven guesses, especially when tired and loaded down with masses of information. Take a break. Come back to your research refreshed and strive to prove your findings are true. Otherwise, you may literally be, 'barking up the wrong tree'!

It is possible that somebody has already researched your family tree, so check this first. Such research might be publicised on the internet, in printed works or deposited with the Guild of One-Name Studies, located at the Society of Genealogists (SoG) in London. (See list of organisations in Appendix F at the end of this book for address details).

Beyond the GRO registers, censuses, parish registers and records, there are many other ways your ancestors' achievements and misdemeanours will have been recorded. Illegitimacy, adoption, migration, educational and occupational records, military, poverty, workhouse and criminal records, religious allegiances, Freemasonry membership, and wills all contain valuable genealogical information.

Using the 10 commandments as a template for identifying particular sins and discovering the genealogical records which could prove such sins existed in your family tree, we can now turn to the records. The first three commandments are to do with our relationship with God.

For this reason, I have grouped the following genealogical records into this category: church affiliation and therefore possible religious spirits, but more seriously, idolatry and Freemasonry.

Much of this research is concerned with finding out clues as to the sins and iniquities of our ancestors, with a view to confessing them and praying for release from their effects. But it is also important to remember the many ways our immediate ancestors have blessed us and how all our ancestors had many good qualities. We need to keep these in mind or learn what they were too, for scripture commands us to:

> Honour your father and your mother, so that you may live long in the land the LORD your God is giving you.   Exodus 20:12, (NIV)

This will then attract God's blessing, giving us a sense of well-being, identity and where we come from. From this, we will find it easier to know where we are going, and therefore our God-given purpose - why we were put on earth by the Lord.

Identifying Generational Sins & Iniquities

Before we deal with generational influences in our lives, it is important to first repent of and pray through our own personal sins and iniquities. Robert Morrissette writes the same thing.[21] As we do that, it will become clearer what negative generational influences there are that need dealing with. Is what you are experiencing having a strong influence on you? Is there a persistent pattern emerging of repeated failings? To your knowledge, did your ancestors struggle with the same issues in their lives?

In dealing with generational sin in our lives, it is important to first pray through what we do know of our familial sins and iniquities. Then we can ask the Lord to reveal what we don't know and pray through what He shows us.

Dr David Wells says that we may find clues as to our generational issues through some family members acting out in their minds or bodies, some aspect of a deceased ancestor's distress, such as an emotional, mental or physical ailment. These can include, amongst other things, anger, depression, hearing voices, schizophrenia and asthma, bronchitis and persistent eating disorders. Sometimes, the unresolved angers, hurts, unrepented of sin and unforgiveness of our dead ancestors (their 'unfinished business'), in some way impinge on our lives in unhelpful ways.[22]

Morrissette advises the following and I would concur wholeheartedly:

> ... identify the source of the generational iniquity. This may take some time. There are several things you can do to accomplish this:

- Recall any family stories you already know.
- Go ask someone who may know your family history.
- Research your family history.
- Ask the Lord to reveal to you what you don't know about your family history.[23]

Dr David Wells advises much the same:

> We may well have to do some careful and time consuming research into our families, so that, with the Holy Spirit's help we may come to a reasonable understanding of the occasions we are researching, and try to understand the circumstances of the people concerned.[24]

In the identification process, it is important to find out **what** events actually happened, **when** they occurred and to **whom**? Within these events, we should ask, **what iniquities** were committed by our ancestors, what **lies** did they believe and what **decisions** did they make as a result?

For example, an event in my father's family which had a profound effect on us, was when my aunt Mary died from spinal meningitis, aged only 15, in June 1943. As she passed away in Wembley Hospital, North London, the air raid siren was sounding the 'All Clear.' My grandparents and father were devastated, so much so that my grandmother had a nervous breakdown and the family lost their faith in God. My father was given compassionate leave and missed his ship that would have taken him to Canada to continue learning to fly in the RAF. He boarded another troopship later on, which took him to South Africa instead, and thence onward by train to Southern Rhodesia to resume his flying training, thereby delaying his entry into the War, which perhaps saved his life.

In prayer, I believe the Lord showed me that my grandparents and Dad had blamed God for taking Mary and then turned away from Him, thinking they could no longer trust Him in times of need or to provide for them. They had thereby decided to take things into their own hands and my father subsequently became a very controlling man. He had not trusted God to help him with wartime flying, even though he was saved from several mishaps, near misses, accidents, and potentially fatal postings. All the other crews he trained with on Wellington bombers either died in accidents or were shot down. Dad seemingly had not recognised the hand of God in all this, who ultimately saved his life. Nor, as far as I know, did he thank God for this. God's saving hand is the reason I am here, and yet I've struggled with unbelief and trusting God (like my father and grandparents), even as a Christian, taking things into my own hands on a number of occasions, resulting in some costly mistakes.

Once the generational iniquities have been identified, the next step is to offer them up to God in **confession**. As descendants of our ancestors, we have the authority to do so. If the Lord shows you, forgive also those who sinned against your ancestors. The result will be freedom from the influence of these iniquities. Thinking, behaviour, and habits will change or become easier to break after such prayer. It will then be important to form new godly thoughts, behaviours, and habits.

Robert Morrissette lays out a four-stage plan of how to do this:

> **Tell the Lord** what happened in your family line.
> **Confess** the sins and iniquities involved.
> **Renounce** any lies and decisions made by your ancestors.
> **Give thanks** for the good your ancestors did and for their good characteristics.[25]

There will be subsequent benefits for your children, if you have any. Gordon Dalbey notes that it is relationship with Father God that ultimately heals generational wounds and enables a father to pass on the Father's heart to his children:

> Knowing the heart of Father God is what heals the father-wound. An honest man knows he doesn't have within himself the wisdom and strength his children need. When he goes to Father God for it

in their behalf, he'll receive the Father's heart. As a man thereby sees his own heart grow for his children, he can understand Father God's heart for himself.[26]

Generational Sins Affecting Job Positions

Generational iniquity is not only passed on by our ancestors. When people change jobs and take on roles' others have had before them, they also take on the spiritual atmosphere left by the previous employee. This can be for good or bad. If you feel oppressed and otherwise struggle with unfamiliar and negative attitudes, emotions and actions in the new workplace that you have not experienced before, it could be a sign that there is an inheritance of iniquity in your workplace. It will need investigating and identifying properly and then confessed and prayed through. Evils spirits can be cast out of buildings.

Generational Sins Affecting Belongings

As well as job positions affecting the new employee, items left by the ex-employee can sometimes also cause problems for the newcomer. If an object was used in some sort of sinful way, then it can end up cursed and then negatively impact its subsequent user. This is also true for second-hand items bought in charity shops or antique stores, for example. It is always wise to confess any sinful practices discerned over such an object, pray the cleansing blood of Jesus over it and dedicate it to God's use and use it in a godly way. If the object was created to be used in specifically idolatrous ways or for satanic use, then it needs to be completely destroyed, and not reused, even after prayer. African witchcraft masks or statues of buddha, bought by tourists, come to mind.

Generational Sins Affecting Land and Property

Sometimes we inherit land and property from our ancestors. With these blessings can also come uninvited problems. If our parents or grandparents were not Christians, on acquiring their properties and possessions, we are likely to come across objects that we somehow do not feel comfortable with. Indeed, the land and buildings may also make us feel uncomfortable. It will not be surprising to realise that our forebears' and / or previous owners' activities in these places will not always have glorified God and so are likely to have left a spiritual residue that will need cleansing. It does not have to be an ancestor's sins that affect a property. It can be any previous owner. Researching the history of the house and its previous owners may throw some light on whatever is negatively affecting the current owner. Reading the books by Nick Barratt [27] or Gill Blanchard [28] on researching the history of your house may well prove useful.

Sometimes a house might even be haunted! Many years ago, I knew a retired teacher, named Bernard, who in his early married life, bought a house in Bedford. After a short while, he noticed that his wife and children were afraid of a certain point at the top of the stairs where they reported feeling a 'chill.' Even the family cat reacted to the spot. The problem persisted until one day, he decided to call in the parish priest. This man duly came round and conducted an exorcism in the house, paying particular attention to the top of the stairs. Bernard felt a force hold him back as the exorcism was conducted. After the priest left, he was spotted by two elderly spinsters who lived nearby. They went up to Bernard and said, *"Oh Mr Shaw, we saw the vicar leave and wondered if everything was alright?"* Bernard explained what had happened, whereupon the two sisters told him that years before, a previous owner of the house had hung himself at the top of those stairs! Need I say more?!

Discernment, confession, repentance and deliverance, the judicious use of anointing oil and 'Holy Water' and a final blessing, will all help to rededicate these places and improve the spiritual atmosphere for either you or to whoever you sell the property to.

When using **anointing oil**, pray a blessing over a quantity of olive oil and that the Lord will use it for His purposes. Then, dip your finger in the oil and wipe it along the door lintels and frames, the windows and boundary fences / corners, asking God to cleanse and bless the room / house you are in. Command any demonic forces to leave, naming them if you discern what they are. Then, ask the Holy Spirit to come in to replace the previous occupants!

'Holy water' is ordinary water that has been similarly consecrated and had salt, also consecrated, added to it in a bottle and the solution re-consecrated. This is not just an old-fashioned religious ritual; it is based on scripture and, rightly used, works to aid in the cleansing process. 2 Kings 2: 19-22 is the scriptural reference for its use:

> Now the people of the city said to Elisha, "The location of this city is good, as my lord sees; but the water is bad, and the land is unfruitful." He said, "Bring me a new bowl, and put salt in it." So, they brought it to him. Then he went to the spring of water and threw the salt into it, and said, "Thus says the LORD, I have made this water wholesome; from now on neither death nor miscarriage shall come from it." So, the water has been wholesome to this day, according to the word that Elisha spoke.
>
> 2 Kings 2:19-22, (NRSV)

The procedure is to go from room to room, sprinkling the water as you go, praying for God to show you if any defilement resides there and then to bind it and command it to go, in the name of Jesus! Then ask the Lord that the water you sprinkle will be used to cleanse that room and bring the fragrance and blessing of Christ into it. Finally, as you go round, bless each room yourself. The same should be done in the grounds of the property. Upon completion, you will notice the changed atmosphere! Jesus now resides there! I have done this numerous times, always with noticeable and beneficial results.

Dealing with Generational Sins and Iniquities

From the Bible, Morrissette and others, we learn that generational sins are dealt with by acknowledgement, confession, renunciation, repentance, forgiveness and giving thanks. However, we also need to break generational curses.

A very experienced minister into freemasonry and the occult, Ken Symington (1947-2022), has much helpful material on his website, including how to work through generational sins and curses.[29] Being biblically based, he too emphasises the importance of identifying with and confessing the sins of ancestors; forgiving them; honouring them; naming the specific areas of sin they were in to; declaring Jesus' death on the cross as the divine exchange for our sin; breaking off any curse from our family line that gave a legal right to the enemy to work in our lives; cutting ungodly soul ties in the generational line; binding the powers of darkness that may have come down the generational line, and telling them to leave; asking the Holy Spirit to fill vacated areas that have been loosed and cleansed and finally, giving thanks to God for what He has done!

In this chapter, I have described what generational sin and iniquity is, outlined what genealogy entails, and given a very brief introduction to the resolution of the effects of generational sin. It is now time to explore, chapter by chapter, key issues in generational sin, how they can be detected in genealogical research and how, as Christians we can pray into their effects, to bring lasting freedom. While there are a number of well-established ways to pray and things to pray for, it is nonetheless important that our prayers are Spirit-led, rather than being done mechanically or in an overly ritualistic manner. What is the Holy Spirit saying?

Further Reading - Select Bibliography

Barratt, Nick. *Tracing the History of Your House.* (2nd ed). Kew: The National Archives, (2006).

Bixler, Otto. *It isn't Free and it isn't Masonry.* Lancaster: Zaccmedia, (2016).

Blanchard, Gill. *Tracing Your House History: A guide for family historians.* Barnsley: Pen & Sword, (2013).

Dalbey, Gordon. *Do Pirates Wear Pajamas?* CA, San Jose: Civitas Press, LLC, (2013).

Fabiano, Catherine & Frank. *Healing Your Past, Releasing Your Future*. Bloomington, MN, USA: Chosen Books, (2012).

Hawkey, Ruth. Freedom from Generational Sin. Chichester: New Wine Press, (1999).

Hickey, Marilyn. *Break the Generation Curse*. Denver, CO: Marilyn Hickey Ministries, (1988).

Morrissette, Robert John. *Generational Restoration*. ID, Coeur d'Alene: Big Blue Skies of Idaho LLC, (2016).

Smith, Patricia A. *From Generation to Generation: A Manual for Healing*. Jacksonville, FL: Jehovah Rapha Press, (1996).

Wells, David. *Praying for the Family Tree*. France, Saint-Benoit-du-Sault: Editions Benedictines, (2006) (On behalf of the Generational Healing Trust).

Wolynn, Mark. *It Didn't Start With You: How Inherited Family Trauma Shapes Who We Are and How to End the Cycle*. New York: Penguin Books, (2017).

Wright, Henry W. *A More Excellent Way*. (Commemorative ed). New Kensington, PA: Whitaker House, (2009).

Chapter 2

Genealogical Evidence for Generational Sexual Sin

Put to death, therefore, whatever belongs to your earthly nature: sexual immorality, impurity, lust, evil desires and greed, which is idolatry.   Colossians 3:5, (NIV)

What is Sexual Sin?

According to the Bible, sexual sin includes fantasy lust, pornography, masturbation, fornication, prostitution, oral and anal sex, bigamy, sodomy, transvestism, adultery, rape, incest, paedophilia, and bestiality. It is any form of sexual activity occurring outside of the covenant of marriage. God wants to restore us to wholeness, but indulgence in sexual sin outside of the will of God will not achieve this, but rather harm us further.

Those sexual sins which have become habitual in your life, or those of any in your ancestors' lives, have also become idols, as indicated in Colossians 3:5.

Biblical Definitions of Sexual Sin

The Bible is explicit in its definitions of sexual sin, with consequent warnings against it. This is for good spiritual, psychological and physical reasons which are there for our protection, not to spoil our fun or rob us of comfort! Out of love, God does not want us to submit to temptation and so injure and ultimately destroy ourselves or others. Basilea Schlink wrote,

> Sin is poison. It not only poisons the whole body, but also the soul and spirit. [1]

Here are two commandments which are relevant to sexual sin:

> Honour your father and your mother
> (Exodus 20:12). The 5th Commandment.

> You shall not commit adultery
> (Exodus 20:14). The 7th Commandment.

GENERATIONAL SEXUAL SIN

Jesus expands the definition of adultery in Matthew 5:27-28 to include lust:

> You have heard that it was said, 'You shall not commit adultery.' But I tell you that anyone who looks at a woman lustfully has already committed adultery with her in his heart.
> Matthew 5:28, (NIV)

Transvestism is listed in Deuteronomy 22:5:

> A woman shall not wear a man's apparel, nor shall a man put on a woman's garment; for whoever does such things is abhorrent to the LORD your God.
> Deuteronomy 22:5, (NRSV)

Other verses include illegitimacy, masturbation and prostitution:

> One of illegitimate birth shall not enter the congregation of the Lord; even to the tenth generation none of his descendants shall enter the congregation of the Lord.
> Deuteronomy 23:2-3, (NKJV)

> If one of your men is unclean because of a nocturnal emission, he is to go outside the camp and stay there. But as evening approaches he is to wash himself, and at sunset he may return to the camp.
> Deuteronomy 23:10-11, (NIV)

> No Israelite man or woman is to become a shrine prostitute.
> Deuteronomy 23:17, (NIV)

Deuteronomy 27:20-23, warn against both incest and bestiality:

> Cursed is anyone who sleeps with his father's wife, for he dishonours his father's bed.
> Then all the people shall say, "Amen!"

> Cursed is anyone who has sexual relations with any animal.
> Then all the people shall say, "Amen!"

> Cursed is anyone who sleeps with his sister, the daughter of his father or the daughter of his mother.
> Then all the people shall say, "Amen!"

> Cursed is anyone who sleeps with his mother-in-law.
> Then all the people shall say, "Amen!"
> Deuteronomy 27:20-23, (NIV)

1 Corinthians 6:9-11, addressed to the Corinthian church, is an all-encompassing passage, covering sexual immorality and some other sins:

> Do you not know that the unrighteous will not inherit the kingdom of God? Do not be deceived; neither the immoral, nor idolaters, nor adulterers, nor sexual perverts, nor thieves, nor the greedy, nor drunkards, nor revilers, nor robbers will inherit the kingdom of God. And such were some of you. But you were washed, you were sanctified, you were justified in the name of the Lord Jesus Christ and in the Spirit of our God.   1 Corinthians 6:9-11, (RSV)

Galatians 5:19-21 and Romans 1:24-27 are similar. The website, www.openbible.info/topics/sexual_sin has many more relevant scriptural passages to do with sexual sin.[2]

Consequences of Sexual Sin – Why is it Harmful?

Sexually transmitted diseases are an obvious consequence of sexual sin and include, bacterial vaginosis (BV), chlamydia, gonorrhoea, hepatitis, herpes, HIV/AIDS & STDs, human papillomavirus (HPV), pelvic inflammatory disease (PID), syphilis, trichomoniasis, chancroid, scabies and more. Infertility can result from some of these diseases.[3]

There can then be unwanted pregnancies, many of them outside of wedlock, leading to abortion. In the UK at present, over ⅓ of all pregnancies lead to abortion. There were 214,869 abortions in England and Wales in 2021. [4] Of those pregnancies which were carried to full term,

> In 2021 there were 304,120 thousand live births to married mothers and 320,710 thousand births to unmarried mothers. [5]

The statistics about **illegitimacy** speak for themselves. In past eras especially, the stigma attached to illegitimacy led many women to give their children up for **adoption**, either voluntarily or by force. Children carrying a sense of rejection from having been rejected by their birth parents and then adopted, perhaps out of county, can struggle later in life with shame. They carry doubts that they are truly accepted by others, fit in, and belong to a particular community. Rejection leads to fear and anger. They can struggle with fears of authority and control, with insecurity, with difficulties believing that God loves them, with developmental, identity and attachment disorders and having a clear sense of occupational identity and purpose. Relationship and marriage problems can also affect them later in life. It is consequentially easier to turn to false comforts.

Addiction to pornography causes men to disrespect women and look at them as sex objects to fulfil their fantasies and can also cause men to sexually assault women. Pornography, however, is also increasingly viewed by women and of course, both men and women can end up in the pornographic industry as models. Pornography often leads to sexual acting out, such as fornication and adultery. Quinn Schipper writes that,

> Perversion may also exploit involuntary inheritances through the bloodline. For example, a propensity toward adultery can often be traced to a generational history of adultery. [6]

The reasons are complex, but very often, the lack of a good father figure in the family is the primary reason these problems develop. This chapter is not the place to expand on this huge topic, even in a limited way, but it is recommended to read the books, *Healing the Masculine Soul* and *Sons of the Father*, by Revd Gordon Dalbey, listed at the end of this chapter. Through these books, the reader will gain a greater understanding and a path to healing. This is also true for the other books listed for further reading.

Harmful Soul Ties formed through Sexual Sin

Soul ties which bind one person to another in an ungodly way are another consequence of sexual sin. This is true for prostitution which is railed against in 1 Corinthians 6:15-20, with clues as to how to become free, as we shall see later:

> Do you not know that your bodies are members of Christ? Shall I then take the members of Christ and make them members of a prostitute? Never! Or do you not know that he who is joined to a prostitute becomes one body with her? For, as it is written, "The two will become one flesh." But he who is joined to the Lord becomes one spirit with him. Flee from sexual immorality. Every other sin a person commits is outside the body, but the sexually immoral person sins against his own body. Or do you not know that your body is a temple of the Holy Spirit within you, whom you have from God? You are not your own, ...
> 1 Corinthians 6:15-20, (ESV)

Curses Resulting from Sexual Sin

As we saw in Deuteronomy 27:20-23, a curse will arise on all forms of incest and bestiality. There is effectively a spiritual curse operating in the lives of those who are illegitimate, as we saw in Deuteronomy 23:2. Deuteronomy 28:15-68 lists all the curses that can or will befall those who do not obey God's commandments and instructions. It is a long list, which includes curses on where the person lives and works, on their food, children, produce, animals, and comings and goings. There will be disasters, panic, frustration, sicknesses and diseases, heat, drought, defeat by enemies, fear, rejection by others, death and even lack of proper burial. There will be a lack of healing for sicknesses, madness, blindness and confusion, abuse, robbery, failure in relationships, including betrothal and marriage, lack of a true home, theft, impoverishment, enslavement, fruitless labour, hunger, thirst, loss of children, humiliation in front of foreigners and lack of advancement. Significantly, verse 46 says, regarding these curses:

> They shall be among you and your descendants as a sign and a portent for ever.   Deuteronomy 28:46, (NRSV)

The chapter goes on the say that the disobedient will be defeated in war and serve their enemies in hunger and thirst and will lack in every way. They will lose their land and be scattered, become broken-spirited and dread even life itself. While this was written as a warning to the people of Israel and effectively prophesied their later scatterings amongst the nations, there is a parallel for all the people of God, not to ignore His guidance and commandments. These scriptures make for frightening and depressing reading, but all is not lost. God has provided the way, through the death and resurrection of Jesus, to find new life, new identity, freedom and healing in Jesus. Jesus became a curse for us, by hanging from the cross! All these curses can be broken! Derek Prince's classic book, *Blessing or Curse: you can choose*,[7] is well worth working through to help in this process.

From Curse to Blessing

Malachi 4:5-6 shows how this curse-reversal process works:

> Behold, I will send you Elijah the prophet
> Before the coming of the great and dreadful day of the LORD.
> And he will turn
> The hearts of the fathers to the children,
> And the hearts of the children to their fathers,
> Lest I come and strike the earth with a curse.
> Malachi 4:5-6, (NKJV)

The book of Malachi is placed at the end of the Old Testament, just before the gospel of Matthew and the story of Jesus' coming. These last two verses of Malachi could be described as the pivotal verses between the Old and New Testaments. So, Elijah can also be interpreted as the prophet John the Baptist, who announced Jesus' ministry and work to restore broken relationships between wayward sons and daughters to their fathers and ultimately, to their heavenly Father.

Once a broken relationship with God has been restored through repentance and initial salvation, the work of undoing the remainder of life's problems begins. Not everything is sorted out at the point of conversion, as any Christian who has been on the journey for any length of time, will testify!

In order to gain further freedom, first it is necessary to know what is holding you back? What things in your life are you struggling with or feel under some sort of oppression, or lack of fruitfulness? A prayerful reading of Deuteronomy and Leviticus, as well as the New Testament letters, such as Corinthians, and the books mentioned and listed, will highlight areas of your life that need attention.

How Far Back?

Suppose these problems originated further back in your family line, even to the 10th generation, as written in Deuteronomy 23:2? If you count a generation as being between 25 and 30 years long, ten generations, including you, (if you are about 80 years of age), take us back about 250 – 380 years. From the year 2023 backwards, that gives us a date period between 1773 and the 1640s (the English Civil War period). While you may know of the misdemeanours in the immediate past, of your parents or grandparents, it is highly unlikely that you will know of any family sexual sins from the 17th century! The only way to find out would be to research your family tree.

What Can You Find Out?

Realistically, the only sexual sins which might be discovered in historical records would be those involving illegitimacy, adoption and perhaps in some criminal records. Any family papers might reveal something else, but the most likely records will be birth, marriage and death certificates, parish registers and records, court and adoption records. Modern DNA testing can also reveal irregularities in the paternal line.

Mention of ancestors may also be found in old **wills**. These might produce information about siblings of your direct ancestors, which might not otherwise be found. As a start, you can search the following websites: www.gov.uk/search-will-probate

Wills made after 1858: www.nationalarchives.gov.uk/help-with-your-research/research-guides/wills-or-administrations-after-1858/

Wills made between 1384 - 1858: www.nationalarchives.gov.uk/help-with-your-research/research-guides/wills-1384-1858/

Evidence for Generational Sexual Sin Illegitimacy

If a child is born out of wedlock, where the parents did not marry or only married after the birth, the child is termed 'illegitimate.' It is quite straightforward to spot an illegitimate birth, because the father's name will not appear on the birth certificate before 1925. After 1969, the surname of the child will appear on the birth certificate. For those born illegitimately, the surname will be that of the mother's maiden name.

Birth, marriage, and death certificates go back to the **beginning of civil registration in 1837** and are kept at the General Register Office (GRO) in Southport. The year and which quarter of the year the event occurred, needs to be found out first. This can be done online via such sites as www.freebmd.org.uk, www.ancestry.co.uk and www.findmypast.co.uk. The quarters of each year are:

(1st quarter): Jan/Feb/Mar,
(2nd quarter): Apr/May/Jun,
(3rd quarter): Jul/Aug/Sep and,
(4th quarter): Oct/Nov/Dec.

At this point, copies of the certificates should be ordered online through: www.gro.gov.uk/gro/content/. In brief, either a pdf or paper version can be purchased. The former is cheaper than the latter. Occupations will also be shown for mothers of illegitimate children. After 1925, the father's surname may appear and if so, the surnames of unmarried parents may probably be different. A search for the marriage certificate will establish whether or not and at what date the parents married. It should not be forgotten that a marriage may have taken place only a few weeks or months before the birth, so even if the child was born **in** wedlock, s/he may have been conceived **out of** wedlock and thus be the product of fornication.

Problems can arise in searching the GRO Registers, especially with cases of illegitimacy. Sometimes parents pretended that their children were legitimate, but were, in reality, born out of wedlock. The child might be given the father's surname, as if the parents were already married. It can then be difficult to trace an earlier marriage for the parents. In fact, you may find the parents' marriage certificate recorded many years later. Maybe the mother married someone else and the child grew up with another man's surname.

Sometimes children pretended they were legitimate when they got married themselves. They might put their father's or grandfathers' name on their marriage certificate, even if their parents never married. On the other hand, children may leave the space for their father's name, blank on the marriage certificate. This is usually an indication of illegitimacy.

The Legitimacy Act of 1926 allowed an illegitimate child to be re-registered as legitimate after the Act was passed. This can be spotted in the, 'When registered' column on the birth certificate, where the birth can be registered years after the actual birth.

Prior to 1837, Church of England **parish registers** or the registers of other denominations will need consulting. These are usually kept at **County Record Offices (CROs)**. However, most of these can now also be viewed online at Ancestry.co.uk or Findmypast.co.uk, for example, making a journey to a CRO unnecessary. Additionally, CROs sometimes have an online record of their parish registers or are in the process of constructing or updating one. Your local CRO will advise.

The registers themselves normally record the baptism / christening of a child, rather than the birth, though sometimes both are recorded, with the birth date being added next to the date of baptism. This was normally conducted within a few weeks of the birth, though christenings sometimes occur several years later in childhood, or even as an adult baptism, especially for Baptists. Again, in the case of an infant or child baptism, only the name of the mother will be recorded if the child is illegitimate. From 1732/3, mothers were required to declare if they were pregnant with an illegitimate child and name the supposed father.

There were other types of **parish records** which identified and dealt with illegitimacy, because before the age of the National Health Service and State benefits, the parish often had to carry the financial burden of providing for a young, out-of-work mother with baby. Ideally, the parish officers would try and trace the reputed father, encourage him to marry the mother and make him agree to pay for the mother's and child's upkeep. In ancient documents, illegitimacy was also termed 'bastardy' or 'base born.' Documents relating to this are known as **'bastardy bonds,'** examinations, warrants and orders, and are concerned with child maintenance. They will be found in the parish registers, churchwardens,' parish constables' and overseers of the poor' accounts, now held in local CROs. They occur from about 1600 up to the late 19th century.

Basically, all Catholic parish registers prior to Henry VIII's **'Dissolution of the Monasteries'** (1535-1538), were kept in the monasteries and as the monasteries were destroyed, so were their mediaeval records.

After the 1834 Poor Law Amendment Act, the poor were looked after by the Board of Guardians, who administered the workhouse system. Records of illegitimacy can then be found in the **local court records,** known as **'Quarter Sessions' records**, where the named father was made to sign a bond saying that he would pay for the child's upkeep and a warrant issued for his arrest if he did not keep up payments. A maintenance order naming him may be in the next quarter sessions' minute book. The quarter sessions courts were so named because they travelled around a jurisdiction, sitting at a particular town or city once a quarter. They were finally abolished in 1972, becoming the Magistrates Courts that we know of today. Again, all these records are now located in CRO's.

Affiliation orders were also records where the unmarried father was ordered to pay the mother of their child for the upkeep of the said child. The mother's name should also be looked for. These documents will appear in the Petty Sessions records of local courts, (now in CROs) and can also appear in local newspapers.

You may find a record of an illegitimate ancestor in a forebear's **will.** As mentioned, wills dated after 1858 are obtainable from the Government website at: www.gov.uk/search-will-probate. In such wills, a clue will be if the father names his heir as his 'reputed' or his 'natural' son or daughter, thereby acknowledging them as his. Again, for will's dated before 1858, see the information guide at the TNA website at: www.nationalarchives.gov.uk/help-with-your-research/research-guides/wills-or-administrations-before-1858/. These earlier wills were proven by church courts and are more complicated.

The important thing to remember in tracing illegitimacy in the family line is to obtain all the available records you can about the person(s) in full. There will be clues about illegitimate births in these records. These could include middle names, the use of a step-parent's name later on, mentions in parish chest records, court records, newspapers, and wills. If all else fails, then DNA testing may produce results.

Records of Adoption

Records of adoption, which came into law in **1927**, after the Adoption of Children Act of 1926, can also help towards revealing the names of birth parents and if there had been illegitimacy in the family. It has been possible for adoptees in the UK to view their birth records since 1975. Those adopted before 11th November 1975, are required to see an adoption counsellor before being given the information on how to apply to see their birth records. However, this will only include the person's original name, their mother's name and the registration district they were born in. Karen Bali's book, *Researching Adoption: An essential guide to tracing birth* *relatives and ancestors*, goes into more detail about this process.[7] The Salvation Army also has information on adoption and fostering and this is kept at **The Salvation Army Social Services Headquarters**, Newington Causeway, London, SE1 6BU. This information (if not restricted) can be supplied to relatives. A more recent development has been the use of social media to help trace birth parents, though being unregulated, this carries risks.

Multiple Marriages or Divorce

If there is evidence from the birth or marriage certificates, parish registers or wills of multiple marriages or divorce, this may be an indication of sexual sin in your ancestry. A careful scrutiny of dates of marriage and subsequent births will be needed to prove or disprove this.

Divorce records may be found at the National Archives, via their website at: www.nationalarchives.gov.uk/help-with-your-research/research-guides/divorce/. Ancestry.co.uk also have records of divorce.

How to Pray into Generational Sexual Sin Issues

To start off, I would recommend praying for protection for yourself and your loved ones and for Jesus to lead and guide you in these prayers. Then pray the 'Lordship Prayer.' The Lordship Prayer and the declarations and prayers following, are used by several Christian ministries, in various forms, which you can find online and whose address details are listed in Appendix F.

Lordship Prayer

"Dear Lord Jesus, I realise my need of You and repent of living my life my own way. I wholeheartedly accept You now as my Saviour, my Redeemer, my Lord, and my Deliverer.

I invite You now to be the Lord of every part and moment of my life, from the time of my conception, right up until now:

Lord of my body, my physical health and behaviour.

Lord of my mind and all my attitudes and mental health.

Lord of all my emotions and all my reactions.

Lord of my spirit and my worship of You.

Lord of my family and all my relationships.

Lord of my sexuality and its expression.

Lord of my will and all my hopes, ambitions, decisions and plans.

Lord of all my work and service for You.

Lord of all my finances.

Lord of all my needs and possessions.

Lord of the manner and time of my death."

Are there any sexual sins in your life, that once confessed and repented of, you still can't gain the victory over? If so, this could be a sign that there is generational sexual sin in your family line, influencing you.

Those sexual sins which have become habitual in your life, or those of any of your ancestors' lives, have become idols. They will need to be confessed as idols and repented of. The psalmist declares in Psalm 79:8-9, (NRSV):

> Do not remember against us the iniquities of our ancestors;
>   let your compassion come speedily to meet us,
>   for we are brought very low.
> Help us, O God of our salvation,
>   for the glory of your name;
> deliver us and forgive our sins,
>   for your name's sake.

Declaration

"Thank you, Jesus, for shedding Your blood and dying on the cross, for the forgiveness of my sins, my ancestors' sins, and my

descendants' sins. You died and rose again that I might be set free to love and to serve You, in newness of life.

While I thank you, Lord, for my ancestors, especially my father and mother who brought me into this world and whom I honour, I do not stand in agreement with them on sinful matters. In these cases, in your presence, Lord, I **confess** and **repent** on behalf of all my parents,' grandparents' and forefathers' involvement in sexual sin. I confess that these are sins against you, which I **renounce** off my life and off the life of my family, which have resulted in curses running through the family line, down to me. Thank you for becoming a curse for me on the cross, so that I might go free. I ask that You would **forgive** my ancestors' involvement in sexual sin as I forgive them also. I claim Your **blood cleansing** from all the effects of generational sexual sin in my life."

Breaking of Soul Ties for Ungodly Ancestral Sexual Behaviour

Once the confession and renunciation has occurred, it will then be necessary to cut off any negative spiritual power of transmission via the generational soul ties, or 'body, soul, and spirit ties,' as some call them. To do this, pray:

"In the name of Jesus, I place the cross and blood of Jesus between myself and each of my family members. I break all the ungodly body, soul, and spirit ties with:
Sexual partners I have had outside of marriage.
Any fantasy images from pornographic materials, whether in magazines, books, or the internet.
My parents, if they had any wrong ties with others.
Between myself and other family members, (name them), who may have developed ungodly ties.
With my grandparents.
With my great-grandparents and,
previous ancestors, (name any relevant ones), going back 10 generations.

I ask you, Jesus, to send out from me any generational spirits of sexual defilement, illegitimacy, abortion etc and draw back to me

anything of my spirit and soul that is residing in father / mother, or any other family members or ancestors I knew."
(For ancestors who have died, we break the whole soul tie).

"I ask that you cleanse my blood line from all sexual defilement passing down to me, from every ancestor, through these soul ties. Cleanse me with your precious blood and fill me afresh with your love and your Holy Spirit, in Jesus' name, I pray."

This prayer will cover sexual sins generally, such as lust, fornication, etc and discernment should be used when waiting upon the Lord for any word of knowledge for a specific revelation. There may be abortion, illegitimacy, and cases of adoption in the family line. This prayer will also be necessary for those ancestral sins which cannot be found in the records.

How to Pray into Abortion

It is not quite so straightforward as to which chapter to include the subject of abortion in, but in the context of the following discussion, it was felt that this was an appropriate place for this subject.

After prayers of confession, repentance, and healing, telling Satan to leave, Dr Kenneth McAll, (1910- 2001), a Christian psychiatrist, used to hold a Eucharist service for the dead with the taking of bread and wine. A name is given the deceased baby, or God is asked for a suitable name for the baby. The spirit and soul of the aborted foetus can then be committed to Jesus. This is because there would have been no funeral service held originally.[9] He recorded over 600 such cases of healing, including those for miscarriage and stillborn babies.[10] In each case, a family member was asked to construct their family tree beforehand, to aid in understanding what had happened in the past which might have led to the patient's problems, many of which were psychiatric in nature. Another two good case studies are provided of people who developed serious psychiatric and medical conditions as a result of earlier abortions. In each case these were cured after the mothers' made confession and their babies were committed to Jesus Christ during a special Eucharist service.[11]

Dr David Wells supports McAll's work and approach, also advocating a committal service to God of those aborted, miscarried and for stillbirths.[12]

How to Pray into Illegitimacy

Was anyone in your family line conceived or born out of wedlock?

Ask the Holy Spirit to remind you of incidences and family stories of any sexual sins in the past in your direct bloodline. As the Lord shows you, write them down, whether the person who committed them was a parent, grandparent, or great-grandparent, etc.

Where there has been proven or even discerned illegitimacy in the family line, this will need **confessing** to the Lord as sin and the power of that **renouncing** off your own life, the lives of your family and the lives of your descendants, if you have any.

One of my genealogy clients was found to have a distant ancestor who was illegitimate, as proven by a 'bastardy bond' dating from May 1813, requiring the reputed father to pay the sum of £8-2-0, to the churchwardens and overseers of the poor of the parish, for expenses incurred incident to the birth and then maintenance of a male bastard child.

How to Pray into Adoption

Where adoption has taken place, there is a good chance there might have been some form of sexual sin involved as the causative factor. This being the case, then there are various prayers and ministry which will be helpful to set the adoptee or descendent of an adoptee free. Bear in mind that not all cases of adoption are to do with sexual sin.

In dealing with the effects of adoption, it will be important to consider the good and bad influences of soul ties, of prenatal and post-natal rejection issues, the effect of attachment and bonding issues, of developmental problems, inner vows, and identity, both false and true and on developing your true identity in Christ. There may be deliverance issues, where wrong spirits have gained access during vulnerable stages of a young person's life.

Remember, that we are all adopted into God's family and into His body, the church. You can pray something like this, *"Father, I thank you that I am now you son / daughter and am adopted into your family. Help me to know and experience your loving acceptance, to dwell and soak in your presence. Cleanse me from all defilement of spirit and soul. Show me any lies I believe about you or myself and renew my mind to think your thoughts. I Jesus' name I ask this."*

John Loren & Paula Sandford of Elijah House Ministries in the US have relevant chapters on healing early trauma in their book, *Growing Pains*, which is listed at the end of this chapter.[13]

Attachment and Bonding

People who have been adopted usually suffer from attachment and bonding issues. Indeed, anyone who has experienced severe rejection early in life will suffer from this condition. Instead of being able to bond naturally with mum and dad, through their love for their child, when that love has not been forthcoming through neglect, lack of care, rejection, the absence of one or both parents, abuse, emotional or legal divorce, death or adoption, then severe emotional deprivation can occur.

The child will become insecure, afraid, unsure of itself, depressed, angry, demanding of attention and affection, unable to sustain healthy relationships, unable to concentrate at school, a poor achiever, aimless or unfocused and lacking in identity. Even though a child may be adopted into a loving family by new parents who really want the child, which will help heal the wounds of rejection, the damage from the past will still need to be faced and prayed through. Love alone may not overcome these earlier wounds, especially if abuse was suffered. Only God can heal such traumas, but He does do so! Prayer ministry may be necessary after the child has come of age and grown up enough to identify where and why they are struggling and to take responsibility for their healing and growth. Through prayer, Jesus can cause a retrospective bonding to occur with parents and also with both Himself and Father God. Time and patience will be needed.

Inner Vows & Bitter Root Judgements

Sometimes, people who have been wounded make inner vows. These could include never to be hurt again, never to trust again, never to forgive. But these self-protective pronouncements and decisions, rather than helping, actually work to enslave the person who made them in ways they could not foresee. Only later will the person find that the same issues occur again and that they do actually find it hard to trust anyone again. This just leads to loneliness and isolation. When the person meets these sorts of brick walls, the way through them is to forgive and to ask God to help them to trust (wisely) again. They need to renounce the inner vows that they made and ask God to break the power of them over their lives.

Additionally, a relative or ancestor who has brought shame on the family because of their sexual sin, may have caused you or another ancestor much pain, resulting in a bitter judgement being made of the person(s). This 'bitter root judgement' may grow to defile your attitudes and relationships with others who may remind you of that relative. When highlighted, this bitter root too needs repenting of, the relative or ancestor forgiven, and Jesus asked to root it out, and replace with His love and grace.

Identity in Christ

It is important to remember that adoption is not something of concern for only a small number of people. As Christians, we are ALL adopted into God's family and must learn a new identity: our identity in Christ! Indeed, Jesus himself was adopted by his earthly father, Joseph. John 1:12-13 says:

> Yet to all who did receive Him, to those who believed in His name, He gave the right to become children of God – children born not of

natural descent, nor of human decision or a husband's will, but born of God. John 1:12-13, (NIV)

We are loved by God more than we can possibly know. We can discover this through the scriptures and in prayer, receive His love and hear His words of affirmation and delight in us. As we rest in His presence, we can soak in his warmth, approval and love. His *rhema* voice and words, heard in our spirits, back up His written, *logos* words in the Bible. As we dwell on these, they will gradually counteract the lies we have been taught to believe about ourselves. God truly is LOVE! He loves us unconditionally! He is truth and his truth-telling will change us as we believe what He says about us, that we are loved and valued.

Binding and Loosing – Deliverance

To conduct self-deliverance, one should pray something like this: - *"I bind and cut myself off from the ruling spirits of lust, fornication, pornography, idolatry, perversion etc, coming down my family line. I bind and loose the spirit(s) of……* [use your discernment to name them] *from me and tell it / them to go, in the mighty name of Jesus!*

Lord, I command my body and brain chemistry to come into godly alignment. I speak to the neurotransmitters in my brain and call them into normal functioning.

Please fill me now with Your Holy Spirit, to replace and infill all the empty places vacated by these other spirits. Renew my mind and put a right spirit within me, that I may praise and serve You now and forever more. And help me to keep the door to the enemy closed!"

The Blessing of Jesus

"I ask, Lord, that you turn all these curses into blessings, as I rest in Your love and presence and as I find my true identity in You. If I am carrying any emotional wounds caused by this generational sexual sin, I ask, Lord, that You surface them and show me, so that I

can give them to You and express them safely, forgive and be healed of them. I ask this in Jesus' name."

In Summary

Give thanks for your ancestors. **Identify** any sexual sin issues in your family line. If found, **confess** these and the influences they have had in your own life. (Lamentations 5:7). **Repent** on behalf of your ancestors, of these sins, by identifying with and owning them as one's own. Ask for and receive God's **forgiveness**. **Cut** soul ties. Seek **deliverance** ministry and / or conduct self-deliverance for any inherited unclean spirits. Seek the **cleansing blood of Jesus** to wash away any stains.

Ask Jesus to **bless you** and **fill you** afresh with His Holy Spirit. Seek to be **obedient** to His guidance and call on your life.

A Recommendation

As mentioned before, the prayers in this chapter are intended just as openers, to help start you on the journey to freedom. In order to work towards complete freedom, I would recommend working through the material and prayers in the ministry books listed at the end of this chapter. It would also be very worthwhile attending one of the excellent training and ministry courses run by Bethel Sozo, Christian Prayer Ministries, Gilgal House Healing Centre, Ellel Ministries, or Sozo Ministries International, here in the UK. This is not an exhaustive list and the reader may hear of other ministries both in the UK and abroad, which can help in this area.

Further Reading - Select Bibliography

Bali, Karen. *Researching Adoption: an essential guide to tracing birth relatives and ancestors.* Bury: The Family History Partnership, (2015).

Dalbey, Gordon. *Healing the Masculine Soul.* London: Word Publishing, (1988).

Dalbey, Gordon. *Sons of the Father*. Eastbourne: Kingsway Communications Ltd, (2002).

Fabiano, Catherine & Frank. *Healing Your Past, Releasing Your Future*. Bloomington, MN: Chosen Books, (2012).

Hawkey, Ruth. *Freedom from Generational Sin*. Chichester: New Wine Press, (1999).

Horrobin, Peter. *Healing through Deliverance*. (rev). Lancaster: Sovereign World, (2008).

McAll, Kenneth. *Healing the Family Tree*. London: Sheldon Press, (1982).

Paley, Ruth. *My Ancestor was a Bastard*. (rev). London: Society of Genealogists Enterprises Ltd, (2011).

Prince, Derek. *Blessing or Curse: You Can Choose*. (3rd ed). Grand Rapids, MI: Chosen Books Publishing Co., (2006).

Sandford, John Loren & Paula. *Growing Pains*. Lake Mary, FL: Charisma House, (2008).

Sandford, John Loren & Paula. *Letting Go of the Past*. Lake Mary, FL: Charisma House, (2008).

Schipper, Quinn. *Trading Faces. Dissociation: A Common Solution to Avoiding Life's Pain.* (2nd ed). OK, Stillwater: New Forums Press, (2005).

Schlink, Basilea. *Praying Our Way Through Life*. Basingstoke: Lakeland, (1970, 1980, 1984).

Wells, David. *Praying for the Family Tree*. France, Saint-Benoit-du-Sault: Editions Benedictines, (2006). (On behalf of the Generational Healing Trust).

Chapter 3

Genealogical Evidence for Rejection and Abandonment Issues, especially Marital and Family Breakdown

Even if my father and mother abandon me, the Lord will hold me close. Psalm 27:10, (NLT)

He was despised and rejected by men, a man of sorrows and acquainted with grief; and as one from whom men hide their faces he was despised, and we esteemed him not. Isaiah 53:3, (ESV)

What are Rejection and Abandonment Issues?

Rejection and abandonment are painful wounds we all experience from time to time. We can also include betrayal by others in this list. Sometimes we will be the innocent party in rejection. At other times we will experience rejection because we have sinned against another and in order to protect themselves, they have perhaps rightly rejected us, or at least our sinful behaviour. Then there are those occasions when we have done the rejecting, both for good and bad reasons. Oftentimes, we do not realise why we behave the way we do, for our motives can be so deeply buried or complex.

Rejection can be experienced through broken friendships, work relationships, redundancies and sackings, engagements and marriages, infidelity, divorce, estranged children, parents and grandparents, loss of children through adoption, church splits, etc, etc. Abuses of various kinds include emotional, verbal, physical, financial, sexual, and spiritual abuse, all of which disrespect the value of the other person and treat them as less than themselves. Our fundamental self-centredness makes this inevitable. Looking back at the 10 Commandments listed in chapter 1, it is easy to see that the breaking of any of them involves some kind of rejection of God.

Consequences of Rejection and Abandonment – Why are they Harmful?

The consequences of all this rejection can include immense pain, hurt, anger, bitterness, vengefulness, and retaliation, even leading to murder. The rejected person may experience confusion, loss of identity, lack of trust, an inability to form and maintain relationships and friendships, isolation, self-rejection and self-loathing, rejection of others, other psychological dysfunctions, disillusion, depression, loss of motivation, emotional breakdown, false comforts and addictions, such as overeating, smoking or pornography, poor life skills, loss of work and career, financial loss, and a general drifting through life, without aim or purpose or hope. Phew – that's quite a list! Suicide and complete separation from God would be Satan's ultimate goal for this unfortunate person.

Rev. Russ Parker, a former director of the Acorn Christian Healing Foundation in Hampshire, writes in his book, *Healing Wounded History,* about the emotional effects on children because of parental abandonment, divorce, or fathers who are emotionally or physically absent. He writes,

> The tragedy is that such patterns, sown in one generation, are reaped and repeated in the lifestyle of the next and so on down the generations unless they are recognised, owned and offered for healing and transformation. A classic example of family repeated patterns can be found in the family of Abraham in the Bible.[1]

Effects on Attachment and Bonding

People who have been adopted usually suffer from attachment and bonding issues. Indeed, anyone who has experienced severe rejection early in life will suffer from this condition. Instead of being able to bond naturally with mum and dad, through their love for their child, when that love has not been forthcoming, through neglect, lack of care, rejection, the absence of one or both parents, abuse, emotional or legal divorce, death or adoption, then severe emotional deprivation can occur.

The child will become insecure, afraid, unsure of itself, depressed, angry, demanding of attention and affection, unable to sustain healthy relationships, unable to concentrate at school, a poor achiever, aimless or unfocused and lacking in identity.

Rev. Russ Parker gives a graphic personal testimony about the effects of emotional abandonment in his own family:

> ...let me share something of my own journey of self-exploration. As a genealogist I have searched my own family tree in some detail. One of the noticeable patterns I have located within the Parker family story is that for at least five generations fathers hardly spoke to or had real dialogue with intimacy with their sons.
>
> ...As I researched my 'fathers' I discovered they were not particularly villainous or unskilled in the art of communication; they were all in their own way popular with their friends and successful in their careers. However, for reasons of history, there was a breakdown of communication within one generation which seems to have been carried down through succeeding generations. Perhaps it is an oversimplification to say that we are usually unable to give to others what we have not received ourselves. Be that as it may, I can nonetheless trace this breakdown in intimacy with sons through at least five fathers. In my own circumstance, I tried to get closer to my father – this was a result of my becoming a Christian and the inspiration I received from the father / son relationship between Jesus and his heavenly Father. My attempt failed. Yet my father was not hostile or even opposed to my attempts; he simply did not seem to know how to respond. I loved him and was frustrated by him.[2]

Russ Parker then goes on to explain how different things triggered his inner need to be fathered and how he found healing. More of his story later.

Inner Vows

Sometimes, people who have been rejected make inner vows. These could include never to be hurt again, never to trust again, never to forgive, never to love. But these self-protective pronouncements and decisions, rather than helping, actually work to imprison the person who made them in ways they could not foresee. Invisible bars lock the person inside themselves. Only later will the person find that the same issues recur and that they find it hard to trust anyone again. This just leads to loneliness and isolation.

Adoption

Where adoption has taken place, there will be roots of experienced rejection from the birth family. Insecurity will be present as the adoptee tries to fit in to the new family, having already gone through at least one foster family before being permanently adopted. Fear may be present, possibly hidden anger too. If the birth family were very dysfunctional, the child may have experienced abuse, which could have been emotional, verbal, physical, sexual, spiritual, or occult in nature. This can result in massive pain, confusion and hurt, including dissociation and fragmentation of the soul and / or human spirit.

However, God is in ultimate control and will do all He can to rescue and send help for this unfortunate person. Jesus wants to save him or her and even if this person is already a struggling Christian, He will guide the seeker to avenues of help. These would include prayer and listening to God, comfort from friends, meals, walks, chats, hugs, time with pets, fellowship with other Christians (not necessarily at church), worship music, pastoral input and support, prayerful reading of Christian healing books, perhaps medication and either lay or professional counselling or ministry.

Even when we have worked through a whole host of forgiveness prayers, repentance and sought counsel and ministry, we may still feel bewildered and stuck in alternating cycles of acceptance followed by rejection from others. This can be the moment when through one way or another, God reveals that we have inherited a tendency to either be rejected and/or reject others. So, we start to think about what our siblings, parents and grandparents went through. Can we see links, connections and patterns forming between the generations? So, we pray into these links, asking God to sever them (as we shall see below). But how far back do they go and do we really know everything there is to know in our immediate family? Sin or repeated rejection by others are such that they produce guilt and shame, which causes people to hide the truth about themselves from each other, much as Adam and Eve tried to hide from God in the garden of Eden. But God is not deceived and out of His love for us, wants to set us free from our sins and sense of shame. To do this, He must bring it into the light through acknowledgement, confession, and repentance, leading to forgiveness, cleansing and freedom. This is achieved both directly with the Lord, but also in confession with select others.

> Therefore, confess your sins to each other and pray for each other so that you may be healed. The prayer of a righteous person is powerful and effective.   James 5:16, (NIV)

We may through reflection, prayer and questioning, discover what generational sins and iniquities lie in our heritage and therefore be able to process them. However, there may be other and more distant sins affecting us that can only be uncovered by diligent research into the genealogical records.

Evidence for Generational Rejection and Abandonment

Records of illegitimacy, adoption, divorce, and multiple marriages and also wills, can give the clearest indication of where there has been rejection and abandonment in the family line.

Records of Illegitimacy

Records of illegitimacy have already been discussed in chapter 2 on sexual sin, so it is not necessary to repeat the same information all over again. Just turn back a chapter and read it again. Suffice it to say that these records can be found amongst the **GRO records** of birth and marriage, searchable online at www.freebmd.org.uk, www.ancestry.co.uk and www.findmypast.co.uk. Certificates can be ordered from: www.gov.uk/order-copy-birth-death-marriage-certificate. The GRO records cover the years from **1837 up to the present**. For records **prior to 1837**, these can also be viewed online at Ancestry.co.uk and FindMyPast.co.uk. A trip to a County Record Office (CRO) will help to locate the Church of England **parish registers** or the registers of other denominations. The originals are normally now kept in local CROs, though, if you decide to make a trip to one, you would be viewing a microfiche or printed copy. Many CRO's also have something called or equivalent to an 'Online Parish Clerk,' where the parish registers have been digitised and can be viewed from the comfort of your own home. If the child is illegitimate, then an infant or child baptism will only have the mother's name recorded in the register, not the father's.

Records of Adoption

As mentioned in chapter 2 on sexual sin issues, records of adoption, which came into law in **1927**, can also help towards revealing the names of birth parents and if there had been illegitimacy in the family. It has been possible for adoptees in the UK to view their birth records since 1975. Those adopted before 11th November 1975, are required to see an adoption counsellor before being given the information on how to apply to see their birth records. However, this will only include the person's original name, their mother's name, and the registration district they were born in. Online information and records can be viewed at: www.gov.uk/adoption-records. Karen Bali's book, *Researching Adoption: An essential guide to tracing birth relatives and ancestors*, goes into more detail about this process.[3] The Salvation Army also has information on adoption and fostering and this is kept at **The Salvation Army Social Services Headquarters**, Newington Causeway, London, SE1 6BU. See: www.salvationarmy.org.uk/contact-us. This information (if not restricted) can be supplied to relatives.

Divorce, Martial Separation and Multiple Marriages

As was also discussed in chapter 2 about sexual sin, evidence of divorce, marital separation or multiple marriages will be a strong

REJECTION AND ABANDONMENT ISSUES

indication of issues of rejection and abandonment in the family line. Broken marriages and divorce affect millions of people, not least the children, with immense suffering caused all round. The evidence for such pain can be deduced from the existence of multiple birth, marriage and death certificates, parish registers or wills. A careful scrutiny of dates of marriage and subsequent births will be needed to further confirm this.

A research guide on divorce records may be found at the National Archives, via their website link: www.nationalarchives.gov.uk/help-with-your-research/research-guides/divorce/. Ancestry.co.uk also have records of divorce.

Prior to 1858, divorces were extremely rare and were tried by ecclesiastical courts, which could grant a **separation from bed and board** (*a mensa et thoro*) on grounds of adultery or life-threatening cruelty. Neither party was allowed to marry again. If the marriage had never been valid in the first place, then a **decree of nullity** could be granted. A further option was for a legal separation to be made, called an **annulment.** This protected the wife's rights and the children's legitimacy. Neither party could marry again until the death of one of them. There are further intricacies to these rules which won't be gone into here.

In very rare cases, a civil divorce could be granted by special Act of Parliament to the very wealthy, who might well have been pursuing a simultaneous action through the ecclesiastical courts. Husbands had to prove a wife's adultery. If successful, the parties were free to marry again. These early divorce records are held in the Parliamentary Archives (PA). (See: www.parliament.uk/business/publications/parliamentary-archives/)

1858 is a key date in divorce law, for it was then that a civil divorce could be obtain from the new Civil Court for Divorce and Matrimonial Causes. This in turn became the Probate, Divorce and Admiralty division of the Supreme Court of Judicature, having merged with other legal departments in 1873. Now, as well as husbands having to prove a wife's adultery, wives were allowed to bring a petition, but they would have to prove their husband's cruelty in addition to infidelity.

Divorce became more accessible during the 1920s with the provision of legal aid and local facilities to hear petitions.

In 1937, in addition to the pre-existing grounds of adultery and cruelty, divorce was extended to include desertion by one party for 3 years, refusal to consummate the marriage and insanity at the time of the marriage.

The **Principal Registry of the Family Division** was created in 1970 to deal with divorce cases, and it keeps records of successful petitions. There are indexed registers of *decrees nisi* and *decrees absolute* granted in England and Wales since 1858. Only members of staff can search these on receipt of an application and payment. (See: www.gov.uk/copy-decree-absolute-final-order). They are not open to the public.

www.findmypast.co.uk has digitised records from the microfilmed TNA records of indexes to successful and unsuccessful divorce petitions dating from 1858 – 1903. www.ancestry.co.uk has images and indexes to the divorce actions between 1858 – 1911. On http://discovery.nationalarchives.gov.uk/, the discovery catalogue for TNA, may be found divorce actions dealt with between 1858 – 1937. Most divorce records after 1938 have been destroyed, unfortunately. However, there are a few Principal Registry cases dated 1938 – 1959, which have survived and been indexed.

Separation and Maintenance Orders

From 1878, wives who had been seriously assaulted by their husbands, could apply for a separation and maintenance order through their local magistrate's court. After 1886, the local magistrates' court could order husbands who had deserted their wives to pay weekly maintenance. These records are now generally held in CROs.

To help in understanding the history of divorce law, here is a table of key dates: -

REJECTION AND ABANDONMENT ISSUES

Prior to 1858   Ecclesiastical Courts granted separation from bed and board (*a mensa et thoro*). Civil divorce also available by Act of Parliament

1858   Civil Court for Divorce and Matrimonial Causes

1873   Probate, Divorce and Admiralty Division of the Supreme Court of Judicature

1920s   Provision of legal aid & local provision

1937   Grounds for divorce widened

1970   Principal Registry of the Family Division of the Supreme Court

Newspapers are also a good source of information about separation and divorce. These can be found in both local and national papers. *The Times* online index has reports of private divorce bills in Parliament prior to 1858 and cases heard in the civil courts from 1858 onwards. (See: www.gale.com/intl/c/the-times-digital-archive).

Wills

We all hope to be included as beneficiaries in our parents' or relatives' wills, but for those who have fallen out with their families, there is the fear of being cut out of a will or not inheriting much. That assumes our relatives made a will. As of 2018, as many as 55% of adults in the UK had not made a will.[4] Who benefits from a will or who doesn't is a cause of great stress in families and potentially, of further fall-outs. Historically, this is the case too. For the researcher looking for evidence of generational rejection in the family line, wills can be very revealing.

Locating a will can be complicated. However, in simple terms, this is the process. To find a will, start by determining the approximate date and place of death and /or probate. A grant of probate needs to be made by a court, before for a person can deal with the deceased's estate. Nowadays, this usually occurs about 6 months after the date of death, though in the past, most grants of probate were made more quickly. If a person does not have a will, then there will be an 'administration' or 'Admon.' Wills divide between those made before 1858 and those made after 1858.

Wills made after 1858

For probate records made in England and Wales, **after 1858**, the quickest way is to look online at: www.gov.uk/search-will-probate. An application for a copy of a will can be made online or by post, using the address provided in the website link. Form PA1S needs to be downloaded, filled in and posted to:

The Postal Copies and Searches Department,
District Probate Registry,
York House,
31 York Place,
Leeds, LS1 2BA

Wills made before 1858

For English and Welsh grants of probate, wills and administrations made **before 1858**, The National Archives (TNA), produces a good online guide for research at: www.nationalarchives.gov.uk/help-with-your-research/research-guides/wills-or-administrations-before-1858/. Before 1858, it was ecclesiastical probate courts which proved wills and administrations and there were more than 300 of them! These divided into two main provinces: The Prerogative Court of Canterbury (PCC) for southern England and the Prerogative Court of York (PCY), for northern England, though wills for any part of England or Wales can sometimes be found in either court's jurisdiction.

The two provinces were divided into a number of dioceses, each with their own bishop's consistory or episcopal courts, which were further divided into archdeaconry courts and then further still into rural deaneries with their courts. Finally, the smallest courts were called 'peculiars.'

Wills in the South of England

For the **south of England**, there are indexes to all the PCC wills and admons held at The National Archives (TNA) covering the years 1384-1858. (See: https://discovery.nationalarchives.gov.uk/) The British Record Society (BRS) has published most of the court indexes in their Index Library series and these indexes are being digitised through The National Wills Index at www.britishorigins.com. Copies of the published volumes of indexes of the BRS are held by the Society of Genealogists (SoG), TNA and County Record Offices (CROs). Failing that, it is necessary the check the estate duty indexes.

Mark Herber [5] says that the first task is to find out which CRO holds records of wills for the area in which the deceased lived. This can be deduced from old county maps, which will give an indication as to the main county town and therefore the location of the relevant CRO. Check online as well, though. The CRO will have digitised or published indexes for the appropriate ecclesiastical court and the archive staff will help to obtain a reference to the right document. Jeremy Gibson and Stuart Raymond have written a useful guide to locating wills.[6]

Wills in the North of England

For the **north of England**, as mentioned, wills prior to 1858 were under the jurisdiction of the Prerogative Court of York (PCY). The province is divided in a similar manner to the PCC and the process for locating a grant of probate and a will is much the same. This area covers the dioceses of York, Durham and Sodor, Carlisle, Chester and Man. The corresponding counties included Northumberland, Co. Durham, Westmorland, Cumberland, Yorkshire, Lancashire, Cheshire and Nottinghamshire. The records are now held at the:

Borthwick Institute for Archives,
University of York,
University Road,
Heslington,
York,
YO10 5DD

See: www.york.ac.uk/borthwick/ and their online catalogue: https://borthcat.york.ac.uk/.
Some copies of wills survive from 1389, though many are missing, but there are published printed indexes up to 1688. There is an almost complete run of registered wills from 1660 up to 1858. There is also an online index through the National Wills Index at www.britishorigins.com.

Wills in Scotland and Ireland (North and Republic)

There is a different process for Scotland and Northern Ireland. **For Scotland**, the website address to follow up on a will is: www.nrscotland.gov.uk/research/guides/wills-and-testaments.
They divide between the years 1514-1925 and 1926-1999. Up to 1925, wills may be located via:
www.scotlandspeople.gov.uk/guides/wills-and-testaments.

For Northern Ireland, the website address is: www.nidirect.gov.uk/information-and-services/search-archives-online/will-calendars. For the **Republic of Ireland**, the following website should be used: www.nationalarchives.ie/.

How to Pray into Generational Rejection and Abandonment Issues

As per other issues, there are various ways we can pray into generational rejection and abandonment and from the discoveries made in the records. To start off, I would recommend praying for protection for yourself and your loved ones and for Jesus to lead and guide you in these prayers. Then pray the 'Lordship Prayer.'

Lordship Prayer

"Dear Lord Jesus, I realise my need of You and repent of living my life my own way. I wholeheartedly accept You now as my Saviour, my Redeemer, my Lord, and my Deliverer.

I invite You now to be the Lord of every part and moment of my life, from the time of my conception, right up until now:

Lord of my body, my physical health and behaviour.

Lord of my mind and all my attitudes and mental health.

Lord of all my emotions and all my reactions.

Lord of my spirit and my worship of You.

Lord of my family and all my relationships.

Lord of my sexuality and its expression.

Lord of my will and all my hopes, ambitions, decisions, and plans.

Lord of all my work and service for You.

Lord of all my finances.

Lord of all my needs and possessions.

Lord of the manner and time of my death."

Declaration

"Thank you, Jesus, for shedding Your blood and dying on the cross, for the forgiveness of my sins, my ancestors' sins, and my descendants' sins. You died and rose again that I might be set free to love and to serve You, in newness of life.

While I thank you, Lord, for my ancestors, especially my father and mother who brought me into this world and whom I honour, I do not stand in agreement with them on sinful matters. In these cases, in your presence, Lord, I **confess** *and* **repent** *on behalf of all my parents,' grandparents' and forefathers' rejection and hurting* of one another, including any abandonment that occurred. I confess that these are sins against you, which I **renounce** off my life and off the life of my family, which have resulted in curses of rejection running through the family line, down to me. Thank you for becoming a curse for me on the cross, so that I might go free. You knew the pain of rejection intimately, especially upon the cross when you experienced the loss of the presence of your Father's love and abandonment by your disciples.

I ask that You would **forgive** my ancestors' unloving behaviour and rejection of one another, as I also forgive them. I claim Your **blood cleansing** from all the effects of generational rejection and abandonment in my life. Thank you that you love and accept me just as I am and love me enough to change my heart and help me change my behaviour. Please fill me afresh with your love and to experience your acceptance. Help me to dwell in your presence and soak in your love. Help me to bond and attach to you. Show me how You truly see and value me and cleanse me from the lies I have believed about myself. In Jesus' name, I pray."

Breaking of Soul Ties for Rejection and Abandonment

"In the name of Jesus, I place the cross and blood of Jesus between myself and each of my family members. I break all the ungodly body, soul, and spirit ties with:
People who have rejected or abandoned me.
With my parents, if they rejected or abandoned me.
Between myself and other family members, (name them), who may have been affected by generational abandonment and rejection.
With my grandparents.
(For ancestors who have died, we break the whole soul tie).
With my great-grandparents and,
with my great-great-grandparents, (name any relevant ones), going back 4 generations.

I ask that you cleanse me from all the effects of rejection and abandonment passing down to me, from every ancestor, through these soul ties."

This prayer will cover the issues mentioned and discernment should be used when waiting upon the Lord for any word of knowledge for a specific revelation. This will be necessary for those ancestral sins which cannot be found in the records.

Going back to Rev. Russ Parker's story of his journey to find healing from wounds of emotional abandonment, he writes:

> The way to healing, I found, was not to demonise my father and the fathers before him, but to own his story as my story and, in confessing it to God, offer it to him for healing. Consequently, the prayer I prayed was 'We (Parkers) are a family where fathers do not speak to their sons. Forgive us, heavenly Father, and help us to change and learn how to love our sons and not repeat the patterns of our family.' I am happy to report that my son and I have a very good relationship where touch and love are commonplace.[7]

How to Pray into Rejection Caused by Illegitimacy

Where there has been proven or even discerned illegitimacy in the family line, this will need **confessing** to the Lord as sin and the power of that **renouncing** off your own life, the lives of your family and the lives of your descendants, if you have any.

Illegitimacy can cause embarrassment, shame, denial, and over-compensation for perceived deficiencies, as well as a sense of rejection by the birth parent(s). It is worth remembering, that Jesus could have been considered illegitimate, for his earthly father Joseph never lay with his mother, Mary before he was born. That was Joseph's fear and why he considered breaking off his marriage pledge to Mary. Under Jewish law, he would have been entitled to do that. However, he did not want to bring disgrace upon Mary and the Holy Spirit urged him not to fear, but to marry Mary. (Matt 1:18-25, Luke 1:26-38, 2:4-5)

Forgiveness towards the parents for their sexual sin and towards the father for possibly abandoning the mother, will be necessary. Sometimes, young children can blame themselves for being rejected or abandoned by their parents when actually, the fault lies with the parents, not the child. The child is not to blame. God can show the adult child the truth of what happened. Receiving God's affirmation, acceptance, and healing for this will gradually resolve the emotional scaring.

How to Pray into Adoption

There are various prayers and ministry which will be helpful to set the adoptee or descendent of an adoptee free.

In dealing with the effects of adoption, it will be important to consider the good and bad influences of soul ties, of prenatal and post-natal rejection issues, the effect of attachment and bonding issues, of developmental problems, inner vows, and identity, both false and true and on developing your true identity in Christ. There may be deliverance issues, where wrong spirits have gained access during vulnerable stages of a young person's life.

Remember, that we are all adopted into God's family and into His body, the church. You can pray something like this, *"Father, I thank you that I am now you son / daughter and am adopted into your family. Help me to know and experience your love and acceptance, to dwell and soak in your presence. Cleanse me from all defilement of spirit and soul. Show me any lies I believe about you or myself and renew my mind to think your thoughts. In Jesus' name I ask this."*

John Loren & Paula Sandford of Elijah House Ministries in the US have relevant chapters on healing early trauma in their book, *Growing Pains*, which is listed at the end of this chapter.

How to Pray into Generational Divorce and Multiple Marriages

As with other issues involving rejection, there will be a foundational need to (sometimes continually) forgive those who hurt you through divorce. Maybe you can't. In that case, ask God to help you be willing to forgive and then to be able to do so. He understands your pain and will help you. He knows the pain can run deep and will take time, even much time to process. Ask Him to make up for 'the years the locusts have eaten,' as the Bible saying goes. (Joel 2:25).

It will be important to repent of judging your parents, if it was them who divorced. Maybe it was your grandparents or great-grandparents? Ask God to forgive them too. You will need to confess the sins of rejection and abandonment in your family line and forgive your ancestors for rejecting each other. Ask God to forgive you for judging them. You may have made inner vows not to love or be like them. These will need renouncing and breaking. In the next section, you will see how to. Then ask Jesus to show you your parents, grandparents or whoever it was, as He understands them. Sometimes it is easier to forgive someone when God shows you what was going on in their lives that made them behave the way they did. You may see patterns of behaviour that you have inherited. In this case, unhealthy generational soul ties will have been formed, which need breaking too. There may be deliverance issues which need appropriate prayer. All of these are covered in this chapter.

Breaking Inner Vows & Bitter Root Judgements

When a person meets an inner psychological brick wall of being unable to form godly friendships and relationships because of mistrust caused by inner vows, the way through them is to forgive and to ask God to help you to trust (wisely) again. You will need to renounce any inner vows that you made and ask God to break the power of them over your life.

Additionally, a relative who has rejected or abandoned you, may have caused you or an ancestor much pain, resulting in a bitter judgement being made of the person(s). This 'bitter root judgement' may grow to defile your attitudes and relationships with others (including your children), who may remind you of that relative. When highlighted, this bitter root too needs repenting of, the relative or ancestor forgiven, and Jesus asked to root it out and replace with His love and grace.

Identity in Christ

It is important to remember that adoption is not something of concern for only a small number of people. As Christians, we are ALL adopted into God's family and must learn a new identity: our identity in Christ! John 1:12-13 says this clearly:

> Yet to all who did receive Him, to those who believed in His name, He gave the right to become children of God – children born not of natural descent, nor of human decision or a husband's will, but born of God.   John 1:12-13, (NIV)

Even Jesus was adopted! – because of Joseph's willingness to be his human father. We are loved by God more than we can possibly know. We can discover this through the scriptures and in prayer, receive His love and hear His words of affirmation and delight in us. As we rest in His presence, we can soak in his warmth, approval, and love. His *rhema* voice and words, heard in our spirits, back up His written, *logos* words in the Bible. As we dwell on these, they will gradually counteract the lies we have been taught to believe about ourselves. God truly is LOVE! He loves us unconditionally! He is truth and his truth-telling will change us as we believe what He says about us, that we are loved and valued. We can also experience this through the love of others.

Establishing Attachment and Bonding

Even though a child may be adopted into a loving family, by new parents who really want the child which will help heal the wounds of rejection, the damage from the past will still need to be faced and prayed through. Love alone may not overcome these earlier wounds, especially if abuse was suffered. Only God can heal such traumas, but He does do so! Prayer ministry may be necessary after the child has come of age and grown up enough to identify where and why they are struggling and to take responsibility for their healing and growth. Through prayer, Jesus can cause attachment and bonding to occur, both retrospectively in the spirit with parents, and with Himself and Father God. Time and patience will be needed for this.

Binding and Loosing – Deliverance

Once all the above prayers have been said and worked through, it is then time to conduct self-deliverance from any evil spirits. Pray something like this: - *"I put the cross and blood of Jesus between myself and... I bind and cut myself off from the ruling spirits of rejection, abandonment, isolation, insecurity, fear, anger, unloving spirits, divorce etc, coming down my family line. I bind and loose the spirit(s) of……. [use your discernment to name them] from me and tell it / them to go, in the mighty name of Jesus!*

Please fill me now with Your Holy Spirit, to replace and infill all the empty places vacated by these other spirits. Renew my mind and put a right spirit within me, that I may praise and serve You now and forever more."

Deliverance ministry can also be sought from suitably trained lay or ordained ministers.

The Blessing of Jesus

"I ask, Lord, that you turn all these curses into blessings, as I rest in Your love and presence and as I find my true identity in You. If I am carrying any further emotional wounds caused by this generational rejection, I ask, Lord, that You surface them and show me, so that I can give them to You and express them safely, forgive and be healed of them. I ask this in Jesus' name."

In Summary

Give thanks for your ancestors. **Identify** any issues in your family line, connected with rejection or abandonment, which may have led to familial sins. If found, **confess** these and the influences they have had in your own life. (Lamentations 5:7). **Repent**, where needed, of these sins in the family line, by identifying with and owning them as one's own. Ask for and receive God's **forgiveness**. **Cut** soul ties. Seek **deliverance** ministry and / or conduct self-deliverance for any inherited spirits of rejection or abandonment. Seek the **cleansing blood of Jesus** to wash away any stains.

Ask Jesus to **bless you** and **fill you** afresh with His Holy Spirit. Seek to be **obedient** to His guidance and call on your life.

A Recommendation

As mentioned before, the prayers in this chapter are intended just as openers, to help start you on the journey to freedom. In order to work towards complete freedom, I would recommend working through the material and prayers in the ministry books listed at the end of this chapter. It would also be very worthwhile attending one of the excellent training and ministry courses run by Bethel Sozo, Christian Prayer Ministries, Gilgal House Healing Centre, Ellel Ministries, or Sozo Ministries International, here in the UK. This is not an exhaustive list and the reader may hear of other ministries both in the UK and abroad, which can help in this area.

Further Reading - Select Bibliography

Bali, Karen. *Researching Adoption: an essential guide to tracing birth relatives and ancestors.* Bury: The Family History Partnership, (2015).

Dalbey, Gordon. *Healing the Masculine Soul.* London: Word Publishing, (1988).

Dalbey, Gordon. *Sons of the Father.* Eastbourne: Kingsway Communications Ltd, (2002).

Fabiano, Catherine & Frank. *Healing Your Past, Releasing Your Future.* Bloomington, MN: Chosen Books, (2012).

Gibson, Jeremy & Raymond, Stuart. *Probate Jurisdictions: where to look for wills.* 6th ed. Bury: The Family History Partnership, (2016).

Hawkey, Ruth. *Freedom from Generational Sin.* Chichester: New Wine Press, (1999).

Herber, Mark. *Ancestral Trails*. (2nd ed.) (Rev). Stroud: Sutton Publishing, (2005).

Horrobin, Peter. *Healing through Deliverance*. (rev). Lancaster: Sovereign World, (2008).

Parker, Russ. *Healing Wounded History*. London: Darton, Longman & Todd Ltd, (2001).

Prince, Derek. *Blessing or Curse: You Can Choose*. (3rd ed). Grand Rapids, MI: Chosen Books Publishing Co., (2006).

Sandford, John Loren & Paula. *Growing Pains*. Lake Mary, FL: Charisma House, (2008).

Sandford, John Loren & Paula. *Letting Go of the Past*. Lake Mary, FL: Charisma House, (2008).

Chapter 4

Genealogical Evidence for Educational Background

Train up a child in the way he should go; even when he is old, he will not depart from it.   Proverbs 22:6, (ESV)

Fathers, do not provoke your children to anger, but bring them up in the discipline and instruction of the Lord.   Ephesians 6:4, (ESV)

The poem, *This Be the Verse*, by the poet, Philip Larkin (1922 – 1985), which I was required to read for A-Level English when aged 17, left me faintly disgusted at its bad language, negativity, and cynicism. However, at 60, even though I still disapprove of the bad language used, the poem's sentiments come across tragically, as partly true to life and relevant to the theme of this book. It seems to best fit in this chapter, whose focus is on education. I have starred the offending words: -

> *They f**k you up, your mum and dad.*
>   *They may not mean to, but they do.*
> *They fill you with the faults they had*
>   *And add some extra, just for you.*
>
> *But they were f**ked up in their turn*
>   *By fools in old-style hats and coats,*
> *Who half the time were soppy-stern*
>   *And half at one another's throats.*
>
> *Man hands on misery to man.*
>   *It deepens like a coastal shelf.*
> *Get out as early as you can,*
>   *And don't have any kids yourself.* [1]

Records of Education

In chapter 7, I will outline in brief the records available for the types of gentry and aristocratic education which existed. In this chapter, I will deal more fully with the subject of education available for all classes of people which can be found in surviving records.

What Generational Sins Related to Education Could be Operating in our Lives?

Within the educational world, cheating, plagiarism, stealing, truancy, bullying, cruelty, intimidation, and injustice are just some of the obvious sins that could have been committed by our ancestors or against them. But have you thought of such things as indoctrination using anti-Christian educational materials, including Darwinism, humanism, social-Darwinism, Marxism, racial prejudice, and colonialism promoting the idea that the British race was somehow superior to other races? Then there might have been deism, or insufficient, neglectful, and biased religious instruction. Where the teaching of the 10 Commandments was neglected, either by family, schooling, or church, this will have had a consequence on the thinking and behaviour of those students thus deprived. In terms of this chapter on education, the 1st Commandment (having no other Gods before me), and 5th (honour your father and mother), seem particularly relevant.

Education for the Better Off

For those who had a more privileged education, there will probably have been an emphasis on the Classics following the renaissance between the 14th and 17th centuries, where the teaching of Latin or Greek was accompanied by an admiration of and identification with the cultures and philosophies of ancient Greece and Rome. Despite having classes in 'divinity' and religious instruction (from a Church of England perspective at this time), this would have inculcated in them a mixing or syncretism with the teachings of pagan Greece and Rome. The 18th century particularly, (during the 'age of enlightenment'), was marked by intellectual questioning, belief in reason, individualism, liberalism, and the growth in human-centred philosophies. Against this backdrop, young men were encouraged to round off their education by going on the 'grand tour' of Europe, where they could see for themselves the wonders of, amongst other places, the ruins of ancient Rome and Athens. Byron, Keats and Shelley were three such young men who rejected Christianity and partook of this experience.

Meanwhile, girls from better off families, if not by private tutor, were often educated in private boarding schools, being taught the Classics, foreign languages, (especially French), music, dancing, and homemaking. Such schools started to appear in the early 17th century and continue to this day. (Prior to the Reformation, girls were taught in the nunneries). Records of these schools will be found in CROs or in the schools themselves.

As inheritors of the expanding British Empire, this type of classical education served as an example to young men and the future leaders of the Empire, how empire 'was done' in the past and how it should be done in the future. It could produce an ungodly mindset of elitism, arrogance, snobbery, brutality, callousness, conquest, and greed for gain (for example in the exploitation of the mineral wealth in colonial territories).

However, in the wisdom of God, as in the days of the Roman Empire, He used the British Empire as a convenient vehicle for missionaries to go all over the world, spreading the good news to previously unreached people groups. For instance, it was largely British Christian influence in mid-to-late 19th century India which led to the outlawing of *suttee*, the practice of widows sacrificing themselves on their deceased husband's funeral pyres.[2] Indeed, as empires go, the British one was known as the most benign of them all. I remember a previous Indian employer under whom I worked in London, counteracting another employee, who had been criticising the British Empire. My boss said that there were good things that the British had brought to India, such as education, hospitals, the railways, administration, and the law.

Examples of a classical education outworked in stone can be seen in the many historic country houses around Britain which are open to the public. Chatsworth House in Derbyshire is one such place. In them, you will usually see architecture in the neo-classical form and artwork, be it paintings, sculptures or furniture having classical themes, rather than or including Christian themes. Christ was not an imperialist! His kingdom is not of this world, though, it must be said that He does wish us to extend His kingdom rule of love, grace and truth on this earth.

> 'Not by might, nor by power, but by my spirit,' saith the Lord of hosts.   Zechariah 4:6b, (KJV)

Records of Grammar and Public Schools

The library of the Society of Genealogists (SoG) in London has a very good collection of grammar and public-school histories and registers, together with an index to them. This can be searched using the online library catalogue. (See: www.sog.org.uk/our-collections/library-catalogue/). Ancestry has a number of such records listed as well. As mentioned, records of girls' boarding schools can be found in CROs and the schools themselves.

Education in the 17th Century

After the Dissolution of the Monasteries between 1536-41 and the ongoing Reformation, when Roman Catholicism was suppressed, only Reformed, Church of England teaching was officially permitted. Dissenting groups such as English Separatists / Independents / Congregationalists, Presbyterians, Puritans and Baptists appeared in the early 1600s, with Quakers following in the mid-17th century.

However, after the Restoration of the Monarchy in 1660, when Charles II (Charles I's son), was welcomed back as King, these dissenting, non-conformist groups were severely persecuted. This was in retaliation for their part in the Civil War against the Crown (1642-51), and the Interregnum (1649-60), led by the religiously Independent Oliver Cromwell, who ordered the execution of Charles I. During this period, the Church of England, which supported the King, had been disempowered. A number of these dissenting groups established their own schools from 1665 onwards because they were barred from teaching in public or private schools by the Five Mile Act of 1665. These schools were illegal and taught only practical subjects, not religion or philosophy.

However, the Toleration Act of 1689 allowed nonconformists (excluding Roman Catholics) to legally establish their own schools. Roman Catholics still had either to be educated at a protestant-run school or at a seminary on the Continent until 1829. Suppression of Roman Catholic teaching was finally abolished with the passing of the Catholic Relief Act of 1829, allowing for the formation of RC schools.

Dame Schools were very much a feature of 17th and 18th century education, though originated in the 16th and continued into the mid-19th century.[3] For a small fee, they provided a basic education to young children in reading, writing and arithmetic and additionally for girls, sewing and knitting. People like Charles Dickens, John Keats and William Wordsworth all attended such schools. Most Dame School records are to be found in CROs.

Records of Dissenting Schools

There is a large collection of nonconformist school records at TNA in the Dr William's Library Collection. Most records of dissenting schools are to be found in the collections of each denomination's central archive or historical society.

Education for the Poor

Charity Schools started to appear in the late-17th Century in poorer urban areas, providing free education for the 'deserving poor'. The idea was to help children out of poverty and give them a better start in life. The SPCK (Society for the Promotion of Christian Knowledge), an Anglican body founded in 1698, set up a great many of these schools. The TNA Discovery website will help locate the records of other Charity schools.
See: https://discovery.nationalarchives.gov.uk/

EDUCATIONAL BACKGROUND

Education in the 18th Century

SPCK run Charity Schools were mainly founded in the 1700's and their surviving records date from 1704 onwards, being located partly in Cambridge University library.[4] These can be searched online at: www.lib.cam.ac.uk/search-and-find. Other places to look are CROs.

In Wales, **Circulating Schools** became very popular during the mid to late 1700s. They taught pupils to read the scriptures in Welsh. The National Library of Wales in Aberystwyth holds records of these. See: www.library.wales/.

Workhouses also contained schools for the education of poor workhouse children. They began in 1723 after the implementation of the General Workhouse Act that year. Children were thus prepared for future apprenticeships which would take the financial burden of looking after them off the parish. Records of these schools can be found in CROs.

A late 18th Century initiative was the foundation of **Sunday Schools,** which became a national phenomenon in 1780 under the leadership of Robert Raikes. These continued well into the 20th century. Some Sunday School records are held in CROs.

Education in the 19th Century

At the other end of the social scale to the grammar and public schools, there was little or no formal mass education for the poor until the early 19th century. At this time, some **factory schools** were set up, following an Act of 1802 which required that free part-time education be provided for both male and female apprentices.

A largely Georgian and Victorian venture were **Ragged Schools**, first set up in 1810 in South London by Thomas Cranfield, to provide free education for poor destitute children. They gained the support of Lord Shaftesbury, who helped in the formation of the Ragged School union in 1844. Records of these schools can be found in CROs and in London Metropolitan Archives (LMA). See:www.cityoflondon.gov.uk/things-to-do/history-and-heritage/london-metropolitan-archives.

The Church of England was responsible for founding **National Schools**, providing elementary education for the poor in 19th century England and Wales.[5] They became increasingly evangelical in focus. Their records can be found in CROs and at the Church of England Record Centre, located at: 15 Galleywall Road, London, SE16 3PB.

A number of **Jewish schools** operated in the 1800s, though some had been founded in the latter part of the 17th century. Jewish school records can be viewed on the JewishGen website at: www.jewishgen.org/databases/uk/schools.htm,[6] on the Family Search website at: www.familysearch.org/en/wiki/England_Jewish_Records,[7] at TNA, and on the Manchester City Council website.[8] They are also housed in some CROs.

Military Schools

Stradling the 18th, 19th and 20th centuries are **military schools** for the sons and daughters of serving Army and Royal Navy (RN) personnel and military academies for young officer recruits. For the Army, were the Royal Military Academy, founded at Woolwich in 1741, and the Royal Military College at Sandhurst, founded in 1812. Individual regiments also had their own schools. For the Royal Navy, there was the Naval Academy in Portsmouth, founded in 1733, which from 1806, was called the Royal Naval College. In 1873, this moved to Greenwich. In 1830, the Royal Naval School was founded to provide an education for the sons of serving RN and Royal Marine (RM) officers. Ten years later, in 1840, this was followed by provision for daughters in the Royal Naval Female School.

Records for such schools may be found at TNA and other places. The Royal Military Academy records are held in the Sandhurst Archives and are subject to a 75-year closure period. See: www.sandhurstcollection.co.uk/. Royal Naval College records dating from 1733 to 1872 are located at the National Museum of the Royal Navy (NMRN), based in Portsmouth.

EDUCATIONAL BACKGROUND

See: www.nmrn.org.uk/collections.[9] For records dated 1873 – 1977, please search TNA.

Compulsory Education

The 1870 Elementary Education Act was passed to introduce compulsory education. Local authorities were required to establish rate-aided board schools in their areas of jurisdiction where there were insufficient numbers of pre-existing voluntary schools. All children aged 5-13 were required to go to school. The country needed a better-educated workforce. At first, these schools were funded by government subsidies, local rates and school fees, (but the latter proved unpopular). In 1918, they were scrapped altogether and primary schools became free. The school leaving age was increased to 14 at this date.

Apart from inherited family papers found at home, records of schools and their pupils, of use to the genealogist may be found in CROs. They range from school log books dating from 1840, admissions registers from 1903, and minute books which record all sorts of information, including the names of individual staff and pupils.

Universities

Oxford and Cambridge Universities were the only two in England until the foundation of Durham University in 1832. Oxford University started teaching in about 1096, with Cambridge University starting in about 1209, but properly founded in 1226. All students up to 1534 were ordained into one of the clerical orders of the Roman Catholic Church. However, after the Reformation, only students from Church of England backgrounds were admitted and this remained the case up to 1871.

Scottish universities were founded later, with St Andrews in 1413, Glasgow in 1451, Aberdeen in 1495, and Edinburgh in 1583. Ireland followed suit with Trinity College Dublin in 1592. Wales opened St David's College, Lampeter in 1828 (Anglican), and University College, Aberystwyth in 1872 (for all).

London University opened its doors in 1836, to students whatever their denomination. It was also the first university to admit women to degree courses in 1868, although Cambridge had already opened Girton College in 1869 and Newnham College in 1871 for women to attend honours examinations.

Up until 1871, Roman Catholic students had to study abroad, and several English colleges were established in France, Belgium, Italy, Spain, and Portugal, at Douai, St Omer, Bruges, Liége, Rome, Madrid, Seville, Valladolid and Lisbon.

University 'Alumni' Records

Records of these Catholic institutions and their English students can be found amongst the archives of the Catholic Record Society. (See: www.crs.org.uk/).

For Anglican students pre-1871, and for all those after this date, the universities kept biographical 'alumni' records. These include names, dates of admission, age, graduation / matriculation dates, degree, and even, in the case of Oxford and Cambridge, names and addresses of fathers, previous school and subsequent career details. There are a number of lists of such university registers, but nowadays, a good place to start searching is on Ancestry.co.uk and the Society of Genealogists (SoG) library in London.

Stuart Raymond lists several of the original publications about university alumni, particularly Oxford and Cambridge.[10] The chief authors of these were A.B. Emden and his *Biographical Register of the University of Oxford* (4 vols) covering the earliest times up to 1540, and I. Foster's, *Alumni Oxoniensis* (8 vols) from 1500-1892. These can now be found online using the title of the volumes. Emden also completed, *A Biographical Register of the University of Cambridge to AD1500*. J. Venn and J.A. Venn compiled *Alumni Cantabrigienses* (10 vols), covering Cambridge students from early times up to 1900. These can also be found online by searching under this title and are also transcribed on to www.ancestry.co.uk. There are other old publications about registers. It is also possible to contact the Oxford and Cambridge colleges direct, in order to research student ancestors, not forgetting the Bodleian Library, Oxford.

The University of Manchester's archives are held in the John Rylands Library on site and details of its alumni may be sought there. (See: www.library.manchester.ac.uk/rylands/). This is true for other universities, which may be contacted for information about past students in your family line.

Apprenticeships

Apprenticeships started in the Middle Ages, and by the 1500s were well established in Britain. They were mainly to provide boys with a solid period of about 7 years of learning a trade under a master, but occasionally girls were apprenticed too. Apprentices were provided bed and board, but not a wage. By 1563, it became compulsory under the Statute of Artificers for those wishing to enter a trade to be first apprenticed, and this was recorded in a written contract. In 1691, the apprenticeship system and contract were extended to cover the poor of each parish. Parish Indentures had existed before this in the 17th century, and these had been legal documents sworn in front of a Justice of the Peace (JP) by the churchwarden and the overseer of the poor, on behalf of the child being apprenticed. Both the JP and master kept a copy. Some of these can nowadays be found in the quarter sessions records in local CROs and municipal record offices.

After 1709, masters had to pay Stamp Duty on premiums received for taking on an apprentice through a formal, legal process. (This was not necessary when fathers took on sons to learn their trade). These Stamp Office returns are kept at TNA in the Inland Revenue (IR) records. They give the names of apprentices (and their father's names up to 1752), and the name, address, trade, and amount paid by the master, plus some indexes to masters. Stamp Duty ended in 1804, though TNA's registers finish in 1811. The SoG has a list of apprentices and masters for the years 1710-1774.

The 1563 Statute of Artificers was repealed in 1814, when it was no longer possible to prosecute anyone who did not finish his apprenticeship, even though he had set up in business. Only about 50% of apprenticeships were completed for one reason or another. Many of those who did not complete their training did so because of disobedience to their masters (though not all) and ended up in crime. The apprenticeship system largely ended in the 20th century because of the all-encompassing reach of national education, although more recently there has been a revival in apprenticeship-based learning. So, it is highly likely that some of our ancestors will have undergone this method of training.

Once an apprentice had completed his training, he would submit a 'master piece' of his work for scrutiny and if passed, he would be considered to have served his apprenticeship. From this point, he would join a town guild which matched his trade and which was responsible for overseeing it.

It is now time to start praying into issues arising from ancestors' educational backgrounds.

How to Pray into Generational Educational Issues

To start off, I would recommend praying for protection for yourself and your loved ones and for Jesus to lead and guide you in these prayers. Then pray the 'Lordship Prayer.' This prayer and the declarations and prayers following, are used by several Christian ministries, in various forms, which you can find online and whose address details are to be found in Appendix F.

Lordship Prayer

"Dear Lord Jesus, I realise my need of You and repent of living my life my own way. I wholeheartedly accept You now as my Saviour, my Redeemer, my Lord, and my Deliverer.

I invite You now to be the Lord of every part and moment of my life, from the time of my conception, right up until now:

Lord of my body, my physical health and behaviour.

Lord of my mind and all my attitudes and mental health.

EDUCATIONAL BACKGROUND

Lord of all my emotions and all of my reactions.

Lord of my spirit and my worship of You.

Lord of my family and all my relationships.

Lord of my sexuality and its expression.

Lord of my will and all of my hopes, ambitions, decisions, and plans.

Lord of all my work and service for You.

Lord of all my finances.

Lord of all my needs and possessions.

Lord of the manner and time of my death."

Declaration

"Thank you, Jesus, for shedding Your blood and dying on the cross, for the forgiveness of my sins, my ancestors' sins, and my descendants' sins. You died and rose again that I might be set free to love and to serve You, in newness of life.

While I thank you, Lord, for my ancestors, especially my father and mother who brought me into this world and whom I honour, I do not stand in agreement with them on sinful matters. In these cases, in your presence, Lord, I **confess** and **repent** on behalf of all my parents', grandparents' and forefathers' sins against You, caused in part by their educational experiences. I confess that these were sins against you, the effects of which I **renounce** off my life and off the life of my family, which have resulted in curses running through the family line, down to me. Thank you for becoming a curse for me on the cross, so that I might go free. I ask that You would **forgive** my ancestors' turning away from you, as I forgive them also.

I confess, repent on behalf of, and forgive any incidents of cheating, lying, bullying or any other sin at school, in apprenticeships, at college or university that my ancestors took part in and I forgive *any incidents of cruelty or unfairness by teachers, masters or lecturers towards my forebears. Where there was any sense of abandonment and rejection from being sent away from family and home to boarding school, resulting in insecurity or an orphan spirit, I also forgive those ancestors who did that to their children. I also forgive any past teacher or lecturer where they taught anti-Christian views or materials to my ancestors and thereby caused them to doubt or turn away from God.*

I claim Your **blood cleansing** *from all the negative educational experiences that have come down to me, in Jesus' name."*

Cutting of Ungodly Soul Ties

Once confession and renunciation for sin has occurred, it will then be necessary to cut off any negative spiritual power transmitting down the family line via the generational soul ties, or 'body, soul, and spirit ties,' as some call them. To do this, a suggested prayer is,

"In the name of Jesus, I place the cross and blood of Jesus between myself, my family and ancestors and I cut the negative body, soul and spirit ties between myself and my father / mother; between myself and other family members, (name them), *who may have developed ungodly ties with me;*
with my grandparents;
with my great-grandparents and,
with my great-great-grandparents and,
with previous ancestors, (name any relevant ones), *going back 4 generations where there has been a spirit of deceit, lying, domination, intimidation, control or witchcraft operating, for instance.*

In Jesus name, I ask that you would send out from me, anything of my relatives' human spirits that have become lodged in mine, and I ask that You draw back to me anything of my spirit and soul that is residing in my father or mother, or any other family members or ancestors I knew." (For ancestors who have died, we break the whole soul tie).

"*I ask Lord, that you would cleanse my blood line and my spirit, soul and body with your precious blood and fill me afresh with your love and your Holy Spirit, in Jesus' name.*"

Wait upon the Lord for any word of knowledge for a specific revelation. This will be necessary for those ancestral sins which cannot be found in the records.

Inner Vows & Bitter Root Judgements

When a person meets an inner psychological brick wall of being unable to trust teachers, lecturers, or educational institutions, this may be because of inner vows made in the past by oneself, or one's ancestors. The way through is to forgive and to ask God to help you to trust (wisely) again. There will be a need to renounce any inner vows and subsequent bitterness, and ask God to break the power of this over one's life.

Identity in Christ

As we spend time in God's written word and in God's presence, He will gradually renew our minds and educate us to think clearly. Not as the world thinks or as we used to think or think about ourselves, but with truth and sober reflection, leading to freedom and clarity. This needs to become a daily activity, which is actually not burdensome at all, but in fact, liberating. The Spirit of God is gradually revealing our true identity, which can only be found in Christ! From this, will flow our new life and work for Him.

Binding and Loosing - Deliverance

To conduct self-deliverance, one should pray something like this: - "*I bind and cut myself off from the ruling spirits of all those educational institutions coming down my family line. I bind and loose the spirit(s) of bullying, intimidation, fear, deceit, rejection, abandonment, orphan spirit, false religion, humanism, Marxism, (any other 'ism!), entitlement, pride, etc,* [use your discernment to name them] *from me and tell it / them to go, in the mighty name of Jesus!*

Please fill me now with Your Holy Spirit, to replace and infill all the empty places vacated by these other spirits. Renew my mind and put a right spirit within me, that I may praise and serve You now and forever more."

The Blessing of Jesus

"I ask, Lord, that you turn all these curses into blessings, as I rest in Your love and presence and as I find my true identity in You. You came to set me free to be me, to renounce the heavy burdens of the past and to carry your yoke, which is light. If I am carrying any emotional wounds caused by generational abuse caused in an educational setting, I ask, Lord, that You surface them and show me, so that I can give them to You and express them safely, forgive and be healed of them. I ask this in Jesus' name."

In Summary

Give thanks for your ancestors. **Identify** any educational issues in your family line, which may have led to familial sins. If found, **confess** these and the influences they have had in your own life. (Lamentations 5:7). **Repent**, where needed, of these sins in the family line, by identifying with and owning them as one's own. Ask for and receive God's **forgiveness**. **Cut** soul ties. Seek **deliverance** ministry and / or conduct self-deliverance for any spirits connected with the education of ancestors. Seek the **cleansing blood of Jesus** to wash away any stains.

Ask Jesus to **bless you** and **fill you** afresh with His Holy Spirit. Seek to be **obedient** to His guidance and call on your life.

A Recommendation

As mentioned before, the prayers in this chapter are intended just as openers, to help start you on the journey to freedom. In order to work towards complete freedom, I would recommend working through the material and prayers in the ministry books listed at the end of this chapter. It would also be very worthwhile attending one of the excellent training and ministry courses run by Bethel Sozo, Christian Prayer Ministries, Gilgal House Healing Centre, Ellel Ministries, or Sozo Ministries International, based in the UK. This is not an exhaustive list and the reader may hear of other ministries both in the UK and abroad, which can help in this area.

Further Reading - Select Bibliography

Fabiano, Catherine & Frank. *Healing Your Past, Releasing Your Future*. Bloomington, MN: Chosen Books, (2012).

Herber, Mark. *Ancestral Trails*. (2nd ed.) (Rev). Stroud: Sutton Publishing, (2005).

Horrobin, Peter. *Healing through Deliverance*. (rev). Lancaster: Sovereign World, (2008).

Prince, Derek. *Blessing or Curse: You Can Choose*. (3rd ed). Grand Rapids, MI: Chosen Books Publishing Co., (2006).

Raymond, Stuart. *My Ancestor was an Apprentice*. London: Society of Genealogists Enterprises Limited, (2010).

Raymond, Stuart. *My Ancestor was a Gentleman*. London: Society of Genealogists Enterprises Limited, (2012).

Chapter 5

Genealogical Evidence for Occupational Background

> *Thou shalt not defraud thy neighbour, neither rob him: the wages of him that is hired shall not abide with thee all night until the morning.* Leviticus 19:13, (KJV)

> *For the Scripture says, 'You shall not muzzle an ox when it treads out the grain,' and, 'The labourer deserves his wages.'*
> 1 Timothy 5:18, (ESV)

Luke 16:1-15, describes the parable of the shrewd manager. Verses 10-13 are perhaps the key ones in this long passage. These three texts (and there are many more), are all concerned with honesty and integrity in the workplace.

> *Whoever can be trusted with very little can also be trusted with much, and whoever is dishonest with very little will also be dishonest with much. So, if you have not been trustworthy in handling worldly wealth, who will trust you with true riches? And if you have not been trustworthy with someone else's property, who will give you property of your own? No one can serve two masters. Either you will hate the one and love the other, or you will be devoted to the one and despise the other. You cannot serve both God and money.* Luke 16:10-13, (NIV)

Records of Occupation

In chapter 7, I outline in brief, the records available for the types of gentry and aristocratic occupations which existed. In this chapter, I will deal more fully with the subject of occupations available for all classes of people which can be found in surviving records.

What Generational Sins Related to Occupations Could be Operating in our Lives?

In the world of work, cheating and theft of property or time would have occurred frequently. Workplace bullying has always been an issue. There was exploitation of poor workers on low pay and a great divide between rich and poor. Unsanitary and unsafe working conditions led to many workplace injuries, ill health, and deaths. Those who would not rest once a week were breaking the 4th Commandment, of not resting on the Sabbath, designed for our benefit.

New 19th century industrialists grew rich from the proceeds of the industrial revolution and advances in technology. Many agricultural labourers were either forced off the land by enclosure acts or the introduction of labour-saving machinery. Others left voluntarily, drawn by the possibility of doubling their wages in the new industries emerging in the towns and cities. The prospect of slightly better terraced housing in the expanding cities acted as a further inducement. It was the time of the rise of the middle classes, who prospered in the growing economy of the 19th century, aided by an influx of wealth from the colonies and opportunities to work abroad. This wealth can be seen reflected in many 19th and early 20th century buildings, whether in city, town or village.

Going back to the subject of **apprenticeships**, as mentioned, only about half of apprentices completed their 7-years' training. For the fortunate ones, they might end up marrying their master's daughter and take over the business in due course. The other half may have fallen foul of their masters, either through their own folly or because of their masters' unfair working conditions. Poverty was likely to follow, and even a life of crime, as it was not possible to secure another apprenticeship if the first one was discarded.

Trade Guilds

In some towns and cities it was not possible to practice one's trade or craft unless membership of a guild had been secured following the successful completion of an apprenticeship. This granted the tradesman 'freedom' of the town or city. There were two types of guild: merchant guilds and craft guilds. These originated in the Middle Ages and continued in the provinces,

declining in the 18th and 19th centuries, with a few exceptions such as the Preston Guild in Lancashire, which has existed for over 830 years and is still in operation! The guild acted as a self-governing body to protect its members and look after their economic interests, determine apprenticeships, set wages and prices, enforce standards, regulate trade, influence bye-laws, and keep outsiders out in order to limit competition. The guild members were therefore important influencers in a town or city landscape, with many becoming burgesses, local government officials and mayors. The guilds thus evolved into municipal corporations and developed the town's magistracy. Their privileges were officially abolished in 1835. Much more could be written about this subject.
See: https://en.wikipedia.org/wiki/Guild.[1, 2]

Guild records may be found in CROs and municipal archives.

Livery Companies in the City of London

In London, guilds became known as livery companies and its members known as 'liverymen,' because of the uniform (or livery) they wore on special occasions. These still exist and operate in much the same way as the provincial guilds did. The earliest Royal charter awarded for incorporation to one of these liveries was to the Worshipful Company of Weavers in 1155 and today, there are 111 livery companies in the City with some 22,500 members. These can be searched online.[3] They are involved in the running of the City and do much charitable work. City officers, sheriffs and the Lord Mayor were all members, and the latter is elected by the liveries.

Some livery company records can be found in the Guildhall Library in the City, at: Aldermanbury, London, EC2V 5AF. (See: https://www.cityoflondon.gov.uk/things-to-do/history-and-heritage/guildhall-library/guildhall-library-catalogue). The records of other liveries can be found with the companies themselves.

The London Metropolitan Archives (LMA) is at: 40 Northampton Rd, London, EC1R 0HB.
(See: https://www.cityoflondon.gov.uk/things-to-do/history-and-heritage/london-metropolitan-archives), which has the original

OCCUPATIONAL BACKGROUND

apprenticeship enrolment books kept by the Chamberlain of London, and these cover the period 1786-1974.

The SoG has indexed the apprenticeship records of over 50 livery companies, dating from 1442 – 1850. These contain the names of the apprentice, the apprentice's father (plus his employment), the master and his livery company. This information can also be found at www.britishorigins.com.

Livery companies may keep the following types of records, useful to the family historian:

* Apprenticeship registers.
* Apprentices admitted to the freedom of the company.
* Apprentices paying orphans' tax (1694 - 1861).
* Stamp Duty payments (1694 - 1949).
* Members elected to company offices.
* Declaration books for oaths of allegiance and the company's rules (1839 - unknown).
* Quarterage books for subscriptions.

If members of livery companies contributed something of significance to the City during their working lives, then they might be awarded the honour of being granted the **Freedom of the City of London**. There are records of these people too, now kept at the London Metropolitan Archives (LMA). The names of these notables appear in the Freedom Admission Papers for 1681-82 and 1688-1783 and in the Freedom Admission Books for 1784-1940. Ancestry.co.uk also has digitised copies of these.[4]

Local **trade directories**, such as Kelly's, would list those in business who had completed apprenticeships, together with their address. They started in London in the mid-17th century and reached their peak in the late 19th century. Directories still continue today in some form or other, though mainly on the internet now, of course. Printed directories covered the whole country and can be found in TNA, the BL, LMA, the Guildhall Library, other metropolitan archives, the SoG, IHGS and CROs for the provinces. (See Appendix E).

As mentioned in chapter 7, the British Library (India Office Collection) in London holds the records of the **East India Company** in which many ambitious and adventurous British people served and gained their fortunes between 1600 - 1874.
(See: www.bl.uk/collection-guides/india-office-records).

Trades Unions

People in trades and crafts often got together to form unions to support one another in times of difficulty. This feature developed in the 18th century and by the late 19th century, there were about 750,000 union members. This has gradually increased to about 6.5 million members in 2020.

Membership records can be found in CROs or with the respective Trade Union. The SoG has some membership records. The most useful for the family researcher will be branch records. They will contain the name, age, occupation, address, names of wives, children, or elderly dependents, as well as benefit and funeral payments made to dependents.

Amongst the many occupations which can be researched in historical records for details of ancestors' work and careers are; agricultural labourers, railwaymen, the police, the military and numerous types of professions.

Agricultural Labourers

In the book, *My Ancestor was an Agricultural Labourer*, by Ian Waller,[5] the author describes in detail, what records survive and where they are kept. Of primary importance will be birth, marriage, and death certificates, which include occupational details of the people listed. Some left wills. The censuses from 1841 onwards also give the occupation of family members. Amongst these, 'Ag. Lab' or Agricultural Labourer will often be found. Agricultural workers included tenant farmers, farm bailiffs, casual farm workers, labourers, horsemen, shepherds, cow hands, gamekeepers, husbandmen, thatchers, and dairy maids. The work of preparing the fields involved ploughing, harrowing and sowing, threshing, flailing and winnowing. Over half of the population of the UK was still involved with agriculture in the early years of Queen Victoria's reign, so most people today will have such ancestors in their family tree. Parish registers also record occupations.

The locations of these farms and villages will be found on old maps, and the National Library of Scotland (NLS) has a full set of old Ordnance Survey maps. These can be viewed for free at: https://maps.nls.uk/. Early 19th century enclosure maps may be seen in CROs.

Much land was owned by local Lords of the Manor, upon which their manorial tenants farmed. Their names can often be found recorded in the proceedings of the manorial courts, and these are now generally kept in CROs or sometimes with local solicitors. The Manorial Documents Register (MDR) will tell you where these manorial records are located.

(See: https://discovery.nationalarchives.gov.uk/manor-search).

Farm work was seasonal and poorly paid, so many 'Ag. Labs' had to supplement their income with various other types of cottage industry, such as straw plaiting or lace making. Poverty was often an overriding experience for labourers which sometimes encouraged a few to go poaching on a landowner's estate. If caught, they would end up before the local magistrate at the Quarter Sessions court. Records of these proceedings will be found in CROs. Such cases would also be reported in the local press, and so it is worth checking the British Newspaper Archive online at:
www.britishnewspaperarchive.co.uk/.

The enclosure Acts of about 1750-1850 forced many agricultural workers off the land. Alongside this, increasing farm mechanization in the 19th century resulted in fewer people being needed to work the land. At the same time, advances in industrialization encouraged a huge number of farm workers to migrate to the burgeoning towns and cities, in search of better paid work and accommodation. Many emigrated overseas to start a new life.

Railwaymen

Before the railways were nationalised in 1948 to form British Rail, (which lasted until 1993), there were four major railway companies: -
* Great Western Railway (GWR),
* London, Midland and Scottish (LMS),
* London and North-Eastern Railway (LNER),
* Southern Railway (SR).

These came into being in 1923, having themselves been formed out of the amalgamation of some 120 separate railway companies that existed after WWI. But even this was a small number compared to the nearly 1000 companies that had grown up in the 19th century. The world's first passenger-carrying train pulled by a locomotive was the Stockton to Darlington railway which opened in 1825. This was followed by the first commercial passenger railway, opening in 1830, on a line running between Liverpool and Manchester.[6] It was a very sought-after occupation to work on the railways, especially to become a train driver!

Records of railwaymen are kept at TNA and the National Records of Scotland (NRS), (See: www.nrscotland.gov.uk/), having originally been collected by the British Transport Historical Commission. The largest part of the TNA collection covers the GWR. Family historians need to know which company their ancestor worked for, before they can research further to find a name. TNA's guide to these will help. Once found, their occupation and income might be listed, and sometimes a full-service record given. For more details, the book, *Tracing Your Railway Ancestors* by Di Drummond explains further, what records there are and how useful they will be.[7]

Police

The nation's police force can be divided up into two for the purposes of family history: the Metropolitan Police Force (Met) for London, and those police forces for the counties outside London.

OCCUPATIONAL BACKGROUND

The Met can be traced back to the Metropolitan Police Act of 1829, initiated by Robert Peel. His men were nicknamed 'Peelers.' Prior to this, there had been an earlier organised police force in London, called the 'Bow Street Runners,' begun in Bow Street, Covent Garden, in 1750 by Henry Fielding, but spreading out from there. It was later in 1919, at the time of the Suffragette movement, that the first female police patrols began.

Historic records for the Met are kept at TNA in the Home Office (HO) and MEPO series. At the moment, they date from 1829 – 1993, though different types of records have differing dates of coverage. There are some gaps. These Met files contain staff records in alphabetical order, including a Register of Joiners, Certificates of Service records, and a Register of Leavers. Names, birth date, rank, warrant number and division, marital status, address, number of children, details of the last employer, date of leaving, and pension records are all given. For more details and how to order, see: www.nationalarchives.gov.uk/help-with-your-research/research-guides/london-metropolitan-police-british-transport-police-railway-police/. There is also an SoG publication: *My Ancestor was a Policeman*, by Anthony Shearman, which will help.[8]

CROs contain the historic records of the different county police constabularies, if they are not held by the forces themselves.

The Military

Other uniformed services, of course, include the military. I have already mentioned in chapter 7, that the officer corps of the **Army**, **Royal Navy**, **Royal Marines** and latterly, the **Royal Air Force**, were attractive occupations for the gentry and aristocracy. But this could also be true for the general population where men and more recently women, have sought to distinguish themselves in the service of their country. (This subject has also been covered in chapter 6 on war trauma, so this topic does not need to be covered in any detail here. Please refer back to chapters 6 and 7). Suffice to say, that historic military records are kept at TNA (not CROs), whilst personnel records since the 1920s are kept by the respective military service. If more recently deceased, only next of kin are entitled to apply to see copies of their relatives' service records. Regimental, naval and air force museums also contain some details of servicemen and women's military careers. Many, if not most historic service records have been digitised and are available online at:

>   www.ancestry.co.uk,
>   www.findmypast.co.uk,
>   www.thegenealogist.co.uk,
>   www.nationalarchives.gov.uk,
>   www.forces-war-records.co.uk,
>   www.thegazette.co.uk.

Royal Service

Apart from the military, there are other personnel who are and were answerable to the Crown: those in royal service. As mentioned in chapter 7, Stuart Raymond goes to some length describing the different types of **royal courtiers** and where the records of these may be found.[9]

Birth, marriage, and death certificates may show an ancestor who worked for the Crown. Within the timespan of the publicly viewable decennial censuses, (1841-1921), it is possible to trace ancestors who worked for the Royal Family to the various palaces where they worked. These would include Buckingham Palace, the Royal Mews, Clarence House, Kensington Palace, St James' Palace, Windsor Castle, Sandringham House, Balmoral Castle, Holyrood Palace in Edinburgh, and Hillsborough Castle in Northern Ireland. The main online source of information specific to **royal household staff** is on FindMyPast. Within this website, look for: 'Royal Household Staff, 1526-1924'. A very interesting list of current and former Royal residences may be seen on Wikipedia.[10] Staff could include gentlemen and ladies in waiting, bodyguards, chaplains, physicians, gentlemen and yeoman ushers, pages, cooks, porters, maids, grooms, gillies, horsemen and stable hands. See also, The Royal Archives website at: www.royal.uk/the-royal-archives for

OCCUPATIONAL BACKGROUND

personnel employed after 1660.

One branch of service where people worked for the Crown was (and is) in the administration of the Crown Estates. These would include constables of castles, bailiffs, stewards, solicitors, surveyors, accountants, receivers, bow bearers, game masters in royal hunting forests, and park keepers.

The Duchy of Lancaster is one such example of a Crown Estate employing many people. (See: www.duchyoflancaster.co.uk). Its main offices are just off the Strand, London, with estates known as 'Surveys,' including Rural, Urban, Foreshore, Minerals, and castles / historic properties. The Rural Surveys are in Cheshire, Lancashire, Staffordshire, Yorkshire, and Southern regions, and cover over 18,000 hectares of land. Lancaster Castle is the Duchy's main property. The Duchy's London office sells books about the history of the Duchy, including two volumes by Robert Somerville, the latter being, *Office-holders in the Duchy and County Palatine of Lancaster from 1603*, published by Phillimore, (1972). This gives details of personnel employed over the last 400 years.

Records of royal service, including with the Duchy of Lancaster, may be seen at TNA, and at British History online at: www.british-history.ac.uk. Within TNA, useful documents might be found in the Patent Rolls (running from 1206 – 1946), and the State Papers Domestic (1547 – 1782). TNA, (not The Royal Archives), holds records of royal service before 1660, as well as some later ones.

A useful set of lists of royal courtiers have been compiled and published by Sir John Sainty,[11] and these are available at the University of London's, Institute of Historical Research, and online at: www.history.ac.uk/publications/office, under, 'Office-holders in Modern Britain.'[12]

Officers of the royal household may be found in a 'Database of Court Officers 1660-1837' at:
www.luc.edu/history/fac_resources/bucholz/DCO/DCO.html[13] Royal Chaplains after 1858 may also be found in *Crockfords Clerical Directory*.

(See: www.crockford.org.uk), and www.theclergydatabase.org.uk for chaplains, 1540-1835. Ancestry.co.uk also has a link to Chapels Royal registers in the section on 'England & Wales, Non-Conformist and Non-Parochial Registers, 1567-1936.'

The Professions

Three main professions are included here and their records described for genealogical research, although there are others. These are the law, medicine, and the clergy.

The Law

The legal profession arose in about the 1200s and from early on, was divided between attorneys, barristers and notaries. The title 'attorney' changed to 'solicitor' in 1875. Both were trained in English schools of common law in London, which developed in the 1300s. Initial barrister's training started in the Inns of Chancery, but progressed onwards in four Inns of Court, which still exist today: Gray's Inn, Lincoln's Inn, Inner Temple, and Middle Temple. They are located around the boundary of the City of London. Upon completion of their training, students were, and are, 'called to the bar.' [14] There had been a fifth Inn of Court – Serjeants' Inn, but this was dissolved in 1877.

TNA houses most records of barristers, attorneys and notaries. Oath rolls of **barristers** sworn into office date from 1673 – 1985. They give the name, Inn and signature of each barrister and are under the KB24 series. (KB stands for King's Bench). Each Inn also maintained a black book, containing names of admissions, appointments, and punishments for misdemeanours. These are also at TNA. Elsewhere, records survive for the Inner Temple as 'Calendars,' dating from 1505 – 1845. These can be viewed online at: www.innertemple.org.uk/who-we-are/history/calendars-of-inner-temple-records-1505-1845/.[15] On the same website, there is also a list of admissions to the Inner Temple, dating in range from 1547 - 1993. See: https://archives.innertemple.org.uk/records/ADM.

Meanwhile, **attorneys** were trained in ten Inns of Chancery

OCCUPATIONAL BACKGROUND

after 1642.[16] These included Clement's, Clifford's, Lyon's, Strand, New, Furnival's, Thavie's, Staple, Barnard's and St George's Inn. The purpose of these declined with the foundation of the Society of Gentlemen Practisers in 1739, and died out after 1825, with the founding of the Law Society of England and Wales. The last Inn – Clement's was sold in 1903. Attorneys' apprenticeship or 'articles' was set at 5 years by an Act of 1728. Having taken the required oath, they would be enrolled with the Court in which they would practice. These courts included the Court of Chancery, the Court of Common Pleas, the Exchequer of Pleas, and King's (or Queen's) Bench. All their records are held at TNA. They include:

* Records of admissions (18th – 20th century)
* Annual certificate of admission (1785 - 1871)
* Law Society: Solicitors Registers of Admission (1790–1884)
* Oaths (1730 – 20th century)
* Affidavits of execution of clerkship (show articles were completed) (1713 – 1837)
* Registers of practicing certificates (1734 – 19th century)

Provincial attorney records may be held in CROs and are searchable on TNA's Discovery website at:
https://discovery.nationalarchives.gov.uk/.

In Ireland, there is an Inn of Court for Northern Ireland and in Eire, the Honorable Society of King's Inn.

Notaries were introduced into England in the 13th and 14th centuries. They recorded matters of legal importance and drew up legal documents, acting as witnesses to signatures made, making sure they were authentic, especially on foreign transactions. They are also commissioners for oaths.[17] They are appointed by the Court of Faculties which is attached to the office of the Archbishop of Canterbury. There are two branches of notaries: general notaries and scrivener notaries. In practice all English and Scottish notaries are practicing solicitors. As mentioned, their records will be found at TNA amongst solicitors records.

Judges in all the higher courts were appointed from

barristers called Serjeants-at-Law, whose records of Admission Rolls, dating from 1689 – 1844, are held at TNA under C216. The other two types of counsel were barristers and King's or Queen's Counsel. Records further include lists of appointments to different places and these cover the period 1570 – 1873, and a list of warrants by name and place to pay half-yearly wages. The latter date from the 13th to 19th centuries. See the E404 series.

The SoG, TNA, British Library and Guildhall Library all have good sets of *Law Lists*. These are divided into sections for judges, counsel (barristers) with their Inn of Court, attorneys (whether London or the provinces) and other groups. The *Law Lists* give names, addresses, qualifications, often include fathers' names as well, the name of a firm or partnership and date of admission. It started in 1775 when it was called the *General Law List* (1775 – 1797), then *The New Law List* (1797 – 1840) and *The Law List* (1841 – now).

Scotland has the *Scottish Law List*, giving similar information, which also includes the 'Faculty of Advocates.' Finally, it is worth checking the alumni records of Oxford and Cambridge Universities, as these give the names of law graduates, their dates of graduation, which Inn they entered, career details, and fathers' names. These have been uploaded on to www.ancestry.co.uk. See the section on 'University alumni records' in chapter 4 for more details.

Medicine

This section will focus on post-Reformation medicine, not on the earlier medieval period. All **physicians and surgeons** after 1511, (the date an Act was passed), had to be licenced by their local bishop in order to practice their craft. By 1750, few were licenced. Surviving licences can be found in diocesan archives around the country. They include the name, parish, date of issue and fee paid. Licensees had to be of good character and have some experience in medicine. Sometimes there will be supporting testimonials written by other medical professionals, to help the applicant. One such source of licences is Lambeth Palace Library in London, which holds

OCCUPATIONAL BACKGROUND

Archbishop's licences granted between 1535-1775. (See: www.lambethpalacelibrary.org/).

The Royal College of Physicians (RCP) in London was founded in 1518, as one of the main governing bodies of the profession. Its library contains records of all its members dating back to its foundation. (See: www.rcplondon.ac.uk/education-practice/library). Of particular interest will be an 11-volume tome called *The Roll of the College of Physicians*, begun by William Munk, which records biographies of its fellows from its inception up to the 2000s, and of licentiates up to 1825. A copy of this work is held at the Guildhall Library in London, while an incomplete one, (up to 1925) is in the library of the SoG. There are also volumes of the *Lives of the Fellows of the* [RCP] at the RCP library.

The Royal College of Surgeons (RCS) of England (founded in 1800) also keeps registers of its members. These date back to 1745, when the earlier Company of Surgeons separated from the Barbers Company. The RCS library (See: www.rcseng.ac.uk/library-and-publications/library/), contains the *Lives of the Fellows of the Royal College of Surgeons*, by Victor Plarr. This includes names, date and place of birth, parents' names, education and qualifications, career details, publications and outside interests, and occasionally other details of ancestry. The Guildhall Library in London also holds this and some membership records. (See: www.cityoflondon.gov.uk/things-to-do/history-and-heritage/guildhall-library).

Within the Guildhall Library are also the records of the **Barber-Surgeons Company**. This came about by the amalgamation of the Barbers Company and the Fellowship of Surgeons by Royal Charter in 1540, and lasted until 1745. The aim was to improve standards in surgery. Trainees underwent a 7-year apprenticeship after which they were examined and if successful, were licensed. The Guildhall Library holds registers of apprentices which date from between 1657 – 1786. They give the name of the apprentice, his father's name, his current parish, county of birth and date of binding. There are also Registers of Freedom Admissions (1522 – 1801), giving the apprentice's name with their master's name, the date and reason for admission, and the amount paid in redemption.

Surgeons were also present on-board ships. From 1629, all ships leaving British ports were required to carry one. Royal Navy surgeons were certificated and these records are kept at TNA in the ADM 106 series. (See: https://discovery.nationalarchives.gov.uk/results/r?_q=surgeons%20certificates&_ser=ADM%20106&id=C1815). They include the surgeon's name, date the certificate was granted, and the ship upon which he served. Surgeons' journals dating from 1793–1880, can be found at: www.nationalarchives.gov.uk/surgeonsatsea/. These journals record the surgeon's name, ship, diseases treated and sometimes, even colourful stories of life on board! These men will also be found in issues of *The Navy List*, alongside other naval officers. Again, see TNA or the SoG library. Army surgeons are likewise listed in *The Army List*.

The **Wellcome Historical Medical Museum and Library** at 183 Euston Road, London, NW1 2BE, contains material dating from 1874 – c.1984. Some of this is of genealogical usefulness. (See: https://wellcomecollection.org/works/k2fae5cz, or phone: 020 7611 2222). One publication held here is *The Medical Directory*, (1870-2015). Earlier editions starting in 1845 are only viewable online within the library, and these go up to 1942. Initially, they included the practitioner's name and address, but later editions also include qualifications, appointments, and publications.

The Institute of Heraldic and Genealogical Studies (IHGS) Library in Canterbury holds an unpublished volume called *Eighteenth Century Medics*, with details of medics from 1710 – 1808. This gives names, parents' names, date of binding, and the name and place of the apprentice's master's practice.

From the Royal College of Surgeons came the foundation of **dentistry** as a separate profession in 1869. Following the Dentists' Act of 1878, *The Dentists' Register* was established in 1879. This

OCCUPATIONAL BACKGROUND

gives names anywhere in the UK, dates, qualifications, location, and any work published by the dentist in question. It can be searched via the British Dental Association (BDA) which has a Dental Museum in London at 64 Wimpole St, W1G 8YS.

(See:https://bda.org/museum/enquiries/PublishingImages/-and-research/was-your-ancestor-a-dentist-factsheet.pdf.
Applications for help should be emailed to: museum@bda.org.

A similar licensing arrangement to that created for physicians and surgeons was also made for **midwives**, and set up in 1603. In order to be licensed by a bishop, midwives had to subscribe to the thirty-nine Articles of Religion (of the Church of England). They had to be diligent, faithful, and willing to help all pregnant women, irrespective of the latter's station in life, and not practice any sort of witchcraft or occult activity. In case of risk to life of new-borns, where a clergyman might not be available, midwives were instructed in how to perform emergency baptisms in front of witnesses. When looking in parish registers for information about baptisms of ancestors, sometimes you will find the word 'private' or 'half' entered for the baptism. This will indicate where a midwife performed it. Midwives' licenses will also include their husband's name or whether they were a widow. Such licences are held in diocesan archives, Lambeth Palace Library, and a very small number are at York Minster Library. The latter covers the northern archdiocese, with records dating between 1665-1673). (See: http://collections.yorkminster.org/).

Apothecaries (now called chemists), can be traced back to mediaeval times in this country. The Society of Apothecaries was formed in 1617. The Apothecaries Act of 1815 allowed the Society to set out what qualifications needed to be gained by apprentices, how to examine them and the power to grant licentiateships. It is now called the Worshipful Company of Apothecaries. Apprenticeship records and freedom admissions to the Society are held internally at: www.apothecaries.org and by the Guildhall Library. These date from between 1617 and the 19th century. The

SoG has a list of apothecaries dating from 1815-1840. There is a more recent publication, *The Register of Pharmaceutical Chemists* dating from 1868 onwards, copies of which are held by the Guildhall Library.

Finally, another important source of biographical information about those trained in medicine, are **university alumni records**. These will be found for the universities of Oxford and Cambridge, Aberdeen, Edinburgh, Glasgow and Trinity College, Dublin, amongst others. Thousands of British Roman Catholic and nonconformist students also trained at the University of Leyden in The Netherlands, which was religiously tolerant. The book, *English Speaking Students of Medicine at the University of Leyden*, written by Robert Innes Smith and published in 1932, includes these people. A copy is held in the SoG Library. See chapter 4 on education for more details of university alumni. Raymond [18] includes a section on the medical profession and related genealogical records in his book.

Clergy

As mentioned in chapter 7, it was normal for the younger sons of gentry to enter the **Church of England** as ordained ministers. In at least the first 50 years after the Dissolution of the Monasteries in the 1530s and the subsequent Reformation, there were few well educated Anglican clergy. What few there were had to serve several parishes at the same time. The situation gradually improved, but with fewer university educated clergy in the north, compared with the south, even up to the early to mid-17th century.

After the Civil War, many Anglican clergymen were ejected from their livings and replaced with Puritan ministers. The situation was reversed upon the Restoration of the Monarchy in 1660 under Charles II. There followed the notorious Five Mile Act of 1665, whereby ministers who had refused to take an oath of allegiance to the king, were forbidden from living within 5 miles of a parish from which they had been expelled. This effectively prevented them from preaching to their erstwhile parishioners.[19] The Five Mile Act was followed by the Test Acts of the 1670s, which severely limited the

OCCUPATIONAL BACKGROUND

ability of Roman Catholics and nonconformists to serve in any public office.[20] Only those who agreed to take communion within the Church of England were permitted. Consequently, there was much poverty amongst dissenting clergy.

The Test Acts were not repealed until 1780 in Ireland (1873 in the universities), and 1828 in England and Wales (1871 for university office holders). The situation in Scotland was slightly different. Tests began there straight after the Reformation and the last test was not repealed until 1889.

Things started to improve in 1704 with the establishment of Queen Anne's Bounty, to provide financial support for ministers on an income of less than £50 a year. Bounty records are kept at TNA. (See: https://discovery.nationalarchives.gov.uk/). TNA also houses something called 'Clergy institution books,' dating from 1556 – 1838. Many such records are also held by CROs.

Diocesan record offices (DROs) hold details of ordination papers and licences to hold livings as a vicar. For those issued through the Archbishop of Canterbury's office, there is the collected works of these, entitled, *The Act Books of the Archbishop of Canterbury, 1663-1859*. This is held at Lambeth Palace Library (See: https://bookscat.lambethpalacelibrary.org.uk/), and at the SoG (which has coverage of earlier dates and also for those of the Archdiocese of York). There is an index to this complied by the British Record Society, (See: www.britishrecordsociety.org/).

A major source of information about Anglican clergy for the period 1540 – 1835, is: www.theclergydatabase.org.uk. This includes curates and chaplains who did not progress on to become vicars or go higher up. For the years since 1858, consult *Crockford's Clerical Directory*. (See: www.crockford.org.uk). This includes clergy for the CofE, Church of Wales, the Episcopal Church of Scotland, and the Church of Ireland. (The latter stopped being listed in 1985).

As mentioned for other careers, university alumni records for Oxford and Cambridge also include biographical entries for Anglican clergy, trained at these universities. These can be found online, extracted from the publications, *Alumni Oxonienses* and *Alumni Cantabrigienses*, available at British History Online (See: www.british-history.ac.uk/), and at: www.ancestry.co.uk, and also at https://venn.lib.cam.ac.uk/ for Cambridge. The SoG sells a book about tracing clergymen in its 'My Ancestor was' series.

The survival of **Roman Catholicism** in England beyond the Reformation depended upon the gentry. This was briefly explained in chapter 7. Trainee priests were often sent to seminaries on the continent, before returning to England to work secretly with the underground Catholic church. The Catholic Relief (or Emancipation) Act of 1829, allowed Catholicism to emerge from the dark and to practice openly. The Catholic Record Society keeps records of seminary alumni. (See: www.crs.org.uk/).

Ministerial adherents of other nonconformist denominations are described in chapter 10 on Religion, together with their respective records.

The SoG and IHGS libraries and bookshops hold records of other occupations not described here. These might throw further light on your ancestors.

It is now time to start praying into the issues arising from ancestors' occupations.

How to Pray into Generational Occupational Issues

To start off, I would recommend praying for protection for yourself and your loved ones and for Jesus to lead and guide you in these prayers. Then pray the 'Lordship Prayer.' This prayer and the declarations and prayers following, are used by several Christian ministries, in various forms, which you can find online and whose address details are included in Appendix F.

Lordship Prayer

"Dear Lord Jesus, I realise my need of You and repent of living my life my own way. I wholeheartedly accept You now as my Saviour, my Redeemer, my Lord, and my Deliverer.

OCCUPATIONAL BACKGROUND

I invite You now to be the Lord of every part and moment of my life, from the time of my conception, right up until now:

Lord of my body, my physical health and behaviour.

Lord of my mind and all my attitudes and mental health.

Lord of all my emotions and all of my reactions.

Lord of my spirit and my worship of You.

Lord of my family and all my relationships.

Lord of my sexuality and its expression.

Lord of my will and all of my hopes, ambitions, decisions, and plans.

Lord of all my work and service for You.

Lord of all my finances.

Lord of all my needs and possessions.

Lord of the manner and time of my death."

Declaration

"Thank you, Jesus, for shedding Your blood and dying on the cross, for the forgiveness of my sins, my ancestors' sins, and my descendants' sins. You died and rose again that I might be set free to love and to serve You, in newness of life.

*While I thank you, Lord, for my ancestors, especially my father and mother who brought me into this world and whom I honour, I do not stand in agreement with them on sinful matters. In these cases, in your presence, Lord, I **confess** and **repent** on behalf of all my parents,' grandparents' and forefathers' sins against You, caused in part by their work experiences. I confess that these were sins against you, the effects of which I **renounce** off my life and off the life of my family, which have resulted in curses running through the family line, down to me. Thank you for becoming a curse for me* on the cross, so that I might go free. I ask that You would **forgive** my ancestors' turning away from you, as I forgive them also.

I confess, repent on behalf of, and forgive any cases of stealing from employers or injustice done to my family on the part of employers who withheld or underpaid wages, or even if they were unjust employers themselves. I also confess, repent on behalf of and forgive any cases of workplace bullying, intimidation, violence, overwork or laziness, and any other sins I am aware of. I claim Your **blood cleansing** from all the negative effects of employment coming down the generations to my life, in Jesus' name."

Cutting of Ungodly Soul Ties

Once confession and renunciation for sin has occurred, it will then be necessary to cut off any negative spiritual power transmitting down the family line via the generational soul ties, or 'body, soul, and spirit ties', as some call them. To do this, a suggested prayer is:

"In the name of Jesus, I place the cross and blood of Jesus between myself, my family and ancestors and I cut the negative body, soul and spirit ties between myself and my father / mother; between myself and other family members, (name them), who may have developed ungodly ties with me;
with my grandparents;
with my great-grandparents and,
with my great-great-grandparents and,
with previous ancestors, (name any relevant ones), going back 4 generations where there has been a spirit of injustice, cruelty, exploitation, bullying, greed, deceit or any other spirit operating. I ask, Jesus, that you send out from me anything of my relatives' human spirits that have lodged in me. and I ask that you draw back to me, Jesus, anything of my spirit and soul that is residing in my father or mother, or any other family members or ancestors I knew."
(For ancestors who have died, we break the whole soul tie).

"I ask Lord, that you would cleanse my blood line and my spirit, soul and body with your precious blood and fill me afresh with *your love and your Holy Spirit, in Jesus' name."*

Wait upon the Lord for any word of knowledge for a specific revelation. This will be necessary for those ancestral sins which cannot be found in the records.

Inner Vows & Bitter Root Judgements

When a person meets an inner psychological brick wall of being unable to trust employers, employees, or work colleagues, this may be because of inner vows made in the past by oneself, or one's ancestors. The way through is to forgive and to ask God to help you to trust (wisely) again. There will be a need to renounce any inner vows and subsequent bitterness, and ask God to break the power of this over one's life.

Identity in Christ

As we spend time reading the Bible and resting in God's presence, He will gradually renew our minds, spirits, souls, and bodies. This needs to become a daily activity, which is actually not burdensome at all, but in fact, liberating. Maybe we have not rested enough and unwittingly or wittingly broken the sabbath. We are out of God's rest for us. Or we have not worked hard enough. As we seek Him for our true identity, He may re-order our priorities, including our work priorities. Maybe God will reveal a different way of doing things, or a solution to a difficult work issue. Maybe we have been toiling at something that brings us no joy, something that our father or mother did, and expected of us, or even a line of work our ancestors did. Maybe our old school pushed us towards a career which was not suitable. Gordon Dalbey has some very helpful material, prayers, and testimonies about this issue in his books.[21, 22] Family expectations can be crushing. We are ill-fitted to the work we are doing and that is why we are unhappy. Maybe Jesus has a new line of work for us or a new calling, something that will be suitable and bring us challenge and satisfaction!

Binding and Loosing - Deliverance

To conduct self-deliverance, one should pray something like this: - *"I bind and cut myself off from any ruling spirits of deceit, bullying, manipulation, control, witchcraft, greed, mammon, intimidation, fear, lying, etc, coming down my family line. I bind and loose the spirit(s) of……. [use your discernment to name them] from me and tell it / them to go, in the mighty name of Jesus!*

Please fill me now with Your Holy Spirit, to replace and infill all the empty places vacated by these other spirits. Renew my mind and put a right spirit within me, that I may praise and serve You now and forever more."

The Blessing of Jesus

"I ask, Lord, that you turn all these curses into blessings, as I rest in Your love and presence and as I find my true identity in You. You came to set me free to be me, to renounce the heavy burdens of the past and to carry your yoke, which is light. If I am carrying any emotional wounds caused by generational abuse caused in an occupational setting, I ask, Lord, that You surface them and show me, so that I can give them to You and express them safely, forgive and be healed of them. I ask this in Jesus' name."

In Summary

Give thanks for your ancestors. **Identify** any occupational issues in your family line, which may have led to familial sins. If found, **confess** these and the influences they have had in your own life. (Lamentations 5:7). **Repent**, where needed, of these sins in the family line, by identifying with and owning them as one's own. Ask for and receive God's **forgiveness**. **Cut** soul ties. Seek **deliverance** ministry and / or conduct self-deliverance for any spirits connected with specific occupations. Seek the **cleansing blood of Jesus** to wash away any stains.

Ask Jesus to **bless you** and **fill you** afresh with His Holy Spirit. Seek to be **obedient** to His guidance and call on your life.

A Recommendation

As mentioned before, the prayers in this chapter are intended just as openers, to help start you on the journey to freedom. In order to work towards complete freedom, I would recommend working through the material and prayers in the ministry books listed at the end of this chapter. It would also be very worthwhile attending one of the excellent training and ministry courses run by Bethel Sozo, Christian Prayer Ministries, Gilgal House Healing Centre, Ellel Ministries, or Sozo Ministries International, here in the UK. This is not an exhaustive list and the reader may hear of other ministries both in the UK and abroad, which can help in this area.

Further Reading - Select Bibliography

Brooks, Brian C.G. & Herber, Mark D. *My Ancestor was a Lawyer*. London: Society of Genealogists Ltd, (2006).

Crail, Mark. *Tracing Your Labour Movement Ancestors*. Barnsley: Pen & Sword Books, (2009).

Dalbey, Gordon. *Healing the Masculine Soul*. London: Word Publishing, (1988).

Dalbey, Gordon. *Sons of the Father*. Eastbourne: Kingsway Publications, (2002).

Drummond, Di. *Tracing Your Railway Ancestors*. Barnsley: Pen & Sword Books Ltd, (2010).

Herber, Mark. *Ancestral Trails*. (2nd ed.) (Rev). Stroud: Sutton Publishing, (2005).

Raymond, Stuart A. *My Ancestor was a Gentleman*. London: Society of Genealogists Enterprises Ltd, (2012).

Shearman, Anthony. *My Ancestor was a Policeman*. London: Society of Genealogists Enterprises Ltd, (2000).

Towey, Peter. *My Ancestor was an Anglican Clergyman*. London: Society of Genealogists Enterprises Ltd, (2015).

Waller, Ian. *My Ancestor was an Agricultural Labourer*. 2nd ed. London, Society of Genealogists Enterprises Ltd, (2019).

Chapter 6

Genealogical Evidence for Trauma Caused by War

> *Blessed be the LORD, my Rock,*
> *who trains my hands for war,*
> *my fingers for battle.*
> *He is my steadfast love and my fortress,*
> *my stronghold and my deliverer.*
> *He is my shield, in whom I take refuge,*
> *who subdues peoples under me.*
> *Psalm 144:1-2, (BSB)*

> *He will cover you with his feathers, and under his wings you will find refuge; his faithfulness will be your shield and rampart.*
> *You will not fear the terror of night, nor the arrow that flies by day, nor the pestilence that stalks in the darkness, nor the plague that destroys at midday.*
> *A thousand may fall at your side, ten thousand at your right hand, but it will not come near you.   Psalm 91:4-7, (NIV)*

The story goes that a squad of American GI's recited Psalm 91 together, every morning in WW2, from the time they landed on the beaches of Normandy on D-Day, right up to the end of the war in Europe 11 months later. None of them was lost, or even received a scratch! Their prayers were answered. But these two scriptures imply that fear is the overriding emotion that accompanies soldiers in battle, together with an encouragement to trust the Lord through it.

An intriguing 2018 article by Jan Grimell in the *Journal of Pastoral Care Counsel*,[1] compares contemporary insights gained from battle veterans suffering from trauma and PTSD, with the biblical accounts of warriors such as Saul, David, Joab and Uriah. He hypothesised that it is possible to discern some war trauma in the behavioural accounts of these men.

What are War Trauma Issues?

Traumas caused by war include, anxiety, nervousness, fear, shock, terror, severe restlessness and agitation[2], obsessions and phobias, grief and loss, depression and despair, nightmares, numerous psychological and psychiatric disorders, flashbacks, Post Traumatic Stress Disorder (PTSD)[3,4], anger, unforgiveness, rage, bitterness, vengefulness, cruelty, emotional shut down or numbness, aimlessness, rigidity, denial, or inappropriate emotional responses, dissociation and fragmentation. Some may carry an abiding sense of injustice.

It can be difficult for veterans who endured violence, or civilians caught up in it to speak about their experiences or relate normally to their families or other people and fit back into 'normal' society after a conflict has finished. They can be lonely and isolated as they find it hard to talk to others about what they went through and know that many others will not truly understand them. So, they remain silent. The insecurities of war can lead to personal insecurity and to the control of others in an attempt to make life safe for themselves.

My paternal grandfather, William Eve, as mentioned in the preface, was a veteran of the trenches in WWI. He never spoke of his experiences to me and I understand, mentioned them very little to the rest of the family. He was socially withdrawn, even rigid, and interacted poorly with my father. Dad was often frustrated with him and so gravitated towards his mother, my grandmother, Alice, instead. Grannie was more sociable and warmer. I am certain that is partly why my Dad related better with his mother than with my Mum, causing her to feel pushed out. I don't think Dad had separated emotionally enough from his mother, to allow him to bond healthily with my Mum. That naturally affected their marriage, which ended in divorce and greatly affected my sister and I. So, you can see how one thing led to another in my family.

Also, there can be pride, egotism, self-idolatry, superiority and arrogance in some veterans who were trained to think they were 'the best' and who achieved so much in combat. Authoritarianism and judgementalism towards others deemed less worthy can then follow. There can be prejudice towards other nationalities, particularly former enemies, indoctrination, wrong thinking and confusion. Scapegoating of others may occur in an attempt to attach blame.

Alternatively, veterans can carry a sense of guilt, regret, failure and shame over acts they committed, or if they were on the losing side. One can imagine that most, if not all of the 10 Commandments are broken in times of war. Some carried a sense of inferiority because they did not experience active combat. Others carried or carry something called 'survivor's guilt,' because they survived when their friends and brothers-in-arms did not. These issues have led many to commit suicide, as for instance, American veterans after the Vietnam War (1955 - 1975).

Physical effects can be sexual licence as people let go of (past) societal standards and seek ungodly comfort, indulging in immoral behaviours, prostitution, rape, (either because of lust or as a form of war on the enemy's women folk) and murder. Illegitimacy is much more common during wartime. So is abortion of unwanted babies. Alcoholism or drug-taking to cover up emotional pain, is a common problem in veterans. Theft of property, is a common war crime. Abuse of others can occur both within the military establishment and once they leave it, as they displace their anger on to others. Many are maimed physically, through loss of limbs, or having a tattoo forcibly imprinted on their bodies, such as happened to concentration camp victims, who still have their individual number visible on their forearms, nearly 80 years later. Dislocation and homelessness are issues both for refugees and for mentally ill combat veterans.

These traumas can lead to demonic spirits of death and murder developing, plus others, or a victim spirit, leading to acting-out behaviour on others, by either the abuser or the abused, or on themselves in the form of suicide.

However, this is not to detract from their many positive attributes: courage, bravery, loyalty, patriotism, respect, obedience, discipline, cheerfulness, humour, inventiveness, strength of character and body, straight-forwardness, intelligence, training and skill, leadership qualities, vision, focus, quick thinking, decisiveness, coolness under fire, compassion, determination, endurance, humility, honour, devotion to duty, and truthfulness. I could go on. It is too easy to focus solely on the negative aspects of a person when considering generational sin and iniquity.

For those with little or no knowledge of their military ancestor's pasts, this next section is written to help you locate those records and to learn about your family's heroes in greater detail. Hopefully, this should equip you with more concrete knowledge and aid discernment into what to pray for in your family tree, in order to be set free from any negative effects of inherited war traumas.

Evidence for Generational War Trauma

Collecting evidence for war trauma in the family and those descendants it affects will probably start with family stories about wartime exploits. The family may remember if their veteran, military or civilian, displayed any emotional or relational upsets because of their wartime experiences. If a married veteran was killed in action, any child of that marriage may have grown up fatherless and consequently suffer from feelings of abandonment and an orphan spirit. (730,854 British children lost their fathers in WWI [5]).

Adult children of surviving war-ravaged parents may well recognise the difficulty their parents may have had in being able to bond and show love towards each other and them, as children. They may feel undervalued and unappreciated and their own feelings misunderstood, trampled over or ignored. They may feel that they couldn't measure up to their parents' expectations and values. This can either lead to a fearful and desperate attempt to be accepted and be like their war-experienced parents, where they never truly individuate from them, or the opposite – full-blown rejection of their parents' values and ideas and walking in the opposite direction, as they try to seek their own (rebellious) identity. But neither is this true individuation, for they still define themselves in terms of how they are _not_ like their parents!

The 1960's hippy and sexual revolution on both sides of the Atlantic and indeed in much of Europe, was a graphic illustration of this rebellion by the sons and daughters against their wartime warrior parents' generation. The rejection of traditional Christian life and values, a rise in seeking after alternative spiritualities, occultism, promiscuity, alcoholism, drug-taking, family breakdown, gang warfare, difficulties relating to authority figures, an increase in mental health issues and many other social problems became rife. We live with the consequences of this in today's society.

The reader of this book may be struggling with their own issues, which they recognise may have been caused by, or originated with their family veteran. Was it a father, mother, uncle, aunt, grandparent or great-grandparent? Any relative who had a significant input into the lives of the children may have passed on some of their own traumas. Or was it a more distant ancestor who was affected? Much to their embarrassment, the reader may recognise that the very wounds inflicted by their parents on to them, they are now inflicting, even unwittingly, on to their own children! All the while growing up, the reader may have vowed _never_ to do this to their children, but nevertheless, they are doing so! Paul had the same difficulty, albeit for different reasons, as related in Romans 7:15.

How do you stop this cycle, this snowball of pain and destruction from continuing down the hill to succeeding generations? The first step is to recognise that there is a problem. Having done that, the next step, with prayer for God's help, is to do something about it. Seek counsel, knowledge, prayer support, confession of wrongdoing, healing prayers and ministry in your home group, local church or outside specialist ministry.

In terms of increased knowledge and understanding of the past and how it affects you now, it will be helpful to write down the experiences and stories of your ancestors. Are there family memorabilia of the war in question? Iraq, The Falklands, Korean War, World War II, World War I, the Boer War, or even further back? Photos, documents, souvenirs?

To gain further understanding of one's ancestors' lives, it will be helpful to research online through some of the following genealogy websites, through military records, unit histories and regimental museums. Try starting with:

www.ancestry.co.uk
www.findmypast.co.uk
www.thegenealogist.co.uk
www.forces-war-records.co.uk
www.nationalarchives.gov.uk
www.cwgc.org
Local regimental museums

These websites will help you find your ancestor's military records, such as the branch of service they served in, whether, Army, Navy, Royal Marines, Merchant Navy or Air Force. They will also tell you which regiment or unit they served in and what medals they were entitled to receive.

Service records of **British Army** officers after April 1922 and 'other ranks' who were discharged from the army, or died in service, after January 1921, are not yet available to the public. However, next of kin may apply to the respective service to view them.

Records of **Royal Navy** and **Royal Marines** are restricted post 1926, except to next of kin.

Merchant Navy records are available up to 1972.

For the **RAF**, service records are restricted access after 1920, except to next of kin.

If you are the next of kin or family, you'll be able to apply to whichever of the services that hold your deceased parent's or grandparents' service records. This should be done through the government website at: www.gov.uk/get-copy-military-service-records/apply-for-someone-elses-records#apply-by-post. From that, you will be given:

- surname, first name, service number, rank and regiment or corps
- date and place of birth
- enlistment and leaving dates
- date of death, if they died in service
- medals
- details about the units they served in

However, details about their military career are only provided 25 years after the date they died, unless the immediate next of kin have given their consent to release this information.

There may be little or no information provided about the person's military service. Home Guard records, for example, might only include their personal details at the time of enlistment.

More general military research can be carried out at The National Archives (TNA), initially online, using one of their guides, at: www.nationalarchives.gov.uk/help-with-your-research/research-guides/?research-category=military-and-maritime [6] Once the basic information about your ancestor's service history is gleaned from these sources, then it will be possible to read up about what their unit was doing in their war and thereby gain a deeper appreciation of the causes of their traumas.

Looking at each service in turn and what records are available, let us start with the British army:

British Army

Publicly available records for the Army date from 1660 – 1949. Most are at The National Archives (TNA) in Kew, Surrey and located in the War Office (WO) series of records. Scottish regiments were incorporated into the British Army in 1707 at the time of the

HEALING ANCESTRAL WOUNDS

Act of Union. The National Army Museum (NAM) in Chelsea, London, (www.nam.ac.uk), does NOT hold individual service papers. It may hold some individual items or photographs that once belonged to or show a soldier ancestor.

When searching for an army ancestor, unless he was an officer, it is very important to try to find out **which regiment** he served in, as otherwise, it will be difficult to locate him. This is particularly true for dates before 1873, when individual regiments kept records, rather than them being kept centrally. Family memorabilia or photos may reveal this, but also a GRO certificate, census return or parish register may do so.

The GRO has several useful indexes for finding an ancestor's regiment. See: www.gro.gov.uk/gro/content/. There is the **Army Regimental Register** covering the period 1761-1924. It records births, baptisms, marriages and burials of soldiers and their families. The **Army Chaplains' Returns** record similar details for overseas stations. Then there are the indexes of war deaths, covering the Boer War, WWI and WWII. They are available online at www.findmypast.co.uk, TNA and the Society of Genealogists (SOG). Another good place to search is online at: www.forces-war-records.co.uk

TNA houses the **monthly returns** of the army, covering the period 1759-1865. These record where each regiment was stationed, month-by-month. If you know where your ancestor was stationed at a particular time, then you might be able to find his regiment that way. There are different records for officers and 'other ranks.' For simplicity, the following descriptions of TNA records are divided into three sections with two sets each:

1) Records for 'other ranks' and officers up to 1913.
2) Records for 'other ranks' and officers in WWI.
3) Records for 'other ranks' and officers in WWII.

Other Ranks, 1760-1913

Soldiers' Discharge Papers give the best information about an individual's service record. They include the soldier's original attestation or joining papers. However, these only exist for soldiers who were discharged, rather than died during service. All these papers have been indexed by name on www.findmypast.co.uk. **Muster rolls** and **pay lists** date from 1732 to 1913. Again, all are in the WO series at TNA. **Description books** exist from 1795-1900 and describe soldiers in cases of desertion. There are also **register of deserters** (1811-1852), an **index to deserters** (1828-1840) (also online at www.findmypast.co.uk) and **casualty lists** (1797-1910).

Each regiment also kept a record of men awarded **pensions**. There are additionally pension records for soldiers discharged through injury, either through the Royal Hospitals at Chelsea or Kilmainham in Dublin. They date from 1681 and 1679 respectively. There is a difference between out-pensions and in-pensions. Out-pensions cover most soldiers, as they went home. In-pensioners were those who lived in the hospitals and these can be located in the hospitals' **Registers and Admissions Books** in the WO series. Chelsea's books cover the years 1702-1933, whilst Kilmainham's cover 1704-1922.

Officers, 1702-1913

The published *Army Lists* are the best place to start researching an ancestor who was an army officer. They list the names and regiments in which an officer served. Both TNA and good local reference libraries have copies of these. From this information, it is possible to build up more from other sources at TNA. This can be from the **commission books**, (1660-1873), which detail officers' careers; from the **Indexed Letter Books**, which cover how an officer bought and sold his commission; the **Commander-in-Chief's Memoranda Papers** (1793-1870), containing applications to purchase and sell commissions, with supporting evidence and letters of recommendation.

A useful source of information for officers are their **service records**, dating from 1764-1915. There are **registers of half-pay** (1713-1870) for retired officers who kept their commission and were available to be called back. **Pensions** paid to widows and payments made to children of deceased officers date from 1713-1913 in TNA's records. They were also made to officers who were disabled on active service and had to leave the army.

WWI Records
Other Ranks, 1914-1920

Only about 40% of soldiers' service records survive from WWI, because many were destroyed by bombing in WWII. **Service records** cover those who were discharged from the army between 1914-1920. It is still helpful to know the ancestor's regiment and ideally, his regimental number. Such details can be found in the **Medal Rolls**, available on www.ancestry.co.uk. Both men and officers may appear in the **honour rolls**, with some biographical information. Many of these are digitised on www.findmypast.co.uk.

Attestation papers (joining papers) give details of name, address and date of birth. **Discharge papers** summarise the soldier's career. **Medical records** and **casualty forms** can give more information about what the soldiers were doing and where. **Pension records** survive for those discharged for medical reasons or for those regular soldiers who finished their full length of service. A gratuity was paid to those survivors who had only signed up for the duration of the war.

Officers, 1914-1920

TNA-held records of WWI officers include those who held a regular pre-war commission, those who held a temporary wartime commission in the regulars, those who were Special Reserve officers, or those who held a Territorial Army commission or temporary commission. However, all these records are reconstructions from other War Office papers, because the originals were completely destroyed in 1940. So, only 217,000 WWI officers have surviving information, out of a total of 247,061 officers who were granted a commission during the war. Like the rest of the British Army's records at TNA, all these are in the WO series.

World War I Deaths

The GRO holds the registers of deaths for 1914-1921. As mentioned, www.findmypast.co.uk has an index to these. The Imperial War Museum in London holds the casualty lists, both in book-form and CD, containing about 700,000 names of *Soldiers Died in the Great War* and *Officers Died in the Great War*. The Commonwealth War Graves Commission (CWGC), www.cwgc.org also has further information about graves and memorials.

As mentioned, **Medal Rolls** will give details of an ancestor's achievements. There were three types of medals granted: campaign medals, gallantry medals and good conduct & long service medals. All are listed in the WO series of records at TNA and can be viewed online at:www.nationalarchives.gov.uk/search/results/?_q=Medal+rolls+WWI, www.ancestry.co.uk, www.findmypast.co.uk and in the *London Gazette*, at: www.thegazette.co.uk, for gallantry awards.

As the different types of individual service records do not provide detailed insights into the activities of an individual, it may be possible to gain more understanding of the possible traumas an ancestor went through, by referring to the **regimental war diaries**. These give an overview of daily operations in each battalion, but rarely mention individuals by name. Again, they are kept at TNA in the WO series. Some are viewable online. Beyond these sources, it is worth visiting the appropriate regimental museum, the Imperial War Museum, and / or the National Army Museum, to read a relevant regimental history and view other items.

WWII Army Records, from 1921 Onwards

As previously mentioned, service records of soldiers who were discharged from the army, or died in service after January 1921, and of British Army officers after April 1922, are not yet available to the public. Next of kin may apply to view them via the **Army Personnel Centre**, at: www.army.mod.uk/people/join-well/army-personnel-centre/. The postal address is: Army Personnel Centre, (Historic Disclosures Section), Mailpoint 400, Kentigern House, 65 Brown Street, Glasgow, G2 8EX. Their website will also direct you to: www.gov.uk/get-copy-military-service-records.

Royal Navy

Records for the Royal Navy are also held at TNA and are in the Admiralty (ADM) series. The National Museum of the Royal Navy

(NMRM) in Portsmouth also holds some service records. See: www.nmrn.org.uk/. It was King Henry VIII who created the Royal Navy as an institution. For ancestors alive and serving between the 16th to 19th centuries, it is important to know when and what ships they served on, because there were no centralised records until 1853.

Ratings

Records of ordinary seamen (ratings) can be gleaned from several naval sources. Muster and pay books and pension records will list individuals. As approximately 1/5 of the entire Navy fought at the Battle of Trafalgar in 1805, the TNA-digitised records of those who served there can be very useful.
See: www.nationalarchives.gov.uk/trafalgarancestors/.

Ship's **muster books** giving details of individuals, date from 1667-1878. Ship's **pay books** cover similar dates. There also survive **Ship's Logs, Captain's Logs** and **Master's Logs**. These give details of voyages, actions and commissions. Seamen's **Certificates of Service** exist for 1802-1894. Publicly viewable **pension records** for ratings exist in one form or another from 1737 to 1921. There are records of in-pensioners at the Royal Greenwich Hospital, from 1704-1869.

Centralised records began in 1853, when new entrants were given a continuous service number and their personal and service details recorded in **Continuous Service Engagement Books**, dating from 1853-1872. These are searchable on the TNA Discovery website: https://discovery.nationalarchives.gov.uk/. From 1873, the **Register of Seamen's Services** lists seamen with a different number system, which was changed again in 1894, giving more information and which is publicly viewable up to 1928. As of 2022, there are **continuous record (CR) cards** for the period 1929-1950. For further guidance, see: www.nationalarchives.gov.uk/help-with-your-research/research-guides/royal-navy-ratings-service-records-1853-1928/.[7]

Seamen's records from about **1926 onwards** can only be viewed by next of kin and those who have been given permission by the next of kin. Online, these can be applied for via: www.apply-deceased-military-record.service.gov.uk/, or in writing to: DNPers, Disclosure Cell, MP G-2, Room 48, West Battery, Whale Island, Portsmouth, PO2 8DX.

Officers

Naval officers' records are easier to locate than those for ratings. The published *Navy Lists*, detailing officers and their careers, date from 1782 up to modern times. There are also a good many other published works, such as *Tracing Your Naval Ancestors*, by Bruno Pappalardo.[8]

Service registers for officers' date from 1756-1931 and those up to 1917 can be viewed on the TNA Discovery website. There are two officers' surveys in the ADM series, taken in the years 1817 and 1846. **Succession Books** show the progression of officers moving from ship to ship, as their careers advanced. **Passing certificates** for lieutenants and **qualifying examinations** for warrant officers and specialist ratings date from 1677 to 1902. As exists for ratings, **Ship's Logs, Captain's Logs, Master's Logs** and **Surgeons' Journals** all give details of officers' lives on board ship. Additionally, there exist **Admirals' Journals** at TNA and **Lieutenants' Logs** at The National Maritime Museum at Greenwich.

Registers of half-pay (a form of pension), date from 1697-1924. **Pension records** proper can also be found in the ADM series. Campaign **Medal Rolls** covering the period 1793-1913 and WWI are located at TNA. www.findmypast.co.uk has digitised the officers' medal roll.

As per for ratings, service records for officers, **post 1924**, are held at the same address in Portsmouth, or online via: www.apply-deceased-military-record.service.gov.uk/.

Casualty records for officers who died in WWI are located on www.ancestry.co.uk. WWI and WWII casualty lists are kept by the GRO and CWGC. TNA holds a **War Graves Roll** for WWI casualties. The website: www.forces-war-records.co.uk is a good source of information.

Royal Marines

TNA holds records for Royal Marines (RM) dating from between 1790 – 1936, in the ADM series. The service was originally formed in 1664. For records of those officers and men who joined the RM **after 1925**, only next of kin and those with their permission can see them, (like the Royal Navy), by applying online via: www.apply-deceased-military-record.service.gov.uk/, or in writing to: DNPers, Disclosure Cell, MP G-2, Room 48, West Battery, Whale Island, Portsmouth, PO2 8DX.

The GRO and CWGC hold records of WWI and WWII deaths. www.findmypast.co.uk has the **Medal Roll** for WWI, as does TNA. The latter also holds records of RM births, marriages and deaths and **pension records**.

Other Ranks

Royal Marines 'other ranks' can be found if the **division** to which they belonged is known. There were four divisions, based in Chatham, Plymouth, Portsmouth and Woolwich. Men would normally join the nearest one to where they lived. These can be found via the **medal rolls** at TNA. If the name of the ship and approximate date on which he served is known, then the *Navy List* might give his division. The ship's home port would be the same as the man's division. As each division was split into numbered **companies**, if the latter is known, then that can also point to the correct division.

The service records for the ancestor can be found once his division is known. These will include **attestation forms** (1790-1925) at TNA, giving personal details. **Description books** (1755-1940) give details about the men's careers. **Records of service** (1842-1936) of individuals can be seen online at TNA. However, for men joining **after 1925**, their records can only be seen by next of kin and those with permission from them, as detailed above.

Officers

Officers' records at TNA date from 1793 – 1925. The

Commissions and Appointments Registers include individuals for the periods 1703-1713 and 1755-1814. They also appear in the *Army Lists* and *Navy Lists*. Most of these can be found online at: www.nationalarchives.gov.uk. Recent officers' records should be applied for, as described in the general section above.

Merchant Navy

The British Merchant Navy accounted for 33% of all merchant ships afloat in 1939 and losses were high in WWII. 30,248 merchant seamen lost their lives during WWII, a higher death rate than any of the armed forces.[9] Nearly 15,000 merchant seamen died in WWI.[10] These figures do not take into account those who survived the wars, but who suffered war traumas, such as being torpedoed.

TNA holds records of Merchant Navy seamen in its Board of Trade (BT) series. They date from 1747-1972. Records of **WWII medals** can be viewed online at: https://discovery.nationalarchives.gov.uk/results/r?_q=seamens+medals&_p=1950.

The GRO has an index of **deaths at sea**, dating from 1837 onwards, often giving the map coordinates of deaths on British registered shipping far out to sea.

TNA also holds records of **musters** of ship's crews and voyages, dating from 1747. From 1835 – 1860, there are **Agreements and Crew Lists** at TNA. After 1860, a digitised index to crew lists has been produced by www.findmypast.co.uk. This is drawn from the actual records which are spread between TNA, the National Maritime Museum at Greenwich, some county record offices (CROs) and also at the Maritime History Archive, Memorial University, St John's, Newfoundland, Canada.

There are **Registers of Service** at TNA, dating from 1835 – 1844. These change to a **Registered Ticket** system, detailing individual seamen from 1844 – 1853 and then a new Register from 1853 - 1857. There is no Seamen's Register for the period 1857 – 1913. A fourth **Seamen's Register** dates from 1913 – 1941. However, the records for 1913 – 1918 were destroyed.

www.findmypast has digitised the survivals. 1941 – 1972 covers the period of a fifth Register at TNA.

Royal Air Force

Records for the RAF and its predecessors, the RFC (Royal Flying Corps) and RNAS (Royal Naval Air Service), are held by The National Archives (TNA), at Kew, Surrey. They date from 1912 for the RFC, 1914 for the RNAS and 1918 for the foundation of the RAF and WRAF. TNA has online guides for research into these records.

> RFC service records are under army War Office (WO) classification numbers.
> RNAS service records are coded under the Admiralty, so have ADM numbers.
> RAF & WRAF service records are categorised under AIR coding numbers.

However, service records of airmen with service numbers higher than 329,000 are kept by the RAF. Also, the service records of those airmen with numbers lower than 329,000, who stayed in the RAF for WWII, will have been kept by the RAF. Next of kin or those with written permission from them, can apply for copies of service records online via: www.apply-deceased-military-record.service.gov.uk/, or in writing to: ACOS Manning, (RAF Disclosures), Room 221b, Trenchard Hall, RAF Cranwell, Sleaford, Lincs, NG34 8HB. (Correct at February 2022).

WWI logbooks, combat reports and **operational record books (ORBs)** kept by each squadron are kept in AIR 1. Similar WWII records are kept in AIR 27. ORBs for 1911 – 1963 are digitised on www.ancestry.co.uk. Other types of operational records are listed elsewhere in the AIR series. Some RAF squadron associations have copies of such records uploaded on their websites for personnel who served on individual squadrons.

The details of **medals** are also kept by TNA. RFC medals awarded are listed in the WO series. RNAS medal awards are listed in the ADM section. RAF medals awarded after June 1918 appear in

AIR 1. Most WWII medal awards are listed in AIR 2. It is worth checking the www.forces-war-records.co.uk website for RAF ancestors.

The RAF Museum in London is also a worthwhile place to conduct research into RAF veterans.

See: www.rafmuseum.org.uk/research/. This holds many casualty cards for both officers and men of the RFC and RAF. WWI casualties in both the RFC and RAF also appear in CD form entitled, *Officers Died in the Great War* and *Soldiers Died in the Great War*. There is also the book, *Airmen Died in the Great War*. The Commonwealth War Graves Commission (CWGC) can help with tracing deceased airmen. The GRO also has an index to WWI deaths.

Having detailed what is generally available in the historical sources to give you leads about researching your military ancestor(s)' pasts, it will then be time to assimilate this new-found knowledge. Once that has been done and you have taken time to ask the Lord to show you what to pray into, it will then be possible to work through the last section of this chapter – the practical and spiritual outworking of prayer and ministry into your past.

How to Pray into Generational War Trauma Issues

As per other issues, there are various ways we can pray into generational issues caused by war trauma and from the discoveries made in the records. Peter Horrobin's book, *Healing from the Consequences of Accident, Shock & Trauma*,[11] is an excellent book detailing how to pray for those who have themselves suffered trauma. It is very relevant for this chapter.

To start off, I would recommend praying for protection for yourself and your loved ones and for Jesus to lead and guide you in these prayers. Then pray the 'Lordship Prayer,' as follows:

Lordship Prayer

"Dear Lord Jesus, I realise my need of You and repent of living my life my own way. I wholeheartedly accept You now as my Saviour, my Redeemer, my Lord and my Deliverer.

I invite You now to be the Lord of every part and moment of my life, from the time of my conception, right up until now:

Lord of my body, my physical health and behaviour.

Lord of my mind and all my attitudes and mental health.

Lord of all my emotions and all my reactions.

Lord of my spirit and my worship of You.

Lord of my family and all my relationships.

Lord of my sexuality and its expression.

Lord of my will and all of my hopes, ambitions, decisions and plans.

Lord of all my work and service for You.

Lord of all my finances.

Lord of all my needs and possessions.

Lord of the manner and time of my death."

Declaration

"Thank you, Jesus, for shedding Your blood and dying on the cross, for the forgiveness of my sins, my ancestors' sins and my descendants' sins. You died and rose again that I might be set free to love and to serve You, in newness of life."

At this point, it will be important to **confess and repent of one's own sins**, which may have been committed out of rebellion against the war-damaged parent who, out of their own brokenness, inflicted pain on you. They may or may not have realised what they were doing. Ask God to forgive you, receive that forgiveness by faith and forgive yourself for whatever you did.

Next, thank God for your ancestors. Then, ask Him to help you **forgive your ancestor**, as difficult as that may be, then make a decision to speak that forgiveness out. If we want our sins forgiven by God, we must be willing to forgive others (Matthew 6:14-15) and keep forgiving until it becomes real in our hearts (Matthew 18:21-35). Peter Horrobin's book on accident and trauma is very clear on these steps.[12] Ask the Lord to bring to the surface any hidden painful memories that may have been shut away and forgotten about. Then ask Jesus to bring his love and comfort to you if you become emotional and want to cry. He can hold you and take the pain, leaving you with just the memory, but without the pain of it.

Sometimes the **demonic** may have attached itself to these painful occurrences and with discernment, it may be necessary to take authority over any evil spirits and to cast them out, in the mighty name of Jesus.

Following that, it may help to ask the Lord to heal any **inner brokenness** by bringing together any broken or split off parts of yourself, to form once again, the whole, inner you. Often through trauma, a person can become dissociated or fragmented in part or whole, where the sheer agony of pain has caused the person to psychologically distance themselves from the traumatic event and bury it alive. They then try to forget what happened to them and get on with their lives. But these buried memories do not die and have a way of causing ongoing problems spiritually, psychologically and physically, until the light of Christ is brought to bear on them. Unusual tiredness may be a symptom of this. Peter Horrobin describes this very well.[13] Finally, any **physical healing** needs associated with the trauma can be addressed through prayer.

The next stage will be to confess the ancestral sins, as if they were one's own:

*"While I thank you, Lord, for my ancestors, especially my father and mother who brought me into this world and whom I honour, I do not stand in agreement with them on sinful matters. In these cases, in your presence, Lord, I **confess** and **repent** on behalf of all my parents,' grandparents' and forefathers' sins. I confess that these were sins against you, the effects of which I **renounce** off my life and off the life of my family. I renounce off my life any curses*

which have resulted from these sins and any curses descending to me through my family line. Thank you for becoming a curse for me on the cross, so that I might go free. You knew the pain of physical violence and trauma intimately, especially as the Roman soldiers crucified You.

I ask that You would **forgive** my ancestors' enemies who hurt them, as I also forgive them. (Have your thought of forgiving Hitler, for instance?!). I claim Your **blood cleansing** from all the effects of generational trauma caused by war in my life. Thank you that you love and accept me just as I am and love and comfort me in all the places that I hurt inside. Please reveal any other painful memories caused by my ancestor's sins. Please fill me afresh with your love and to experience your comfort, safety and restoration. Help me to dwell in your presence and soak in your love. You have not abandoned me. I ask that you would prove to me that you really are my protector and shield against the attacks of the enemy. [Do read Psalm 91 after this prayer]. Set me free from any lies I came to believe that you are not strong enough to save and deliver me. In Jesus' name, I pray."

An interesting example of healing from an ancestral war death is related by the Christian psychiatrist, Dr Kenneth McAll (1910 – 2001), in his book, *Healing the Family Tree*.[14] A man who had joined the RAF after a difficult upbringing, had got into the occult and became seriously frightened by the occurrence of automatic writing he learned, which repeatedly spelled out the words, 'German murder'. After becoming a Christian and seeking help, it turned out that through drawing up his family tree, he discovered that his great uncle had been blown up by a German landmine during the Great War, and so there had not been a proper funeral service. During a Eucharist service, the great uncle was committed to Jesus, the man confessed his sins and occult behaviour, and was set free. He subsequently completed his Bible college training well.

In another example of McAll's work, quoted by Stephen Baker, in his booklet, *Healing Present Hurts Rooted in the Past*,[15] was the case of an elderly and retired Anglican clergyman in the north of England, who had lost a leg in WWI. This man suffered years of phantom pains from his missing leg, which made him short-tempered and difficult to be with. He had lost a number of housekeepers for this reason, until one day, a new Christian housekeeper recommended that he invite Dr Kenneth McAll to help out.

Dr McAll duly came and asked him to tell his story, learning that all the man's palls in their artillery position had been killed by the same shell which took off his leg. He asked if there had been a funeral for them, and was rebuffed for asking such a question, because they had been in the middle of a battle at the time and in any case, there was nothing left to bury! The men had been blown to bits. Nevertheless, McAll insisted that they hold a requiem service at that very moment, in order to forgive and to seek forgiveness for those events of so long ago, and to commit the clergyman's palls to God. This they did, taking the Eucharist at the same time. A year later McAll learnt from the man's son that, from that very moment, all the pain had left his father's leg, and he was able to live out the last few months of his life peacefully and contentedly.

Rev Patricia Smith in her book goes so far as to say:

> ...the more experience we have in praying with people for generational healing, the more we find that some things in the family line simply will not be solved by intercessory prayer alone. These are actions so sinful, hurts so deep that only the greatest power available to the Christian will heal them. This is the power that is present to us in the celebration of the Holy Eucharist.[16]

McAll's work is supported by Dr David Wells, who recommends a committal service be held for the uncommitted dead, i.e., those who died during wartime without having had a funeral service, those lost at sea, or suicides who, in the past, were not given Christian burials. A memorial service may not have been sufficient to lay the dead to rest,[17] [or to comfort the bereaved]. This quote from Wells' booklet is helpful:

> Healing in the whole family often follows the committal of the unmourned or unrecognised individual with all the associated sin, pain and distress to God, preferably done by at least one member of that family.[18]

We need to also pray for wrong soul ties with our forebears to be broken:

Breaking of Soul Ties for Inherited War Trauma

"In the name of Jesus, I place the cross and blood of Jesus between myself and each of my family members. I break all the ungodly body, soul and spirit ties with:
My parents, if they experienced the effects of war. (For ancestors who have died, we break the whole soul tie).
With my grandparents, if they suffered war trauma.
With my great-grandparents and,
with my great-great-grandparents, (name any relevant ones), *going back 4 generations.*

I also break any ungodly body, soul and spirit ties, particularly with regards shock and trauma, with any other veterans or individuals who suffered from any war and who had a significant input into my life.

I ask that you would cleanse me from all the effects of trauma, shock, loss, grief and bereavement, passing down to me from every ancestor, through these soul ties."

This prayer will cover the issues mentioned and discernment should be used when waiting upon the Lord for any word of knowledge for a specific revelation. This will be necessary for those ancestral issues which cannot be found in the records.

Breaking Inner Vows & Bitter Root Judgements

When a person meets an inner psychological brick wall of being unable to form godly friendships and relationships because of mistrust caused by inner vows not to trust again, the way through them is to ask God to show you what inner vows were made and against whom. Then forgive the person(s) who broke your trust, renounce the inner vow and ask God to break the power of this inner vow over your life. Finally, ask God to help you to trust (wisely) again.

Additionally, a war-ravaged relative may have caused you or an ancestor much pain, resulting in a **bitter judgement** being made of the person(s). This 'bitter root judgement' may grow to defile your attitudes and relationships with others (including your children), who may remind you of that relative. When highlighted, this bitter root too needs repenting of, the relative or ancestor forgiven, and Jesus asked to root it out, and replace with His love and grace.

Binding and Loosing – Deliverance

Once the above prayers have been said and worked through, it is then time to conduct self-deliverance from any evil spirits. Pray something like this:

"I put the cross and blood of Jesus between myself and... I bind and cut myself off from the ruling spirits of anxiety, fear, intimidation, insecurity, confusion, mistrust, anger, hate, murder, isolation, death, etc, coming down my family line. I bind and loose the spirit(s) of....... [use your discernment to name them] from me and tell it / them to go, in the mighty name of Jesus!"

Lord, I command my body and brain chemistry to come into godly alignment. I speak to the neurotransmitters in my brain and call them into normal functioning.

Please fill me now with Your Holy Spirit, to replace and infill all the empty places vacated by these other spirits. Renew my mind and put a right spirit within me, that I may praise and serve You now and forever more."

Deliverance ministry can also be sought from suitably trained lay or ordained ministers.

The Blessing of Jesus

"I ask, Lord, that you turn all these previous curses into blessings, as I rest in Your love and presence and as I find my peace and security in You. If I am carrying any further emotional wounds caused by this generational trauma, I ask, Lord, that You surface them and show me, so that I can give them to You and express them safely, forgive and be healed of them. I ask this in Jesus' name."

In Summary

Give thanks for you're the lives of your ancestors. **Identify** any war trauma issues in your family line, which may have led to familial sins. If found, **confess** these and the influences they have had in your own life. (Lamentations 5:7). **Repent**, where needed, of these sins in the family line, by identifying with and owning them as one's own. Ask for and receive God's **forgiveness**. **Cut** soul ties. Seek **deliverance** ministry and / or conduct self-deliverance for any spirits encouraged to take up residence because of trauma. Seek the **cleansing blood of Jesus** to wash away any stains.

Ask Jesus to **bless you** and **fill you** afresh with His Holy Spirit. Seek to be **obedient** to His guidance and call on your life.

A Recommendation

As mentioned before, the prayers in this chapter are intended just as openers, to help start you on the journey to freedom. In order to work towards complete freedom, I would recommend working through the material and prayers in the ministry books listed at the end of this chapter. It would also be very worthwhile attending one of the excellent training and ministry courses run by Bethel Sozo, Christian Prayer Ministries, Gilgal House Healing Centre, Ellel Ministries, or Sozo Ministries International, here in the UK. This is not an exhaustive list and the reader may hear of other ministries both in the UK and abroad, which can help in this area.

Further Reading - Select Bibliography

Fowler, Simon. *Tracing Your Army Ancestors: A Guide for Family Historians*. (2nd ed). Barnsley: Pen & Sword Books Ltd, (2013).

Hawkey, Ruth. *Freedom from Generational Sin*. Chichester: New Wine Press, (1999).

Hawkey, Ruth. *Healing the Human Spirit*. Chichester: New Wine Press, (1996).

Herber, Mark. *Ancestral Trails*. (2nd ed.) (Rev). Stroud: Sutton Publishing, (2005).

Horrobin, Peter. *Healing from the Consequences of Accident, Shock & Trauma*. Lancaster: Sovereign World, (2016).

Horrobin, Peter. *Healing through Deliverance*. (rev). Lancaster: Sovereign World, (2008).

Pappalardo, Bruno. *Tracing Your Naval Ancestors*. Kew: Public Record Office, (2003).

McAll, Kenneth. *Healing the Family Tree*. London: Sheldon Press, (1982).

Smith, Patricia A. *From Generation to Generation: A Manual for Healing*. Jacksonville, FL: Jehovah Rapha Press, (1996).

Spencer, William. *Air Force Records: A Guide for Family Historians*. (2nd ed). Kew: The National Archives, (2008).

Wells, David. *Praying for the Family Tree*. France, Saint-Benoit-du-Sault: Editions Benedictines, (2006). (On behalf of the Generational Healing Trust).

Wills, Simon. *Tracing Your Merchant Navy Ancestors: A Guide for Family Historians*. Barnsley: Pen & Sword Books Ltd, (2012).

Chapter 7

Genealogical Evidence for Generational Poverty and Wealth

> My brothers and sisters, believers in our glorious Lord Jesus Christ must not show favouritism. Suppose a man comes into your meeting wearing a gold ring and fine clothes, and a poor man in filthy old clothes also comes in. If you show special attention to the man wearing fine clothes and say, "Here's a good seat for you," but say to the poor man, "You stand there" or "Sit on the floor by my feet," have you not discriminated among yourselves and become judges with evil thoughts?
>
> Listen, my dear brothers and sisters: Has not God chosen those who are poor in the eyes of the world to be rich in faith and to inherit the kingdom He promised those who love him? But you have dishonoured the poor. Is it not the rich who are exploiting you? Are they not the ones who are dragging you into court? Are they not the ones who are blaspheming the noble name of him to whom you belong?   James 2:1-7, (NIV)

James, the brother of Jesus also wrote:

> Now listen, you rich people, weep and wail because of the misery that is coming on you. Your wealth has rotted, and moths have eaten your clothes. Your gold and silver are corroded. Their corrosion will testify against you and eat your flesh like fire. You have hoarded wealth in the last days. Look! The wages you failed to pay the workers who mowed your fields are crying out against you. The cries of the harvesters have reached the ears of the Lord Almighty. You have lived on earth in luxury and self-indulgence. You have fattened yourselves in the day of slaughter. You have condemned and murdered the innocent one, who was not opposing you.   James 5:1-6, (NIV)

These are strong words.

Both poverty and wealth can run in the same family and both can be a curse to those with experience of them.

The obvious place to start researching the financial background of your ancestors is by observing and asking them! Your parents and maybe grandparents should be able to give you a clear idea of their start in life and the sort of family, house, neighbourhood, education and working life they had. This will have strongly influenced their identities and how they thought of themselves. They will know whether they came from a poor, middling or wealthy background. Photos, paperwork, artifacts and household records will confirm what they tell you.

Birth, Marriage and Death Certificates

For further evidence of your family's earlier financial and social standing, the best place to start researching in the genealogical records are birth, marriage and death certificates, either kept at home or located at the GRO. See: www.gov.uk/order-copy-birth-death-marriage-certificate.

Census Returns

These will not only give the names, ages, (and therefore approximate dates of birth), but also the home address, occupations and possibly religious background of your ancestors. Thus, a good idea of the relative wealth or poverty of your forebears will be gleaned, and possibly an indication about their attitudes and beliefs. Look to ancestry.co.uk or Findmypast.co.uk to find this out.

Old Maps

From the street address given on the census returns, it is possible to find the buildings on old maps of where your ancestors lived. Depending on the size of the building, this would give an idea of the relative poverty or wealth of the localities they lived in, which mere street addresses cannot do. There is a free searchable website of old Ordnance Survey maps in various scales, kept by the National Library of Scotland at https://maps.nls.uk/, spanning the years 1855

– 1971. Properties with individual house names are a likely indicator of a higher valuation.

Newspaper Reports

Typing in the names of your ancestors into the British Newspaper Archive website at: www.britishnewspaperarchive.co.uk/ may produce an article written about them. It may record an achievement, list an occupation, detail a criminal trial or conviction of an offence, and otherwise give details about the appearance, family, social standing, address, views and wealth of the individual. To locate such articles, you will need to know an approximate date, town or county, to be able to check the digitised newspapers listed. This is an expanding online project, so if you find gaps in the newspaper records, it may be worth re-checking at a later date to see if further dates of newspapers have been added.

Criminal Records

Poverty can lead people into a life of crime, but a life of crime can keep people poor as well. Envy and the lust for wealth, but achieved outside societally approved ways, can also draw people towards crime. Sometimes wealth can lead to arrogance and a belief by some of the wealthy that their behaviour is above the reach of the law and that they can do what they like to gain and secure further wealth. For example, in tax avoidance schemes.

So, it is worth exploring Britain's extensive criminal records for any ancestors who succumbed to the temptations and illicit thrills in breaking the law. If your ancestor did end up on the wrong side of the law, there is a good chance of finding him or her in the court records as well as newspaper reports. This topic is covered in some detail in chapter 8. There will probably be a restriction of about 75 to 100 years on accessing court records, but those of the first half of the 20th century and certainly earlier than that, will be available. So, it will be worth checking both 19th and 18th century records of the Quarter Session Courts and the Assize Courts.

Such records are increasingly found on the main genealogical websites:
www.ancestry.co.uk
www.findmypast.co.uk
www.thegeneaologist.co.uk

As well as:
www.nationalarchives.gov.uk www.oldbaileyonline.org

Look also in local County Record Offices (CROs), and Borough Record Offices (BROs), whose websites can be found online.

I will now consider the subjects of poverty and wealth separately.

POVERTY

Settlement and Removal Orders

A good source of English and Welsh records on poverty in the local parish are those termed, **settlement and removal orders** and the **settlement certificates** they generated. These are usually kept in CROs, but may be in diocesan record offices (DROs), or even the original parish church. They contain the names of all the family, the date, the parish where they were legally settled and the names of its churchwardens and overseers of the poor. These certificates came out of the Act of Settlement and Removal (1662), which was designed to prove entitlement to poor relief. The poor were effectively forced to stay in the parish of their birth or later settlement. It is known as the 'Old Poor Law.' Settlement certificates proved which parish a family belonged to and therefore which parish was legally obliged to provide for the poor residing there. The overseers of the poor, a body of the parish church, issued the certificates and administered relief. Settlement rights largely depended upon the place of birth, but also on the residency of a husband, should a woman marry into his parish.

In subsequent years, people could also gain settlement if they could prove they had resided in the parish for a period of 40 days, or were paying the parish rate, were apprenticed in the parish, were serving as a parish officer, or working in the parish as an unmarried servant for one year. Further concessions were made on a temporary basis at harvest time, when itinerant workers were allowed into the parish to work the fields, so long as they returned to their own parishes afterwards. More details are given on the GenGuide web page. [1]

A **Settlement Examination** by the parish authorities and a Justice of the Peace took place in cases of illegitimacy, vagrancy, suspected illegal immigration (very topical now!), and sickness. Such persons were likely to become a financial burden on the parish and so a right to settlement had to be proved. Surviving **Examination Papers** are likely to be found in local CROs, in the vestry minutes and Quarter Sessions records. They will contain the names of applicants, parentage, names of children, a date, locations where the family had lived and the verdict of the magistrate. Where such people were not accepted, then a series of **Removal Orders** were generated and the poor were removed, forcibly or otherwise, from the parish, back to their own parish of settlement. Treatment could be harsh and poverty was effectively regarded as a crime, with the poor sometimes passed from pillar to post. One can only imagine the effect such treatment had on the self-respect and morale of these unfortunates and their descendants. The settlement and removal laws were repealed in 1876.

Many poor agricultural workers left the land in the late 18th and early 19th centuries to work in the new industrial towns, moving especially from the south to the north. To save the parish from further expense, many pauper children from the south were apprenticed to masters in the midlands and north, gaining settlement there, but often dying young from the dreadful conditions they had to endure. These 'pauper apprenticeship' papers can be found in local and metropolitan archives. Some children were even sent abroad.

When researching pauper families, thought should be given

to the subject of **bastardy bonds** issued in connection with illegitimate children, as covered in chapter 2 on generational sexual sin.

Under the New Poor Law of 1834, more properly called the Poor Law (Amendment) Act, the responsibility for poor relief was taken away from the vestry, and parishes were united in groups or Unions under a Board of Guardians. These built or reused existing buildings as **workhouses** to accommodate the poor and put them to work. (Up until this time, there had existed 'houses of correction' and later, 'houses of industry'). However, the parish was still responsible for settlement matters up until 1865. After various further changes, the Boards of Guardians were abolished by the Local Government Act of 1929, when county councils and boroughs took over their responsibilities. After 1930, only the aged and infirm were cared for in workhouses, which finally closed in 1948, becoming either hospitals or care homes for the elderly.

Workhouse Records

Records of the workhouse system date from the years 1834 – 1948, when the final abolition of the poor law took place and the National Health Service was founded. These records are located in CROs and metropolitan record offices. The poor, who normally entered their local workhouse, first had their names recorded in the **admission and discharge registers**. These are quite detailed and will be helpful for family historians wanting to prayerfully understand their past.

Details include the names of inmates (families were usually broken up when they entered the workhouse), age, place of birth, date of admission and discharge, marital status, place of settlement, occupation details, any other income sources, physical fitness, reason for seeking workhouse relief, names of relatives and church denomination. Workhouse staff are also listed and its principal officers are named in local county directories (again, kept in CROs).

In addition, there are the **indoor relief lists**, sometimes compiled every six months, which include pauper names, dates of birth and how long they had lived in the workhouse. There are also **registers** of births, baptisms, deaths and burials that occurred in these institutions.

Other forms of evidence for parish support of the poor can be found in the **poor rate books**, vestry minutes and parish books, churchwardens' and overseers' accounts, all now kept by local CROs. Before workhouses came into being, the usual method of (outdoor) support was through **direct gifts** in cash or kind given to, or for the care of the poor on a weekly or monthly basis. Sometimes this was to help the poor find work. Those receiving help were listed by name and the numbers in each family noted, their residence, the amount of bread, soup and clothing given and on which dates, plus any payments given to the vestry for this help. Sometimes the provision of medicine is listed and when the pauper died, his or her few meagre possessions were itemised for sale, so that the parish could recoup some of its expenses.

The National Archives

The National Archives (TNA) at Kew in Surrey hold a variety of records relating to poverty. www.nationalarchives.gov.uk/a2a/ is its website, with the A2A (Access 2 Archives) element showing links to other repositories. Amongst TNA's collections include those on almshouses, charity and ragged schools, emigration, friendly societies and burial clubs. Amongst other, lesser sources of information about poverty are:

Barnardo Homes (Orphanages)

The charity, Barnardo's used to run orphanages. The descendants of such orphans may contact Barnardo's who run a genealogy service called 'Making Connections' which is able to trace the records of relatives' ancestors who were former Barnardo children, looked after in Britain, Australia and Canada. These were sometimes called 'child migrants.' Barnardo's also provide counselling, advice, support and access to post-adoption services for adopted adults, birth parents and relatives. The address is: Making

Connections, Barnardo's, 140 Balaam Street, London, E13 4RD. (See: www.barnardos.org.uk/services/making-connections).

Charity Schools

Records of other schools for the poor are to be found again at TNA, CROs and borough record offices. Many schools were started by the SPCK - the Society for Promoting Christian Knowledge. Its historical records are housed at the University of Cambridge's Manuscripts Department. (See: www.lib.cam.ac.uk). It is best to start by searching the A2A website for individual charitable schools.

Ragged Schools

Ragged schools were schools for the poorest of children. They were founded in 1844 and were a feature of 19th century life in working class districts, being finally abolished in 1902 and replaced by local education authorities.[2] Records, including school registers, are to be found at TNA, CROs and metropolitan record offices. Barnardo's also keeps records, including photographs of many ragged school pupils dating from 1866 onwards.

Emigration

Many poor families were helped to move to Canada and the USA between 1776 – 1890, by the Poor Law unions and lists of emigrants are kept at TNA. Its research guide, 'Emigrants – Domestic Records Information' will help with this. Other institutions also keep records of child migration.[3]

Friendly Societies

These societies were started to provide mutual welfare and financial assistance and many of the people who benefitted would have been poor. According to Robert Burlison (2009), it is estimated that about one in two adult working males belonged to a friendly society at the beginning of the 20th century.[4] Wikipedia has a useful article describing them.[5] Records at TNA cover the period, 1785 – 1966 and include membership lists. There are more friendly society records kept in local CROs or metropolitan ROs. The A2A website at

TNA will help researchers to find which record office holds the files of individual friendly societies. Some friendly societies still keep their historic records and the contact details for these can be found at: www.fca.co.uk.

Local, Parochial Charities

Other records of the poor may be found in the many local charities that existed in the 19th century. These can be found by searching the A2A website of TNA.

Almshouses

TNA contains records for **almshouses**, those charitable institutions which provided accommodation for good living, poor elderly folk. The magnificent Abbots Hospital in Guildford is such an example, founded in 1619 by George Abbot, the then Archbishop of Canterbury, as a gift of accommodation for the town's elderly poor, *'out of love to the place of my birth.'* It is still running on its original endowment from over 400 years ago! (See: www.abbotshospital.org/)[6] The A2A website shows that its records are held at Surrey History Centre (SHC), and those records which used to be held at Guildford Muniment Room are now also held at SHC in Woking.

Almshouse details can also be found at the following website: www.british-history.ac.uk, which is the online version of the famous Victoria County History series of publications. The Almshouse Association (www.almshouses.org) represents almshouses in the UK.

Burial Clubs

Burial clubs were formed in the 19th century to help poor families with the cost of funeral and burial expenses. Members paid a weekly sum to the club and this went towards the cost of a funeral. (See: https://historyhouse.co.uk/articles/burial_clubs.html).[7] Records of these clubs may be seen at TNA: https://discovery.nationalarchives.gov.uk/.

Ireland

Irish Poor Law records dating from the early 19th to early 20th century are held in both parts of Ireland. Northern Irish records are stored at PRONI – the Public Record Office of Northern Ireland. (See: www.nidirect.gov.uk/campaigns/public-record-office-northern-ireland-proni). The address is: 2 Titanic Boulevard Titanic Quarter, Belfast BT3 9HQ.

For Republic of Ireland (Eire) records, which are kept at The National Archives of Ireland, see: www.nationalarchives.ie/. The postal address is: Bishop Street, Dublin 8, Ireland, D08 DF85.

There are also locally kept records in the different county record offices around the country. Ireland also took a decennial census, so these should be consulted too.

Scotland

Scotland had its own sets of Acts of Settlement and poor laws, separate from the English and Welsh system. The Poor Law (Scotland) Act, 1845, set up parochial boards to administer poor relief. The orphaned and destitute under the age of 14, infirm and elderly, could all apply for relief from parish charities. The **kirk** (Scottish for church) would record in their minute books what money was received, what relief disbursed and what refused. In cases of illegitimacy, absent fathers were ordered to pay for the support of their children and wives by the **sheriff courts**, the equivalent of the quarter sessions courts in England.

Almshouses or poorhouses were built mainly in burghs (autonomous municipal corporations) in Scotland since medieval times, and after the 1845 Act, over seventy more were built for the 'combinations' of Poor Law unions. As in England, registers of inmates, amongst other records, were kept and some of these survive in local record offices. Some health board archives have poorhouse records where those later became hospitals.

Many of these records are kept at The National Archives of Scotland. (See: www.nrscotland.gov.uk/). Its address is: HM

General Register House, 2 Princes Street, Edinburgh, EH1 3YY. Similar to the A2A website at TNA, the Scottish Archive Network aims to make available online many thousands of record collections in more than 50 Scottish archives on SCAN.
(See: www.scan.org.uk/aboutus/indexonline.htm).

More information on all these sources of poor records can be found in Robert Burlison's book, *Tracing Pauper Ancestors*.[8] This includes information on other more minor records which may contain the names of poor ancestors, such as subscription charities, industrial schools and reformatory training ships.

WEALTH

As mentioned earlier, wealth can also be a snare to those who have it. The Bible warns us of the dangers that can come from the love of mammon in our lives and how it will take us away from God. See Jesus' own words in Luke 16:9-13:

> I tell you, use worldly wealth to gain friends for yourselves, so that when it is gone, you will be welcomed into eternal dwellings.
> 'Whoever can be trusted with very little can also be trusted with much, and whoever is dishonest with very little will also be dishonest with much. So, if you have not been trustworthy in handling worldly wealth, who will trust you with true riches? And if you have not been trustworthy with someone else's property, who will give you property of your own?'
> 'No one can serve two masters. Either you will hate the one and love the other, or you will be devoted to the one and despise the other. You cannot serve both God and money.'
>
> Luke 16:9-13, (NIV)

In scripture it is also written:

> Then Jesus said to his disciples, "Truly I tell you; it is hard for someone who is rich to enter the kingdom of heaven. Again, I tell you, it is easier for a camel to go through the eye of a needle than for someone who is rich to enter the kingdom of God."
> When the disciples heard this, they were greatly astonished and

asked, "Who then can be saved?"
Matthew 19:23-25; Mark 10:23-26; Luke 18:24-27, (NIV)

But the Bible also records Jesus' reassuring words:

"What is impossible with man, is possible with God!"
Luke 18:27, (NIV)

With wealth can come arrogance, a sense of entitlement, haughtiness, callousness, independence from God, reliance on money, possessions and position (in society), greed, idolatry (and the breaking of the 1st and 2nd Commandments, about having no other gods before the Lord), over-confidence in the intellect that may have helped the person to become rich, competitiveness, mistrust of others (who oppose the rich), lack of peace from all the effort entailed in becoming and maintaining wealth, property and possessions and a whole host of other evils. Of course, this is not always the case and some wealthy individuals and families can be very godly, donating much time and money to charitable causes, Christian or otherwise.

Thinking in relational terms, the wealthy and over-busy often do not have much spare time to attend to their spouses or children's needs. Love is limited in such households and often performance related, with 'love' demonstrated by the simple expedient of gift giving, or buying off with presents. Love comes to be associated with things, not the time needed for warm interpersonal affection, communication and touch. Such children, now emotionally stunted adults, can either grow up to do the same to their children or else, maybe at the other extreme, rebel, reject their parents and upbringing and go off the rails, blaming God in the process for letting it happen.

Children from wealthy backgrounds, historically were relegated to the care of nannies or governesses or packed off to boarding school, only seeing their parents in holiday time. Winston Churchill is a famous example of such a child, abandoned to this system of childcare and upbringing. Is it any wonder that he grew up craving the attention he was not properly given as a child and being unable to relate to God as a loving Father?

These problems naturally filter down the generations, as unfathered, and / or unmothered children who are brought up to value possessions over people, are ill-equipped to parent their own children with either human or God's love. Should such a one be found by Jesus, the journey of godly parenting and renewal of the mind can now begin, but can take much time. Indeed, it might have begun before conversion, when the afflicted seeks counselling or psychotherapy for the growing awareness of their mounting problems and dysfunction.

Part of that journey may include discovering what went on in their past and in their family's past. This is the place where genealogy can now help in the quest for truth and answers.

Two books which can help those on such a quest are, *My Ancestor was a Gentleman*, (2012) by Stuart Raymond and *Tracing your Aristocratic Ancestors* (2013) by Anthony Adolf. I will summarise their findings. There is a huge amount of information available on noble and gentry ancestors. Apart from birth, marriage and death records, census returns, newspapers and the like, as previously outlined, researchers should look into the following materials: the origins of their surnames, into personal records and family histories, heraldry, the heraldic 'visitations,' Burke's Peerage, estate and legal records, loyalty oaths and poll books and, last but not least, educational and career records.

Surnames

Research into surname origins and where they are distributed (See: https://named.publicprofiler.org/), can give an indication of whether you have gentry or aristocratic forebears. Surnames were widely in use by the 14th century. Recognised surname dictionaries should be used rather than online sources which contain many errors. Reaney and Wilson [9] divided up surnames into four categories: topographic (where someone came from), patronymic or matronymic (from the father's or mother's name), occupational (their job), and nicknames (based on some personal physical or moral characteristic). Anthony Adolph [10] says that aristocratic surnames are more likely to be either topographic or patronymic in origin. The *Oxford Dictionary of National Biography* has many aristocrats and gentry in and can also be looked up online at: www.oxforddnb.com. Beware, surnames do sometimes change and sometimes, first and middle names display aristocratic origins.

Personal Records

It goes without saying, that personal records passed down the family may well indicate wealth, gentry or an aristocratic background.

Family Histories

Before embarking on fresh research into your family tree, it is worth checking to see if anyone else has researched your family. Occasionally, the results of these researches are lodged with the Society of Genealogists' library in London. The SoG is linked to the Guild of One Name Studies, whose website is: https://one-name.org/. This guild has members who research the origins of particular surnames and lodge the results with the SoG.

The British Library has many books relating to gentry and aristocratic genealogy and biographies. For instance, *Who's Who* and *Who Was Who*. Its online catalogue is: www.bl.uk/catalogues-and-collections/catalogues. Stuart Raymond's book has a good list of useful biographical dictionaries.[11] Obituaries of aristocrats and gentlemen can be found in old newspapers, digitised on the British Newspaper Archive at: www.britishnewspaperarchive.co.uk/, as well as in *The Times* newspaper online at: www.thetimes.co.uk. Old editions of local papers can be found in local libraries. Another important source of obituaries can be found in *The Gentleman's Magazine*, which was published between 1731 – 1907. Stuart Raymond indicates that this can be searched via specialist publications and repositories, such as the Harleian Society, British Record Society and the Bodleian Library, Oxford.[12] The David Wilson

Library at the University of Leicester also holds copies of *The Gentleman's Magazine*.

Care should be taken if relying upon previously published gentlemen's or aristocratic family trees, as these are sometimes inaccurate. Such was the interest in proving lineage back to an illustrious or royal ancestor, even Adam himself (!), that professional care was not always taken, with mistakes, assumptions, ignored illegitimacy and even inventions made which, with modern scrutiny, can be shown to be false.

Heraldry

The topic of names and published family histories links neatly into the subject of heraldry. It is almost certain that all aristocratic and gentry families will have a coat of arms, otherwise known as 'armorial bearings.' The body responsible for awarding and recording coats of arms is the College of Arms, (founded in 1484 by King Richard III), at 130 Queen Victoria Street, London, EC4V 4BT. Their website is: www.college-of-arms.gov.uk/. Heraldry is useful for identifying individuals and which families they married into and at what approximate date.

Heraldic Visitations

These refer to the visits the heralds of the College of Arms made to the nobles, knights and gentlemen who bore arms in each county during the Tudor and Stuart periods. Lists of such people, some of which survive, were compiled by the sheriffs of each county to enable the visitations. These were to identify which families were entitled to lay claim to a coat of arms, and they also became known as 'armigerous' families. Starting in 1498/9, the major series of visitations were conducted in c.1580, 1620 and 1666. The heralds recorded the evidence and from that, compiled pedigrees, from which might be granted the right to arms for those who did not previously have any. The earliest parts of some pedigrees are more likely to be inaccurate, as some families sought to make connections going back to mythical ancestors such as Brutus, supposedly the heroic founder of the British race and grandson of Aeneas from the

Trojan Wars! [13]

Numerous copies of these arms can be seen in the British Library and other places, such as the SoG and IHGS, rather than the originals in the College of Arms, which is not open to the public. However, it is also possible to commission a herald to make a search of the records held at the College of Arms.
(See: www.college.of.arms.gov.uk).

The Harleian Society, (See: https://harleian.org.uk/) has published the heraldic visitation returns, though care should be taken as to the accuracy of published material there and elsewhere due to incomplete recording, falsifications, copying mistakes and editorial changes.[14] There are a few published guide books to the visitations, held in various libraries and by the societies mentioned above. Anthony Adolph includes a number of these in his book.[15] He also briefly lists contact details for Welsh, Irish and Scottish visitation records.

Welsh records may be seen via the Harleian Society website (But see also The National Library of Wales in Penglais Road, Aberystwyth, SY23 3BU, whose website is:
https://archifau.llyfrgell.cymru/index.php/visitation-records-5).[16]

Apart from at the College of Arms, **Irish records** are also held at The National Library of Ireland, Genealogy Advisory Service, whose address is: 7-8 Kildare Street, Dublin 2, DO2 P638. (See: www.nli.ie/en/genealogy-advisory-service.aspx). [17]

Scottish visitation records are held at New Register House, 3 West Register Street, Edinburgh, EH1 3YT.
(See: www.nrscotland.gov.uk). The Scottish Record Society also contains such records. (See: www.scottishrecordsociety.org.uk/) [18]

Burke's Peerage

This is a published genealogical guide to mainly the British nobility, begun in 1826 and now available online too, at www.burkespeerage.com/. Drawing on earlier works compiled by other genealogists, it includes the peerage, baronetage, knightage and landed gentry of the United Kingdom and the prominent families of Ireland, as well as other dominions and countries. It therefore covers the wealthy end of various countries. *Burke's Peerage* is now in its 107th edition, the latest edition being published in 2003. Later editions of *Burke's* are more accurate than earlier editions, though still not perfect. See Anthony Adolph's book for more details. [19]

There are other variations of *Burke's Peerage*, including *Burke's Extinct Peerage* for peerages and baronetcies which are no longer extant, so it is worth checking the latter publication if no noble ancestor is found in the former.

Estate and Legal Records

Estate and legal records were kept in the 'muniment' room of every aristocrat and gentleman. These were needed to store records relating to title deeds, land conveyances and the efficient running of the owner's estate(s), including leases relating to tenants. It was important to keep a check on which tenants owed rent, how much and when it was due. There might also be letters, journals, instructions and litigation matters kept.

Many of these records are likely to have been passed in modern times to official repositories for safe keeping, such as local County Record Offices (CRO's), Borough Record Offices (BROs), The National Archives (TNA), the British Library, or other institutions. Legal records are also likely to be found in central court archives. Stuart Raymond describes these in some detail.[20] One important guide to major collections of estate records he recommends is:

> *Principal family and estate collections: family names A-[Z]*. 2 vols. Guides to sources for British history 10. London: HMSO, (1996)

Manorial Records

Of some use to gentry ancestry may be manorial records. The gentry may have held a manor or manors and so been titled, 'Lord of the manor.' He appointed a steward and other officials under him, to manage his manorial lands and tenants. They would meet at regular intervals to hold a Court Baron, Customary Court, Court Leet and the 'View of Frankpledge' to elect officers and deal with felonies such as thefts, disputes between tenants and breaches of the peace. Manorial issues were recorded on rolls of parchment and records of these survive from the 12th to 20th centuries. The manorial system was finally abolished in 1925, though nominally, lordships of manors have continued up to the present day.

The **Manorial Documents Register** (MDR), held at TNA, lists what manorial records survive for England and Wales and where they are kept. This and a guide to it are on the website. (See: https://discovery.nationalarchives.gov.uk/manor-search).

Some Irish manorial records are held at TNA, whilst those for Northern Ireland can be searched via the Public Record Office of Northern Ireland (PRONI) in Belfast, at: www.nidirect.gov.uk/campaigns/public-record-office-northern-ireland-proni, and for Eire, in The National Archives of Ireland in Dublin at: www.nationalarchives.ie/. Scotland did not have quite the same system, but 'Scotland's People' does have records of Scottish landed families containing similar information. (See: https://catalogue.nrscotland.gov.uk/nrsonlinecatalogue/welcome.aspx). A directory of Scottish archives can be consulted on the Scottish Archive Network at www.scan.org.uk.

Wills and Probate

An important source of information for tracing aristocratic and gentleman ancestors is to be found in records of wills and probate. These can be very informative, naming whole families as well as servants, the faith and wishes of the testator, giving details about the extent of the estate, and the goods and chattels thereof. The latter will be found in inventories accompanying the will. If no will was made, then a 'letter of administration' was.

Up to 1858, wills were proved in ecclesiastical courts, but in civil courts after this date. The records of these earlier wills (plus letters of administration) are now held either in CRO's (in diocesan

archive bundles), in diocesan archives themselves, or at TNA. The gentry preferred to have their wills proved in the higher courts, meaning either the Prerogative Court of Canterbury (PCC) or the Prerogative Court of York (PCY), rather than the lower ecclesiastical courts. Pre-1858 PCC wills can be found at TNA and online at: www.nationalarchives.gov.uk/help-with-your-research/research-guides/wills-1384-1858/. PCY wills, pre-1858, can be found at the Borthwick Institute for Archives in York, or online at: https://borthcat.york.ac.uk/index.php/are-you-looking-for-a-will.
For post-1858 wills and letters of administration in England and Wales, again, see the TNA online catalogue to proceed from there.

For Northern Irish wills and probate records pre- and post-1858, see PRONI at: www.nidirect.gov.uk/campaigns/public-record-office-northern-ireland-proni.

For Irish Republic wills and probate see the National Archives of Ireland at: www.nationalarchives.ie/.

For Scottish wills and probate, pre-1925, see Scotland's People at: www.scotlandspeople.gov.uk/guides/wills-and-testaments. and for post-1925 wills and probate, see the National Records of Scotland at: www.nrscotland.gov.uk/.

Again, both Stuart Raymond and Anthony Adolph go into more detail in their books,[21, 22] though, of course, there are many, much more detailed books and guides to wills and probate in the British Isles. Increasingly, more and more records of wills and probate can be found on both www.ancestry.co.uk and www.findmypast.co.uk.

Other Estate Records

Of further use in tracing gentleman and aristocratic ancestors are the various large-scale surveys that have been carried out over the last 300 years. These include the **enclosure awards and maps** of land, dating from about 1700 - 1900, giving the names of mainly gentry landowners and their tenants.

Tithe awards and maps, similarly giving the names of

landowners and tenants, were made after the passing of the Tithe Commutation Act of 1836, which abolished the giving of tithes to the church (10% of income) and replaced it with rental payments to landowners. These can be found in CROs and TNA.

The **Return of owners of land** was compiled in 1873 to record everyone who owned more than one acre of land and therefore records every aristocrat and gentleman landowner. London and Middlesex were not included in this survey. www.ancestry.co.uk has records of this return.

Finally, **Lloyd George's Finance Act** of 1909-1910 led to the recording of all landowners and occupiers and their properties. These details are now held in CROs and TNA. Both Stuart Raymond and Anthony Adolph include **court records** in their texts, as the wealthy often got into **legal disputes** over property rights and other matters of concern to them. The central London courts at this time included the Court of Chancery, the Court of Chivalry, the Court of Common Pleas, the Court of Exchequer, the Court of Requests, the Court of Star Chamber and the King's Bench. Cases of litigation in any of these courts may be found in the records held at TNA, but it is not my intention to go into any more detail about these. [23,24]

Loyalty Oaths and Poll Books

I have decided not to go into records of 17th century loyalty oaths and later taxation and poll books from the 18th to 19th centuries, as the preceding records should easily be enough to find wealthy ancestors. This is not intended as a treatise on all genealogical records!

Records of Illustrious Education and Careers

Chapters 4 and 5 deal in more detail about the subjects of education and occupations, but for now, the following can be said about these types of records for the aristocracy and gentry. Firstly, educational records:

Education

Gentry sons, by and large, were increasingly educated in grammar schools or public schools from the sixteenth century onwards. Many aristocratic children had private tutors at home, but later, were also educated in public schools. The most famous of these are Eton and Harrow. In Britain these are private, fee-paying schools, unlike in America, where the term 'public' school refers to a free state school. Registers of these children were kept by the schools themselves, of which many can be found in the library of the Society of Genealogists (SoG) in London. (See: www.sog.org.uk/our-collections/). Some are to be found on www.ancestry.co.uk.

Having left school, many of these (mainly) boys went up to university, which in earlier centuries was limited to Oxford (from 1096), Cambridge (from 1209), St Andrews (from 1413), Glasgow (from 1451), Aberdeen (from 1495), Edinburgh (from 1583), Trinity College Dublin (from 1592), St David's College, Lampeter (from 1828), Durham (from 1832), and London (from 1836). Women were not admitted to the universities (London being the earliest) until 1868. University College, Aberystwyth opened in 1872.

Records of university 'alumni' were kept from early on, though not all gentry and aristocrats matriculated and therefore do not appear in these lists. Many of these lists have been published and can be found in the SoG and on www.ancestry.co.uk. The latter has both Oxford and Cambridge University alumni recorded, taken from original university publications listed by Stuart Raymond.[25] University educational records are covered in more dealt in chapter 4, whilst the next section – occupations, is covered more fully in chapter 5, where it focuses on a wider variety of work for all types of people.

Occupations

Apart from managing their estates, typical gentry occupations were as clergy in the Church of England, the law (both solicitors and barristers), as courtiers to the crown, Justices of the

Peace, Parliament, medicine, the military (Royal Navy and Army, but more recently, the RAF) and even in trade, as merchants, bankers or craftsmen! The East India Company proved a popular route for sons of gentlemen. It should be noted, that sometimes membership of the Freemasons was sought to enable men to gain social connections as a route to gain position and wealth. This topic is covered in chapter 12.

Clergy

It was typical for the younger sons of gentry to enter the **Church of England** as ordained ministers, partly because this position, it has been written, would ensure that they could carry on living as gentlemen, but at minimal cost to their fathers! A major source of information about Anglican clergy for the period 1540 – 1835 is: www.theclergydatabase.org.uk. For the years since 1858, consult *Crockford's Clerical Directory*. (See: www.crockford.org.uk/)

Having said that holy orders in the Church of England was a popular route for the gentry, it is also true that the survival of **Roman Catholicism** in England after the Reformation, depended upon the gentry. Younger sons of the Catholic gentry were often sent to seminaries on the continent to be trained there, before returning secretly to England to work as clandestine priests. Many Catholic gentlemen lived in Lancashire. With the Catholic Relief (or Emancipation) Act of 1829, Catholicism was finally given full freedom again to operate. The Catholic Record Society keeps records of seminary alumni. (See: www.crs.org.uk/).

Royal Service

Stuart Raymond goes into some length describing the different types of **royal courtiers** and where the records of these may be found.[26] Chief amongst these locations are The Royal Archives for people post-1660, (See: www.royal.uk/the-royal-archives), TNA, and British History online at: www.british-history.ac.uk. Securing a position at Court or within the administration of Crown Estates very often depended on having the right contacts within Court circles and having the ability to pay to be taken on into whatever role was vacant.

The Law

Many gentry sons entered the law. This was a lucrative profession for them. Their education in the law was often finished at the Inns of Court in London and fortunately, there is a database of admissions to one of these Inns, the Inner Temple,
at: https://archives.innertemple.org.uk/records/ADM.[27] The SoG, TNA, British Library and Guildhall Library all have good sets of *Law Lists*, which frequently include father's names as well. University alumni records also provide useful information about graduates who went into the legal profession. For a wider description of the legal profession as it relates to gentry, see Stuart Raymond.[28] and the section on the law as an occupation in chapter 5.

The Military

The officer ranks of the **Royal Navy, Royal Marines, Army** and much later, the **Royal Air Force**, were an obvious choice for young men of the aristocracy and gentry, who, before 1871, purchased their commissions. There is a wealth of information on these occupations both in print form and on the internet. I have covered this subject matter in chapter 6 on war trauma, so it is best to look back there for more details. However, as a little bit of extra information and to include the briefest of summaries, you may be interested in this:

Army records at TNA may be divided up into two periods: the Civil War soldiers, both Royalist and Parliamentarian (1642-1660) and those officers who served from the early 1700s until WWI. Both Ancestry.co.uk and Findmypast.co.uk have good records for WWI. Forces War Records at www.forces-war-records.co.uk has a very good selection of military records spanning several centuries, up to and including WW2. Stuart Raymond goes into some detail about military gentry ancestors.[29]

Records of Civil War officers' details may be looked up on

TNA's website: https://discovery.nationalarchives.gov.uk/. TNA also keeps the records of military personnel for later centuries, up to the 1920s. Army officers are listed in the *Army Lists* from 1740 onwards, while naval officers may be found in the *Navy Lists* from 1797 onwards. Anthony Adolph points out that there are good biographical dictionaries for past RN officers, such as *The Commissioned Sea Officers of the Royal Navy 1660-1815*, by Syrett and DiNardo, (1994).[30] Royal Marines officers' records are held at TNA and date from 1793-1925. The Imperial War Museum in London holds the casualty lists of soldiers who died in the Great War of 1914-18. After the 1920s, the relevant military service must be approached for records of officers by their next of kin.

Medicine

Few sons of the aristocracy entered medicine, but many younger sons of the gentry did, becoming either physicians or surgeons. This profession only became more organised in the 19th century with better training. The Royal College of Physicians in London has been one of the main governing bodies of the profession since 1518 and its library contains records of all its members dating back to its foundation. The Royal College of Surgeons of England also keeps registers of its members. These date back to 1745. The Guildhall Library in London also holds some membership records. (See: www.cityoflondon.gov.uk/things-to-do/history-and-heritage/guildhall-library).

Apothecaries (now called chemists), formed the Society of Apothecaries in 1617, now called the Worshipful Company of Apothecaries. Its apprenticeship and membership records are held internally at: www.apothecaries.org and by the Guildhall Library. There are other publications which list the past members of the various branches of medicine. See Stuart Raymond's book for these.[31] Chapter 5 on occupations in this book deals more fully with the medical professions.

Trade

For those younger sons of the gentry and aristocracy who went into trade, the usual route was to gain an apprenticeship with a master for a period of 7 years. For the gentry, this would likely be in London. Surviving records of apprenticeship indentures (when they signed up) are kept in borough record offices, TNA, the SoG and in London livery company archives.

See: https://discovery.nationalarchives.gov.uk/ which lists where any particular record is kept around the country. Once in business for themselves, they would have their names and businesses entered into the trade directories of the time. These can be found in CROs, borough record offices, TNA and the BL.

The British Library (India Office Collection) in London holds the records of the **East India Company** in which many gentry sons served and gained their fortunes between 1600 - 1874.
(See: www.bl.uk/collection-guides/india-office-records).
Stuart Raymond describes in further detail, records of trade.[32]

I have not described all the types of records that may be searched when trying to find aristocratic and gentry ancestors. For example, while Anthony Adolph writes about the subject of genetics and DNA testing to find and make connections with aristocratic ancestry,[33] I have not done so. The subject is very briefly mentioned in relation to King Richard III in my introductory chapter. The records which are included in this chapter are the main ones useful for your purposes.

Having done your research into locating poor and / or wealthy forebears, it is now possible to move on to the section about how to pray into your findings.

How to Pray into Generational Poverty & Wealth Issues
A Question:

Are there any issues in your life, such as recurring poverty, mishandling of money, attitudes that betray a lack of trust in God's provision, a 'poverty spirit' or independence from God, arrogance, haughtiness, expensive tastes and indulgencies that your pocket cannot afford, etc, etc, that once confessed and repented of, you still can't gain the victory over? If so, this could be a sign that there is generational curse, familial attitudes and expectations or other problems coming down your family line, influencing you.

Marilyn Hickey states [34] that:

> Poverty breeds immorality, shame, carelessness, and crime. The curse starts in one generation and just grows and grows, making itself worse with each new generation. Where did that curse come from? "The curse causeless shall not come." There must have been sin!

To start off, I would recommend praying for protection for yourself and your loved ones and for Jesus to lead and guide you in these prayers. Then pray the 'Lordship Prayer.' This prayer and the declarations and prayers following, are used by several Christian ministries, in various forms, which you can find online and whose address details you can find in Appendix F.

Lordship Prayer

"Dear Lord Jesus, I realise my need of You and repent of living my life my own way. I wholeheartedly accept You now as my Saviour, my Redeemer, my Lord and my Deliverer.

I invite You now to be the Lord of every part and moment of my life, from the time of my conception, right up until now:

Lord of my body, my physical health and behaviour.

Lord of my mind and all my attitudes and mental health.

Lord of all my emotions and all my reactions.

Lord of my spirit and my worship of You.

Lord of my family and all my relationships.

Lord of my sexuality and its expression.

Lord of my will and all of my hopes, ambitions, decisions and plans.

Lord of all my work and service for You.

Lord of all my finances.

Lord of all my needs and possessions.

Lord of the manner and time of my death."

A Recommendation:

Those unhelpful activities and attitudes which may have become habitual in your life, or those of any of your ancestors' lives, may have become idols. They will need to be confessed as idols and repented of. Any pleasure or excitement gained from them needs also to be repented of and taken to God in prayer for Him to remove the pleasure of sinning.

If fear of being without has a place in your life, then this fear needs to be repented of too and renounced. Pray for an increasing level of trust in God's provision to grow in your life. Ask God to renew your mind and give you hope and belief that you can pay your way honestly through life and for Jesus to show you how. God will not let you down!

If you find that you look down on the poor, despite the fact of knowing that the poor have a special place in Jesus' heart, then this too needs repenting of and asking God to change your heart. Do you support the needy in any practical ways, such as donating to or volunteering at a foodbank?

Declaration

"Thank you, Jesus, for shedding Your blood and dying on the cross, for the forgiveness of my sins, my ancestors' sins and my descendants' sins. You died and rose again that I might be set free to love and to serve You, in newness of life.

While I thank you, Lord, for my ancestors, especially my father and mother who brought me into this world and whom I honour, I do not stand in agreement with them on sinful matters. In *these cases, in your presence, Lord, I **confess** and **repent** on behalf of all my parents,' grandparents' and forefathers' mistrust, rejection, cursing or indifference towards You, because of their experiences of either poverty or wealth. I confess that these are sins against you, which I **renounce** off my life and off the life of my family, which have resulted in curses running through the family line, down to me. Thank you for becoming a curse for me on the cross, so that I might go free. I ask that You would **forgive** my ancestors' turning away from you, as I forgive them also, either because of lack of teaching, unbelief and despair caused through poverty or through wrong teaching, idolatry, self-idolatry, pride and the cares of worldly wealth.*

*I also forgive any cases of injustice done to my family on the part of employers who withheld or underpaid wages, or the police, the judiciary, the courts or any authority involved in my family's lives, who may have treated them badly. I claim Your **blood cleansing** from all the negative effects of generational poverty and wealth in my life, in Jesus' name."*

Cutting of Ungodly Soul Ties

Once confession and renunciation for sin has occurred, it will then be necessary to cut off any negative spiritual power transmitting down the family line via the generational soul ties, or 'body, soul and spirit ties,' as some call them. To do this, a suggested prayer is,

"In the name of Jesus, I place the cross and blood of Jesus between myself, my family and ancestors and I cut the negative body, soul and spirit ties between myself and my father / mother; between myself and other family members, (name them), *who may have developed ungodly ties with me;*
with my grandparents;
with my great-grandparents and,
with my great-great-grandparents and,
with previous ancestors, (name any relevant ones), *going back 4 generations where there has been a spirit of poverty, idolatry or self-*

idolatry operating. I ask you, Jesus, to send out from me every generational spirit of poverty, fear, despondency, despair, bitterness, idolatry, self-idolatry, pride, deceit, arrogance, freemasonry, etc and draw back to me anything of my spirit and soul that is residing in my father or mother, or any other family members or ancestors I knew."
(For ancestors who have died, we break the whole soul tie).

"I ask Lord, that you would cleanse my blood line and my spirit, soul and body with your precious blood and fill me afresh with your love and your Holy Spirit, in Jesus' name."

Wait upon the Lord for any word of knowledge for a specific revelation. This will be necessary for those ancestral sins which cannot be found in the records.

Inner Vows & Bitter Root Judgements

When people have been crushed by poverty and see no escape, they sometimes conclude they will never be free to make ends meet. They may have made what is called, a 'bitter root judgement' out of the bitterness of their hearts. This same attitude can be passed down to their children. Or they may make inner vows never to let their children suffer in the same way and cause their children to grasp after advancement, achievement and wealth, excluding God and the care of others in the process. Some well-known millionaires have come from such backgrounds. They can be tough, suspicious and unforgiving of those seen as not as successful and guard their wealth ferociously. Some become philanthropic and generous to others, while others hoard their wealth, without compassion for or trust of the weak and poor.

But these self-protective pronouncements and decisions, rather than helping, actually work to enslave the person who made them in ways they could not foresee at the time. Only later will the person find that negative issues recur again and again. Their poverty or wealth imprisons them. The old memory may be forgotten, but when they reach out to someone and want to get close, they actually find that their inability to trust works to isolate them still, leading to loneliness.

When the person meets these sorts of brick walls, the way through them is to repent of and renounce these bitter root judgements and to ask God to help them to live wisely. They need to renounce the inner vows that they made and ask God to break the power of these vows over their lives. They may need to forgive several people from the past and ask God to show them who they can trust. It is better to give than to hoard wealth. Poverty can also trap people into holding on too tightly to what they have, so that they fear to give anything away. But God is no man's debtor.

> Jesus sat down opposite the place where the offerings were put and watched the crowd putting their money into the temple treasury. Many rich people threw in large amounts. But a poor widow came and put in two very small copper coins, worth only a few cents. Calling his disciples to him, Jesus said, "Truly I tell you; this poor widow has put more into the treasury than all the others. They all gave out of their wealth; but she, out of her poverty, put in everything—all she had to live on."
> Mark 12:41-44, Luke 21:1-4, (NIV)

Identity in Christ

As Christians, we have a new identity. We are no longer enemies of God, alienated from Him, from others and from ourselves. While some of our ancestors may have been crushed and alienated from society through their poverty, this heritage need not define us. Similarly, if some of our ancestors rejected God because of their love of money and wealth, their attitudes and behaviour need not be repeated in us. We are now accepted as beloved sons and daughters of the King of Kings! We have worth and value and therefore a new, godly reason and purpose for living. As Christians, ALL are set free and adopted into God's family and need to learn a new identity: our identity in Christ! John 1:12-13 says this clearly:

> *Yet to all who did receive Him, to those who believed in His name, He gave the right to become children of God – children born not of*

> *natural descent, nor of human decision or a husband's will, but born of God.* John 1:12-13, (NIV)

We are loved by God more than we can possibly know. We can discover this through the scriptures and personally through prayer, receive His love and hear His words of affirmation and delight in us. As we rest in His presence, we can soak in his warmth, approval, and love. His *rhema* voice and words, heard in our spirits, back up His written, *logos* words in the Bible. As we dwell on these, they will gradually counteract the lies we have been taught to believe about ourselves. God truly is LOVE! He loves us unconditionally! He is truth and His truth-telling will change us as we believe what He says about us; that we are loved and valued.

Binding and Loosing - Deliverance

To conduct self-deliverance, one should pray something like this: - *"I bind and cut myself off from the ruling spirits of poverty, fear, failure, despair, anger, resentment, idolatry, self-idolatry, pride, arrogance, deceit, cynicism, freemasonry, etc, coming down my family line. I bind and loose the spirit(s) of……. [use your discernment to name them] from me and tell it / them to go, in the mighty name of Jesus! I break the curse of the spirit of poverty or mammon love operating in my family line, even down to me.*

Please fill me now with Your Holy Spirit, to replace and infill all the empty places vacated by these other spirits. Renew my mind and put a right spirit within me, that I may praise and serve You now and forever more."

The Blessing of Jesus

"I ask, Lord, that you turn all these curses into blessings, as I rest in Your love and presence and as I find my true identity in You. You came to set me free to be me, to renounce the heavy burdens of the past and to carry your yoke, which is light. If I am carrying any emotional wounds, or wounds of neglectful parenting caused by generational poverty or idolatry through inherited wealth, I ask, Lord, that You surface them and show me, so that I can give them to You

and express them safely, forgive and be healed of them. I ask this in Jesus' name."

In Summary

Give thanks for your ancestors. **Identify** any issues to do with poverty or wealth found in your family line, which may have led to familial sins. If found, **confess** these and the influences they have had in your own life. (Lamentations 5:7). **Repent**, where needed, of these sins in the family line, by identifying with and owning them as one's own. Ask for and receive God's **forgiveness**. **Cut** soul ties. Seek **deliverance** ministry and / or conduct self-deliverance for any spirits encouraged to take up residence by poverty or wealth. Seek the **cleansing blood of Jesus** to wash away any stains.

Ask Jesus to **bless you** and **fill you** afresh with His Holy Spirit. Seek to be **obedient** to His guidance and call on your life.

A Recommendation

As mentioned before, the prayers in this chapter are intended just as openers, to help start you on the journey to freedom. In order to work towards complete freedom, I would recommend working through the material and prayers in the ministry books listed at the end of this chapter. It would also be very worthwhile attending one of the excellent training and ministry courses run by Bethel Sozo, Christian Prayer Ministries, Gilgal House Healing Centre, Ellel Ministries, or Sozo Ministries International, here in the UK. This is not an exhaustive list and the reader may hear of other ministries both in the UK and abroad, which can help in this area.

As well as family and friends who might help, your local church will be there for you. There are also numerous charities, such as the Salvation Army and foodbanks, with perhaps the best in the UK being Christians Against Poverty (CAP), who can and do help people order their finances and get out of debt. Local councils are there to assist too. There is always help to hand.

Further Reading - Select Bibliography

Adolph, Anthony. *Tracing Your Aristocratic Ancestors: a guide for family historians.* Barnsley: Pen & Sword Family History, (2013).

Burlison, Robert. *Tracing Your Pauper Ancestors: a guide for family historians.* Barnsley: Pen & Sword Family History, (2009).

Raymond, Stuart A. *My Ancestor was a Gentleman.* London: Society of Genealogists Enterprises Ltd, (2012).

Chapter 8

Genealogical Evidence for Criminal Ancestry

For the ways of a man are before the eyes of the Lord,
And He watches all his paths.
His own iniquities will capture the wicked,
And he will be held with the cords of his sin.
He will die for lack of instruction,
And in the greatness of his folly he will go astray.
Proverbs 5:21-23, (NASB)

One of the criminals who hung there hurled insults at him: "Aren't you the Messiah? Save yourself and us!" But the other criminal rebuked him. "Don't you fear God," he said, "since you are under the same sentence? We are punished justly, for we are getting what our deeds deserve. But this man has done nothing wrong."
Then he said, "Jesus, remember me when you come into your kingdom."
Jesus answered him, "Truly I tell you, today you will be with me in paradise."   Luke 23:39-43, (NIV)

Crime as Defined in the 10 Commandments

The Bible's 10 Commandments list five separate items, numbered six to ten, which either are, or can lead to criminally-defined behaviour:

6) You shall not murder
7) You shall not commit adultery
8) You shall not steal
9) You shall not bear false witness against your neighbour
10) You shall not covet

These form the basis of Britain's Christian-based criminal code, which stretches back to the time of King Alfred the Great's law code in the 9th Century.

Crimes in Britain's Past

From the Middle Ages until 1967, crimes were divided into felonies or misdemeanours. In the 18th century, the most common crimes were theft of property, (called larceny), including burglary and robbery, prostitution, public drunkenness and scandalous behaviour. These were treated very harshly. There were some 220 capital offences for felonies by mid-century, known as the 'Bloody Code',[1] with hanging the usual mode of execution. Most of these capital offences were abolished in the early 1800s. Lesser punishments for misdemeanours included whipping, fines, imprisonment with hard labour or transportation overseas for either 7 or 14 years. Transportation began in 1617 to the new American colonies and later, also to the West Indies. With the outbreak of the American War of Independence in 1775, transportation to America ended, but a new avenue for convicts was opened with the First Fleet sailing from Portsmouth to Australia in May 1787.

The most common crimes in the 19th century were petty theft, committed by males. The most common crimes committed by females were linked to prostitution, including soliciting, drunkenness, being drunk and disorderly and vagrancy. Company frauds and financial scandals were also quite commonplace.[2] Transportation as a punishment to the colonies, especially Australia, came to an end in 1868. Over 160,000 people were transported to Australia between 1787 and 1868.

The last execution in the UK was carried out in 1964, whilst the death penalty was finally abolished for all categories of crime, as recently as 2004.[3]

Other forms of misdemeanour straddling the centuries were those linked to sexual misconduct and the unmarried. Illegitimacy, or 'bastardy' as it was known, and the effect of children born out of wedlock could cause considerable financial problems for the local parish before the Poor Law Amendment Act was passed in 1834. After that date, responsibility for the poor passed to the Board of Guardians and the new system of workhouses. The reputed fathers of illegitimate children were brought before the courts and required to pay for the upkeep of their children, thereby helping the mothers, and relieving the burden on the local parish rates. However, this topic is covered more fully in chapter 2 on sexual sin and chapter 7 on poverty. The reason for including it here is because old court records are full of documented cases of illegitimacy, bastardy orders and bonds, ensuring the father paid maintenance for his child's upkeep.

Consequences of Crime – Why is it Harmful?

Crime not only harms its victims and society, but also the perpetrator. Physical, emotional and spiritual harm can result. Later, I will explain about the damage of harmful soul ties being formed through crime. Other consequences will be a guilty conscience or a seared conscience, a loss of social conscience towards those sinned against, shame, mistrust, cynicism, broken personal boundaries, lack of responsibility, distorted emotions and thinking, deceit, rebellion, broken family relationships due to imprisonment, loss of honest earnings, the inability to find work with a criminal record, poverty and the modelling of a crooked lifestyle to any children of the criminal. No doubt there are other consequences.

It is the issue of modelling a life of crime to the next generation and early learning of it by the children that is of especial concern here. While children should not be held accountable for their parents' sins (Deuteronomy 24:16), there is a greater risk that those taught how to become criminals, either consciously or unconsciously by their parents, may indeed want to emulate them. This will perpetuate this distorted training in the children, who will thus incur the penalties for their own sins. A generational weakness and temptation to commit crime (an iniquity) has been set up. Demonic spirits invited in by the sinful forefather or mother can then be passed on to the children quite unwittingly, almost condemning the descendants to act out in similar ways as they grow older. This is a principle which neatly leads us on to the next issue of curses being passed down the family line.

Curses Resulting from Crime

Deuteronomy 27:11-26 describes the curses that would be incurred by the people of Israel when they broke the law of Moses. Amongst these curses are those for dishonouring a father or mother (v.16), moving a neighbour's boundary stone (v.17), misleading a blind person on the road (v.18), depriving the alien, orphan or widow of justice (v.19), various familial sexual sins (v.20-23), striking down a neighbour in secret (v.24) and taking a bribe to shed innocent blood (v.25). So, these curses cover sins, including sexual sins, against the family and crimes against others and their property. All of them violate some boundary or other, whether personal or property.

The effects of these curses are described in the next chapter of Deuteronomy 28:15-68. The curses would affect the wrongdoer whether they are in the city or field (v.16), the basket and kneading-bowl (v.17), the fruit of the womb or ground, cattle and calves, sheep or lambs (v.18), going in or out (v.19), disasters, panic, frustration (v.20), disease, drought and crop failure (v.21-22), climate and soil problems (v.23-24), war, defeat and death (v.25-26), sickness of body and mind (v.27-28), blindness, insult and robbery (v.29), relationship breakdown, inability to live in your own house or enjoy the wine from your own vineyard (v.30), the theft or killing of livestock (v.31), the loss of your children to 'another people' (v.32), having your produce eaten by an unknown people, being abused and crushed (v.33), seeing sights that drive you mad (v.34), you will be afflicted with untreatable boils all over your body (v.35), banishment or enslavement in another country full of idols (v.36), and eventually being led by the Lord to a place where the people there completely reject the wrongdoer (v.37).

Verses 38 – 68 carry on in the same vein, expanding upon these curses – lack of food and drink, despite planting, children taken into captivity, foreigners in power over the Israelites while the latter descend lower and lower, destruction, serving enemies, the land besieged, cannibalism even, severe diseases, banishment from the homeland, no rest or peace, a 'languishing spirit' and dread, as slaves in a foreign land. (Echoes of Egypt).

Furthermore, these curses can be passed down the family line from parents to their children, grandchildren and so on. Quinn Schipper [4] succinctly defines the meaning of a generational curse:

> A generational curse is a form of involuntary inheritance through the bloodline of lineage and ancestral sin. Ill effects such as poverty, barrenness, chronic or hereditary infirmity, addiction, mental illness, failure, and hindrances to spiritual growth often distinguish this type of curse.

A prayer for the renunciation of generational curses, based on Schipper's example, is given in Appendix D.

From Curse to Blessing

> Behold, I will send you Elijah the prophet
> Before the coming of the great and dreadful day of the LORD.
> And he will turn
> The hearts of the fathers to the children,
> And the hearts of the children to their fathers,
> Lest I come and strike the earth with a curse.
> Malachi 4:5-6, (NKJV)

This scripture from Malachi, the last book of the Old Testament, prefigures the work of Jesus, our Messiah, who came to undo the curses of our inheritance and grant us salvation, as described in the very next book, Matthew, the first book of the New Testament.

These pivotal verses show that where fathers and their children are estranged, there will be a curse at work. This truth is graphically illustrated in a story relayed by Gordon Dalbey, in his book, *Sons of the Father*.[5, 6] There was an occasion in a men's penitentiary in the US, when Mother's Day was approaching. A nun, working in the prison, wanting to help these men, responded to their requests for Mother's Day cards and so ordered hundreds from a card manufacturer. These duly arrived and the prisoners were invited to come to collect them in time to send on to their mothers. All the cards were collected and sent. Buoyed by this pastoral success, she looked ahead in the calendar to find the date for Father's Day and ordered enough Father's Day cards for every prisoner. When the time came, a similar announcement was given for prisoners to come and collect their Father's Day cards. Not one prisoner ever came. Tragically, years after, those same cards were still in boxes in the chaplaincy office.

This story speaks volumes about the consequences of broken relationships with our earthly fathers and how the pain of this can lead to rebellion and a life of crime. However, this one reason and example demonstrates exactly why Jesus came. Only He can turn the hearts of fathers to their children and the hearts of the children to their fathers and, ultimately, their Father in heaven. He comes to bless and to heal.

Harmful Soul Ties formed through Crime

Soul ties were designed by God to be good and for our blessing. They were designed to knit us together in godly relationships for, as God said in Genesis 2:18:

> 'It is not good for the man to be alone. I will make a helper suitable for him.'

So, He put Adam into a deep sleep and took out a rib from his side to form Eve. In 1 Samuel 18:1 and 3-4, (NIV), we read of how the souls of David and Jonathan were knit together as one:

> After David had finished talking with Saul, Jonathan became one in spirit with David, and he loved him as himself.
>
> ...And Jonathan made a covenant with David because he loved him as himself. Jonathan took off the robe he was wearing and gave it

to David, along with his tunic, and even his sword, his bow and his belt. 1 Samuel 18:1, 3-4, (NIV)

These are examples of godly soul ties. One might add, the relationships Jesus had with his disciples were also godly!

However, because of the fall, all human relationships have become tainted and so there will be a mixture of both godly and ungodly ties in most relationships. This is true where a person or an ancestor has got involved in crime, thus contaminating his or her family relationships, friendships or work relationships.

One such marital relationship, tainted by crime in the Bible, was between the weak King Ahab and his dominant Queen, Jezebel. In 1 Kings 21:1-16, we read about a man named Naboth who owned a vineyard, close to King Ahab's palace, in the city of Jezreel. Ahab wanted this land for himself. However, because Naboth had inherited this land from his ancestors, it was special to him so he would not sell it, even to the king. It was also forbidden to do so under Mosaic law. So, Ahab went into a sulk. Seeing him thus, Jezebel took action and arranged for Naboth to be falsely accused of cursing God and the king. This gave her the pretext to have Naboth arrested and executed and his vineyard given to Ahab. This crime did not go unpunished, for eventually both Ahab and Jezebel were killed for their many sins.

In modern parlance, one can think of the expression, 'As thick as thieves,' to describe the unholy bonds that are formed between criminals or between criminals and those they 'train' up. The 1968 musical, 'Oliver', based on Charles Dickens' 1838 novel, 'Oliver Twist', comes to mind. In it, the elderly villain, Fagin, brings up numerous orphaned, young street urchins in the nefarious art of pick-pocketing, in return for being a 'father-figure' who gives them a roof over their heads and food for their bellies.

More seriously though, such 'nurture' and training will bond the child to the adult and result in the child seeing crime as a 'good' or 'normal' thing, confusing and ultimately dulling their consciences to what is right. Such training cannot end well.

Historical Records of Crime

What are the surviving, publicly-viewable records of past crimes in this country? There are a surprising number of records that do survive and which are held in various archives and repositories across the land. In fact, for the family historian who discovers a criminal ancestor, he or she will quite possibly learn more about their forbear than any other of their ancestors, because of the detailed nature of many of these records. This section will briefly describe what these records are and where they are held.

Basically, there are court records, newspaper records, prison records and transportation records. Many of these can be found on three main genealogical websites: www.ancestry.co.uk, www.findmypast.co.uk and www.thegenealogist.co.uk, as well as the British Newspaper Archive, www.britishnewspaperarchive.co.uk and the *London, Edinburgh and Belfast Gazettes* at www.thegazette.co.uk. However, there are a number of other important sources of information to be researched. These include local County Record Offices (CROs); The National Archives (TNA) and the Old Bailey website (www.oldbaileyonline.org) for many London trials. There are numerous books detailing their locations, such as Jeremy Gibson's *Quarter Sessions for Family Historians,* (2008).[7]

Before describing what these records are, I will start with a brief description of the structure of the British court system that existed in more recent centuries, as these all created their own records.

The Structure of Historical Courts

Skipping over the earlier mediaeval courts, the court system from the 16th century until 1971 was divided into three. The lowest court was the **Petty Sessions**; the middle one, the **Court of Quarter Sessions**, and the higher one was the **Court of Assize**. Since 1971, these have been termed magistrates' courts, county courts and the High Court.

The Petty Sessions Court met locally twice a month and

dealt with minor criminal matters, such as domestic disputes, vagrancy, financial debts, public order offences and the breaking of the Sabbath.

The Quarter Sessions Court met every three months (i.e. four times a year), on a rotating county basis and dealt with middling issues, such as petty larceny, offences against bye-laws, licencing laws, tax and tithe avoidance, poor law offences including settlement and removal orders for poor families, single parent families and vagrants, bastardy orders and bonds to make reputed fathers of illegitimate children pay maintenance. They also dealt with suppression of riots to preserve the peace, arresting of offenders, and trying suspects in all cases (in earlier times) below treason. Two of my clients had ancestors who were tried for offences in the quarter sessions courts.

The Assize Courts had higher authority and worked on a circuit basis covering several counties each, with two assize judges working in pairs. They tried the more important cases or felonies that carried the death penalty, but also had some overlap with the Quarter Sessions in matters of larceny (or theft). Serious offences included murder, rape, infanticide, highway robbery, assault, rioting, recusancy and treason. Anyone who was transported before 1718 or was transported for 14 years after this date would have been tried at an assize court. After 1718, anyone who was transported for less than 14 years could have been tried at either an assize or quarter sessions court. Until 1832, sheep stealing was punishable with death and so until this time, such cases were tried by the assize courts. After 1832, when it was treated less seriously, the Court of Quarter Sessions dealt with cases of sheep stealing.

About 70% of all criminal cases tried at the assizes were for larceny or related offences. Witchcraft cases and religious recusancy trials (of Roman Catholics), were especially common during the reign of the protestant Queen Elizabeth I (1558 – 1603). The assizes also had authority in matters of local government. They dealt with the suppression of local alehouses, and corporate matters in towns.

Frequently, appeals against settlement and removal orders of paupers and bastard children in disputes between counties, were brought before the assizes. Matrimonial separation and desertion issues were also handled. There is far more that could be written about the assize courts, indeed any of the courts, but not in a book chapter of this necessarily short length.

Types and Locations of Records

Petty Sessions records are kept by local CROs. However, their survival prior to the 19th century is not good. Some are digitised on www.ancestry.co.uk and www.findmypast.co.uk and newspaper reports about cases at the time may be found via www.britishnewspaperarchive.co.uk.

Quarter Sessions records are mainly kept in local CROs, though some are increasingly found on www.ancestry.co.uk and www.findmypast.co.uk and some have been published by local history societies. Many CRO quarter sessions records are still unindexed and only catalogued with scant details. They include those involving **bastardy disputes** where illegitimate children were concerned. The reputed fathers were required to pay for the maintenance of their children's upkeep, thus aiding the mother, so that the parish would not have to bear the cost. Before the Poor Law Amendment Act of 1834, justices of the peace worked closely with the parish officials, especially the overseers of the poor. A **bastardy order and bond** would be issued by the court to order the father to pay a regular sum for the child's upkeep, with a bond to appear before the court, together with a bondsman who would make sure he did, on pain of incurring a larger fine if they did not attend, or if the father did not pay. The father's name should appear on the bond, together with his bondsman, the mother's name and the sex (not name) of the child concerned, as well as the amount of the bond.

There are also **recognizance books,** similar to bastardy bonds, (recording a form of bail and where a person was required to attend court and give evidence, with a pledge of money that could be forfeited for non-attendance), **estreats** (a copy of a court record for use in the enforcement of a fine or forfeiture of a recognizance), **writs, indictments, conviction registers, calendars of prisoners** held in gaols, **debtors' papers**, records of **insolvency** and **prison discharge** and contracts for the **transportation** of felons.

The book mentioned previously, *Quarter Sessions for Family Historians*, by Jeremy Gibson provides a summary of the surviving records for each county and where they are held.[8] Many 19th century court cases were reported in the local press and the British Newspaper Archive is well worth checking for such reports. (See: www.britishnewspaperarchive.co.uk/)

Assize records, as mentioned, contain details of more serious crimes. However, they are quite similar to those produced by the quarter sessions courts. There survive **calendars of prisoners** (or gaol books) to be tried, **indictment files, crown minute books, presentment (or process) books, recognizances, depositions, informations, coroner's inquests, civil minute books and order books.** These terms are explained by searching online or checking more detailed works on the assize courts and by the archive repositories holding them.

Most English assize records are now kept at The National Archives (TNA) in Kew, West London. The National Library of Wales in Aberystwyth holds the equivalent Court of Great Sessions records, dating from 1543-1830. (See: www.library.wales/collections/learn-more/screen-sound-archive/discover/search-the-catalogue). **Welsh records** after 1830 are at TNA. See later in the chapter for help in locating Scottish and Irish historic criminal records.

Survival rates of documents vary and few assize records have been published. Some assize records are to be found in local CROs. Prior to 1733, the records are in Latin, but afterwards, they are in English. It is best to start by searching the minute books, gaol books or agenda books for specific trials of named individuals. Descriptions may include the name, age, address and occupation of the accused. Sometimes, even a photograph may be included.

When searching TNA records for an ancestor, it will be necessary to know the name, and the county or circuit which tried him/her and the approximate date. The Criminal Registers for England and Wales cover the period, 1805-1892 and these provide the verdicts and sentences meted out to offenders. Bear in mind, though, that calendars of prisoners' records (dating from 1868) of less than 75 or 100 years old, are closed to the public.

London

About 1/6th of the population of England and Wales lives within the London area. So, the London courts were kept busy! Cases within the City of London were tried at the **Old Bailey** and also sometimes, the **Guildhall**. Prisoners were kept at Newgate gaol.

The Old Bailey's records survive from 1684 and are almost complete from 1744 up to the early / mid-20th century. They can be viewed through the Old Bailey's own website at: www.oldbaileyonline.org, as well as on www.findmypast, the Guildhall Library and the British Library, where they are known as the Old Bailey Session Papers.

When the **Central Criminal Court** (CCC) was established in 1834, taking over from the Old Bailey sessions, it still carried on meeting at the Old Bailey. It covered crimes committed within the **City of London**, Middlesex, and the parts of Surrey, Kent and Essex nearest London. The CCC also tried crimes committed abroad and on the high seas. Its records, post 1834 are to be found at TNA. www.findmypast.co.uk has CCC calendars of prisoners from 1855-1931 listed online.

Guildhall cases covering the **City of London** and Southwark now have their records administered by the London Metropolitan Archives (LMA). See: www.cityoflondon.gov.uk/things-to-do/history-and-heritage/london-metropolitan-archives).

Between 1618 and 1844, cases within the **City of Westminster** were dealt with by the Westminster Sessions of the Peace. The Middlesex Sessions dealt with Westminster cases after 1844. These were equivalent to the quarter sessions, with the exception that they met every month, not every quarter. The Westminster records are also at LMA.

Transportation

Transportation as a punishment fascinates the modern family historian. Briefly, between 1617 and 1782, convicts were transported to the American colonies and the West Indies. During the American War of Independence (1775-1783), convicts were required to do hard labour for about 3 years within Britain or other British-held colonies, such as Antigua, Bermuda and Gibraltar, when convicts began to be confined on floating prison hulks. After America was 'lost,' i.e., became independent, convicts were transported to Australia for the first time in May 1787. Prison 'hulks' continued in use until 1857 as a means of holding prisoners between sentencing and their transportation. Transportation to Australia lasted until 1868, by which time, as mentioned earlier, over 160,000 people had been sent there.

Records of transportation for the period, 1617-1782 are listed in the State Papers Domestic at TNA. For the period 1787 – 1867, you should look at the convict transportation registers, the contracts for the transportation of convicts (1842-67) and **prison hulk registers** (1776-1857), Treasury Board Papers and Treasury Money Books at TNA. Both ancestry.co.uk and findmypast.co.uk have records of convicts transported to New South Wales and Van Diemen's Land (later called Tasmania).

Prisons & Prisoners

Many towns, plus cities and boroughs had their **own gaols** and the records of these will be with local CROs or at TNA. Some of these are on ancestry.co.uk and findmypast.co.uk. TNA has a register of **habitual criminals** in England and Wales (1869-76), and one for London (1881-1959), kept originally by the Metropolitan Police.

Captions, Transfer Papers & Licences

TNA also has a series of records called **Captions** (1843-71) which were court orders, recording the name, crime and sentence given upon conviction. There are 19th century **transfer papers** in TNA which record a convict's move from one government prison to another. For good behaviour, prisoners might be granted a **licence** to be freed on parole and these survive in TNA for the period (1853-87). These are also available online at ancestry.co.uk and findmypast.co.uk.

Petitions & Pardons

Late 18th and 19th century **Petitions** for clemency raised either by the convict, or their victim's relatives to deny clemency, and **pardons** given by the judges, are to be found at TNA.

Other Jurisdictions

This chapter primarily focuses on English and Welsh records, but for **Scotland**, the websites containing relevant information on historic criminal records would include:
www.nls.uk/family-history,
www.nrscotland.gov.uk/research/guides/crime-and-criminals
www.scottishindexes.com/ScotlandsCriminalDatabase.aspx

For **Northern Irish** historic criminal records, you can start by looking at:
www.nidirect.gov.uk/information-and-services/public-record-office-northern-ireland-proni/search-archives-online
www.publicrecordsearch.co.uk/northern-ireland/

For **Irish Republic** historic criminal records, search:
www.nationalarchives.ie/legal-records/court-records-held-in-the-national-archives/
www.familysearch.org/search/collection/2487287
https://timeline.ie/tracing-irish-ancestors-online/irish-crime-records/

Remember to try the British Newspaper Archive at: www.britishnewspaperarchive.co.uk/ for reports of trials. Both ancestry.co.uk and findmypast.co.uk will be useful in tracing Welsh, Scottish and Irish criminal records.

As can be seen from even this brief summary of the available historical records about crime, there is a wealth of information to be sought which could throw light on the activities of an ancestor caught up on the wrong side of the law. The reader will be able to determine through prayer, whether those long-distant behaviours and mind sets which fuelled their ancestors might have been passed down the family line to themselves.

Evidence of Crime on the Family Line

In his book, *Healing the Family Tree*, Dr Kenneth McAll [9] writes about a 73-year-old lady who suddenly developed violent and unprovoked outbursts of temper towards her younger sister. Their mother had also displayed similar behaviour before she had died four years previously, aged 96. This lady was always apologetic, but couldn't understand her behaviour. Dr McAll was called to help and drew up a family tree to help try to understand the reason. Together, they found a pattern going back six generations, whereby the eldest daughter in each generation had displayed similar behaviour as this lady! It had started in about 1750, when there had been a murder in the family. The eldest daughter at that time, (presumably distraught by the murder), became an alcoholic and destroyed much of the family's belongings, before drinking herself to death at the age of 40.

The lady's niece had also been having psychiatric treatment for some months for violent behaviour. To resolve this inherited pattern, Dr McAll, together with two clergymen, medical people and a family member, held a Eucharist service to pray for the family and those departed. Both ladies were healed and had no further attacks.

In another case, Dr McAll asked some parents to construct a family tree for their adopted son, who was in prison for repeatedly stealing. As he was adopted, they didn't know about his family tree and explained how he had been chosen to replace their baby boy who had died at birth. When, during a Eucharist service for him, they named their baby and committed him to the loving care of Jesus, their adopted son suddenly changed in prison, was reformed, released and later gained and held a responsible job.

The reader may know of instances in his or her own family or another person's family, where there has been a pattern of inherited misdemeanours or criminal activity.

How to Pray into Generational Criminal Activity Issues

To start off, I would recommend praying for protection for yourself and your loved ones and for Jesus to lead and guide you in these prayers. Then pray the 'Lordship Prayer.' This prayer and the declarations and prayers following, are used by several Christian ministries, in various forms, which you can find online and whose address details are listed in Appendix F.

Lordship Prayer

"Dear Lord Jesus, I realise my need of You and repent of living my life my own way. I wholeheartedly accept You now as my Saviour, my Redeemer, my Lord and my Deliverer.

I invite You now to be the Lord of every part and moment of my life, from the time of my conception, right up until now:

Lord of my body, my physical health and behaviour.

Lord of my mind and all my attitudes and mental health.

Lord of all my emotions and all my reactions.

Lord of my spirit and my worship of You.

Lord of my family and all my relationships.

Lord of my sexuality and its expression.

Lord of my will and all of my hopes, ambitions, decisions and plans.

Lord of all my work and service for You.

Lord of all my finances.

Lord of all my needs and possessions.

Lord of the manner and time of my death."

Are there any cases of breaking the law in your life, whether caught out or not, that once confessed and repented of, you still can't gain the victory over? If so, this could be a sign that there is generational criminal activity in your family line influencing you.

Those dubious activities which have become habitual in your life, or those of any of your ancestors' lives, have become idols. They will need to be confessed as idols and repented of. Any pleasure or excitement gained from rebellion and breaking the law, needs also to be taken to God in prayer for Him to take away the pleasure of sinning and repented of. If laziness or fear of being without the basic necessities of life led to stealing, then this behaviour and fear needs to be repented of and renounced and for God's love and trust of His provision to grow in your life. Ask God to renew your mind and give you hope and belief that you can pay your way honestly through life. God will not let you down!

There are also numerous charities, such as the Salvation Army and foodbanks, with perhaps the best in the UK being Christians Against Poverty (CAP), who can and do help people order their finances and get out of debt. The local church will always try to help. Local councils are there to assist too. There is always help to hand.

Declaration

"Thank you, Jesus, for shedding Your blood and dying on the cross, for the forgiveness of my sins, my ancestors' sins and my descendants' sins. You died and rose again that I might be set free to love and to serve You, in newness of life.

*While I thank you, Lord, for my ancestors, especially my father and mother who brought me into this world and whom I honour, I do not stand in agreement with them on sinful matters. In these cases, in your presence, Lord, I **confess** and **repent** on behalf of* all my parents,' grandparents' and forefathers' involvement in any criminal activity. I confess that these were sins against you, which I **renounce** off my life and off the life of my family, and which have resulted in curses running through the family line, down to me. Thank you for becoming a curse for me on the cross, so that I might go free. I ask that You would **forgive** my ancestors' involvement in criminal activity as I forgive them also. I also forgive any cases of injustice to my family on the part of the police, the judiciary, the courts and any authority involved. I claim Your **blood cleansing** from all the effects of generational criminal activity in my life, in Jesus' name."

Prayer of Committal of the Dead

It may be helpful to hold a prayer of committal, including a Eucharist service, sharing the bread and wine (or fruit juice), when committing the (perhaps criminal) dead to God. The examples quoted above, from the successful ministry of Dr Kenneth McCall, would indicate that this can be of lasting benefit to the living descendants.

How to Pray Further into Criminal Ancestry

Where ancestors have been before the courts for sexual offences, details of these and prayers for setting yourself free are to be found in more detail in chapter 2. Negative soul ties being formed through sin and their effect on succeeding generations, need to be addressed.

Cutting of Ungodly Soul Ties

Once confession and renunciation for sin has occurred, it will then be necessary to cut off any negative spiritual power transmitting down the family line via the generational soul ties, or 'body, soul and spirit ties,' as some call them. To do this, a suggested prayer is,

"In the name of Jesus, I place the cross and blood of Jesus between myself, my family and ancestors and I cut the negative

body, soul and spirit ties between myself and my father / mother; between myself and other family members, (name them), *who may have developed ungodly ties with me;*
with my grandparents;
with my great-grandparents and,
with my great-great-grandparents and,
with previous ancestors, (name any relevant ones), *going back 10 generations where there has been sexual crime involved. I ask you, Jesus, to send out from me every generational spirit of sexual licence, lying, deceit, theft, violence, murder etc and draw back to me anything of my spirit and soul that is residing in father / mother, or any other family members or ancestors I knew."*
(For ancestors who have died, we break the whole soul tie).

"*I ask Lord, that you would cleanse my blood line and my spirit, soul and body with your precious blood and fill me afresh with your love and your Holy Spirit, in Jesus' name."*

Wait upon the Lord for any word of knowledge for a specific revelation. This will be necessary for those ancestral sins which cannot be found in the records.

Inner Vows & Bitter Root Judgements

When people have been wounded, they sometimes make inner vows to protect themselves from being hurt again. These could include the decision to retaliate and take revenge, never to forgive the offender and never to trust again. But these self-protective pronouncements and decisions, rather than helping, actually work to enslave the person who made them in ways they could not foresee at the time. Only later will the person find that the same issues occur again and again. The old memory may be forgotten, but when they reach out to someone and want to get close, they actually find that their inability to trust works to isolate them further, leading to loneliness.

When the person meets these sorts of brick walls, the way through them is to forgive and to ask God to help them to trust (wisely) again. They need to renounce the inner vows that they made and ask God to break the power of these vows over their lives.

Additionally, a relative with a criminal record may have caused you or an ancestor much pain, resulting in a bitter judgement being made of the person(s). This 'bitter root judgement' may grow to defile your attitudes and relationships with others who may remind you of that relative. When highlighted, this bitter root too needs repenting of, the relative or ancestor forgiven, and Jesus asked to root it out and replace with His love and grace.

Identity in Christ

As Christians, we have a new identity. We are no longer enemies of God, alienated from Him, from others and from ourselves. While some of our ancestors may have been alienated from society through their criminal acts, rejected, imprisoned, even transported, or executed, this heritage need not define us. We are now accepted as beloved sons and daughters of the King of Kings! We have worth and therefore a new, godly reason and purpose for living. As Christians, ALL are set free and adopted into God's family and must learn a new identity: our identity in Christ! John 1:12-13 says this clearly:

> *Yet to all who did receive Him, to those who believed in His name, He gave the right to become children of God – children born not of natural descent, nor of human decision or a husband's will, but born of God.* John 1:12-13, (NIV)

We are loved by God more than we can possibly know. We can discover this through the scriptures and personally through prayer, receive His love and hear His words of affirmation and delight in us. As we rest in His presence, we can soak in his warmth, approval and love. His *rhema* voice and words, heard in our spirits, back up His written, *logos* words in the Bible. As we dwell on these, they will gradually counteract the lies we have been taught to believe about ourselves. God truly is LOVE! He loves us unconditionally! He is truth and his truth-telling will change us as we believe what He says about us; that we are loved and valued.

Binding and Loosing - Deliverance

To conduct self-deliverance, one should pray something like this:

"I bind and cut myself off from the ruling spirits of rebellion, deceit, cynicism, violence, murder, lust, fornication, perversion, witchcraft etc, coming down my family line. I bind and loose the spirit(s) of....... [use your discernment to name them] *from me and tell it / them to go, in the mighty name of Jesus!*

Please fill me now with Your Holy Spirit, to replace and infill all the empty places vacated by these other spirits. Renew my mind and put a right spirit within me, that I may praise and serve You now and forever more."

The Blessing of Jesus

"I ask, Lord, that you turn all these curses into blessings, as I rest in Your love and presence and as I find my true identity in You. You came to set me free to be me, to renounce the heavy burdens of the past and to carry your yoke, which is light. If I am carrying any emotional wounds caused by generational criminal ancestry, I ask, Lord, that You surface them and show me, so that I can give them to You and express them safely, forgive and be healed of them. I ask this in Jesus' name."

In Summary

Give thanks for your ancestors. **Identify** any criminal ancestors in your family's past. If found, **confess** these crimes in your family line and any influence they have had on your own life. (Lamentations 5:7). **Repent,** where needed, of these sins, by identifying with and owning them as one's own. Ask for and receive God's **forgiveness**. **Cut** soul ties. Seek **deliverance** ministry and / or conduct self-deliverance for any resulting spirits. Seek the **cleansing blood of Jesus** to wash away any stains.

Ask Jesus to **bless you** and **fill you** afresh with His Holy Spirit. Seek to be **obedient** to His guidance and call on your life.

A Recommendation

As mentioned before, the prayers in this chapter are intended just as openers, to help start you on the journey to freedom. In order to work towards complete freedom, I would recommend working through the material and prayers in the ministry books listed at the end of this chapter. It would also be very worthwhile attending one of the excellent training and ministry courses run by Bethel Sozo, Christian Prayer Ministries, Gilgal House Healing Centre, Ellel Ministries, or Sozo Ministries International, here in the UK. This is not an exhaustive list and the reader may hear of other ministries both in the UK and abroad, which can help in this area.

Further Reading - Select Bibliography

Dalbey, Gordon. *Sons of the Father*. Folsom, CA: Civitas Press, (2012).

Hawkey, Ruth. *Freedom from Generational Sin*. Chichester: New Wine Press, (1999).

Gibson, Jeremy. *Quarter Sessions for Family Historians*. (5th ed). Bury: Family History Partnership, (2008).

McAll, Kenneth. *Healing the Family Tree*. London: Sheldon Press, (1982).

Prince, Derek. *Blessing or Curse: You Can Choose*. (3rd ed). Grand Rapids, MI: Chosen Books Publishing Co., (2006).

Schipper, Quinn. *Trading Faces. Dissociation: A Common Solution to Avoiding Life's Pain*. (3rd ed). Stillwater, OK: Quinn Schipper, (2020).

Wade, Stephen. *Tracing Your Criminal Ancestors: a guide for family historians*. Barnsley: Pen & Sword Family History, (2009).

Chapter 9

Genealogical Evidence for Generational Mental Illness

> *That day David fled from Saul and went to Achish king of Gath. But the servants of Achish said to him, "Isn't this David, the king of the land? Isn't he the one they sing about in their dances: "'Saul has slain his thousands, and David his tens of thousands'?"*
>
> *David took these words to heart and was very much afraid of Achish king of Gath. So he pretended to be insane in their presence; and while he was in their hands he acted like a madman, making marks on the doors of the gate and letting saliva run down his beard.*
>
> *Achish said to his servants, "Look at the man! He is insane! Why bring him to me? Am I so short of madmen that you have to bring this fellow here to carry on like this in front of me? Must this man come into my house?"* 1 Samuel 21:10-15, (NIV)

> *On hearing this, Jesus said to them, "It is not the healthy who need a doctor, but the sick. I have not come to call the righteous, but sinners."*   Mark 2:17, (NIV)

Definition of Mental Illness

It is a well-known fact that repeated sin can and does lead to mental health problems. For one thing, as we all know, sin robs us of peace with God, with others and with ourselves. That is just the beginning of a potential downward spiral. The 10 Commandments are there for a reason! Not to spoil our fun, but to protect us, and others from harm!

The definition of mental illness or insanity has changed over the centuries and it can therefore be difficult to pin down as an exact, measurable science. However, for the sake of this chapter and the scope of the useful genealogical research needed to prove the existence of mental illness in the family line, I will only cover the years back to the mid-18th century. Kathy Chater lists three broad strands to these illnesses; the curable *neuroses*, the (apparently) incurable *psychoses* and those physically affected with *mental retardation,* which is also incurable.[1]

The *neuroses*, previously called neurasthenia or nerves, include chronic anxiety, hypochondria, depression and obsessive-compulsive disorder (OCD). These people are aware they have a problem and may be willing to seek help.

The *psychoses* include(d) personality disorders, bipolar disorder (formerly called manic depression), schizophrenia, autism, and Asperger's Syndrome and affected people who were not in touch with reality.

Those with *mental retardation* might have included mongolism (now called Down's Syndrome), which was more common in children who were / are born to older mothers in their 40s. Then there is Alzheimer's Disease, previously termed *senile dementia*.

Those who were either not treated or treated unsuccessfully for venereal disease, were diagnosed before the 1940s as having *General Paralysis of the Insane (GPI)*. In earlier times, they were treated with either mercury or arsenic, themselves poisons!

Problems Developing from Generational Mental Illness

Patterns of thought and behaviour often go down family lines and these can include health issues. They can be of a physical, psychological or spiritual nature. So, mental illness in an ancestor may affect and manifest in a similar way in some of the descendants.

Dr Kenneth McAll in his book, *Healing the Family Tree*, graphically describes how unhealthy **bonds of control** can develop between, say, mothers and children, which can greatly inhibit the offspring from developing normally, leading in some cases, to mental illness.[2]

In one case study, Dr McAll recalled a lady, the daughter of a clergyman, who was incarcerated in a psychiatric hospital for having attempted on numerous occasions to gouge out the eyes of her children. Dr McAll asked the clergyman to draw up his family tree to try and discover what might be influencing his daughter from the past. It turned out, that generations before, the family had lived in a castle. They were able then to go on a tour of that castle and amongst other things, see the dungeons. In those dungeons, they saw various instruments of torture, including those which would have been used to gouge out eyes.

The clergyman and Dr McAll, with the permission of the bishop, were going to hold a Eucharist for the dead, but shortly after, the father heard from the hospital over 100 miles away that his daughter had stopped having her obsessional thoughts of gouging out eyes on the very day that they had made the decision to hold a Eucharist! Later on, they found out that an aunt, who was also in a psychiatric hospital, albeit a different one, was miraculously healed at about the same time. So instead of holding a Eucharist, they held a service of thanksgiving instead.

If you suspect that there may be some history of mental illness in your family line, beyond your immediate known family, but do not know of any details, then the next section in this chapter may help you find out some information about your ancestors' lives.

Evidence of Mental Illness in your Family Line

The general rule of thumb in genealogy is to start with your immediate family and work backwards. What family stories do you already know? Do they indicate an inherited component to mental illness or disturbance in your family? Ask your eldest relatives first about what they remember of their lives and those of their parents and grandparents. Are there any family papers which might give a clue as to what went on in the past? This section will only consider the main types of records of interest in locating a mentally ill ancestor.

General Registration Records

Sometimes, a gap in the birth order of an ancestor's children, as noted from the birth certificates, may indicate that a parent may have been sent away to an asylum. Of course, this might have been for other reasons. Until the law changed in 1937, it was not possible to get a divorce on the grounds of the spouse being

mentally ill. Up until then, it was only possible if a spouse was proved to have been insane at the time of marriage. **Divorce records**, from 1858 – 1972 are held at TNA.
(See:www.nationalarchives.gov.uk/help-with-your-research/research-guides/divorce/).

Then look at or order relevant **death certificates** for your ancestors, from the General Register Office (GRO). Nowadays, this is done online, via: www.gro.gov.uk/gro/content/. These go back to 1837, when civil registration began. The reason for a death will be given on the death certificate and sometimes, suicide is given as the cause (as happened in my Great-Great Grandfather's case). If it was signed by a coroner, then an inquest took place. From this, it should be possible to trace the **coroner's report** in the local County Record Office (CRO) or Borough Record Office (BRO), in the area where the suicide happened. They keep the original reports amongst the Quarter Sessions Records (the legal papers generated by the forerunners of today's magistrates' courts, up to 1971). Coroners had to hand over their reports to the Quarter Sessions between 1752 – 1860.[3] The National Archives (TNA) also hold coroner's reports. The whereabouts of these reports can be found by checking a copy of *Coroner's Records in England and Wales*, by Gibson and Rogers.[4]

More modern coroner's inquest reports are kept under the control of the coroner for 75 years, but are normally sent to the local CRO after 5 years. However, they are still under restricted access for 75 years. The family may apply for permission directly to the coroner to view the relevant report if it is still closed. However, bear in mind that most reports may have been destroyed if they are greater than 15 years old, unless they pre-date 1875.[5]

Local Newspapers and Suicides

In the case of a suicide, the local newspapers will probably have reported it and any inquest that took place into it. Checking this route may well be quicker than searching for a coroner's report. Chater [6] says newspapers are the best source of information on an inquest from the late 19th century, up to the middle of the 20th century. This is less so these days, because of the changes in technology and the decline in the numbers of newspaper staff. Dramatic, newsworthy suicides may even be reported in the national press. CROs and local libraries will have copies of old local newspapers. It is worth checking *The British Newspaper Archive* online at: www.britishnewspaperarchive.co.uk. This has the facility to type in any search term, such as a name, for any particular newspaper, in any county that has been digitised, on any particular date, month and year. Failing that, a local library or CRO will have copies of original local newspapers.

Census Records may indicate cases of mental illness. The 1851 census onwards has a column for recording the deaf, blind, dumb and lunatic. This is a good place to remind readers that the terminology for mental illness has changed over the years. From the 18th to 20th centuries, words for mental illness, as well as epilepsy, included, 'persons of unsound mind', lunatic, idiot, mentally handicapped, mentally retarded, cretin, moron, and imbecile. Thankfully, these terms are no longer used officially as they carry negative meanings now. However, names of asylum inmates are usually not given, only their initials, or first name and initials. So, identifying an ancestor in an asylum has to be done using other records to supplement them. This changed on the 1911 census, when full names are given. Most names are given on the 1921 census, though some institutions only have inmates' initials provided.

County and Borough Record Office Records

Workhouses were normally the first place where lunatics were assessed and therefore workhouse records will reflect this. They are likely to be in the minutes and the overseer of the poor accounts. These are kept in local CROs and BROs. Some start as early as 1764. Workhouse records were closed for 65 years, but as workhouses as a whole were abolished in 1930, it means that their records have now been open since 1995. There are a number of websites devoted to the history of workhouses and their records. See for example: www.workhouses.org.uk/records/.[7]

CROs and BROs also hold **Poor Law Union** records dating back to 1834. These can help find mentally sick patients in both the parish and Quarter Sessions records. Also held will be the admission and discharge books for lunatics originally kept in the old Victorian asylums, from 1834 - 1909.

Those kept by TNA are in the MH series. Some patients' files have survived for the period 1849 – 1960, though there is a 75-year confidentiality ruling, so as of 2022, those after 1947 are closed. Almshouse records in CROs and BROs may also be worth checking.

Bethlem Hospital

The Bethlem Hospital was the first hospital dedicated for the poor insane, way back in 1247, although mentally ill patients are not mentioned until 1377. Most of the earliest patients were physically, rather than mentally sick. The premises have moved several times in London over the centuries and Bethlem Hospital is now located in Beckenham, Kent, where it has been since 1930.[8] It remained the only public asylum until the beginning of the 18th century. Amongst many types of records, it has patient admissions registers and casebooks from 1683 - 1932, the incurable patient admissions register, dating from 1723 – 1919 and discharge and death registers, 1782 – 1906. (See: https://search.findmypast.co.uk/search-world-records/london-bethlem-hospital-patient-admission-registers-and-casebooks-1683-1932).[9] TNA holds the records for dangerous lunatics incarcerated in Bethlem Hospital. These are in the Home Office (HO) series of records. TNA also lists what records are available on its Hospital Records Database.[10]

Private madhouses, where families paid for their relatives to stay, began to be established from the late 17th century. By today's standards, they were completely unprofessional with minimal genuine care. CROs and BROs hold records of private madhouse licences in their Quarter Sessions records. The *Access to Archives* (A2A) service can be checked online for these. It contains catalogues of the different county record offices and local archives. (See: https://discovery.nationalarchives.gov.uk/). TNA has a list of private madhouses in a County Register, together with their owners and patients, dating between 1798 – 1812, in the MH series.

However, **public asylums** for the poor (after the Bethlem Hospital), started in 1713 with the Bethel Hospital in Norwich. A number of such establishments were built throughout the rest of the 1700s, but records for these are very sketchy or non-existent. From 1845, the provision of public asylums became mandatory and this led to the building of large institutions in attractive rural locations, outside of the cities.

Many asylum records are online. If you know where your ancestor lived or died, and that he or she had spent time in an asylum, then the name and location of asylums are usually listed on the online databases of local CROs, BROs or at TNA. TNA also hosts the *Hospital Records Database*, which is a joint venture with the Wellcome Trust.
(See: www.nationalarchives.gov.uk/hospitalrecords/).

One such asylum was the Camberwell House Asylum, destined to become the second largest in London. The Wellcome Collection's library in London (https://wellcomecollection.org/) houses some of its patient admission records (1847 – 1888). The Royal College of Psychiatrists' library, also in London, houses other patient and clinical records (1846 – 1865).
(See: www.rcpsych.ac.uk/about-us/library-and-archives/library).

English and Welsh Asylums

There was an Index of English and Welsh Lunatic Asylums and Mental Hospitals made in 1844, which numerous websites make reference to, such as: http://studymore.org.uk/4_13_TA.HTM.[11]

Records for the Criminally Insane

Transcripts of the **criminal trials** for the insane, held at the Old Bailey, for London and Middlesex cases, are available to view online at: www.oldbaileyonline.org. These cases date from 1674 –

1913. For trials held in the county Assizes outside of London, **local and national newspapers** will hold accounts of these.

Broadmoor in Crowthorne, Berkshire, was specifically built in 1864 to house the criminally insane. It was the first such asylum. Criminal lunatics at the Bethlem Hospital were then transferred to Broadmoor. Some criminal records are relevant for the criminally insane. TNA holds the records for Broadmoor and transfers of prisoners to it between 1882 – 1921, as well as quarterly returns up to 1876. However, Broadmoor's own archives are now in Berkshire Record Office, (www.berkshirerecordoffice.org.uk), but they are closed for 100 years.

Some TNA records of insane prisoners from 1846 onwards are in the MH series. CROs and BROs contain details of payments made for criminally insane paupers held in county asylums. These are in the **Poor Law Union** records.

The Wiltshire and Swindon History Centre (www.wshc.org.uk/) holds the records of 'harmless' criminally insane inmates of the largest private asylum (**Fisherton House Asylum)**, in the UK, near Salisbury, Wiltshire, dating from 1813. It changed its name to Old Manor Hospital in 1924 and closed in 2003.[12]

Other such specialist asylums built in the 20th century included Rampton in Retford, Nottinghamshire. There was also Moss Side and Park Lane, both on the same site near Liverpool, but merged and renamed Ashworth Hospital in 1989.[13] There is also the State Hospital in Carstairs, Scotland, serving both Scotland and Northern Ireland. They are now termed, 'high security psychiatric hospitals.' However, the records for these latter institutions are closed for 100 years and so not generally available for viewing.

Other Records at TNA

One set of TNA records are called *Chancery Lunatics* and these are to be found in the C series of records dated post-1853 and in the Ind 1 series pre-1853. They date from the 17th century up to 1932. They are so-named after the Court of Chancery in London, which was responsible for trying cases of lunacy for the wealthy insane, together with their decrees and judgements.

There are **Court of Protection** records in the J series and records of those who **escaped** from lunatic asylums in the MH series. There are other MH series records which will not be listed in this book. Some **wills and probate** records may indicate that the person making the will was of unsound mind, if it was contested and therefore took a long time to prove in court. Records of wills made in the church courts prior to 1858 are now generally held either at TNA for Prerogative Court of Canterbury (PCC) wills, or the Borthwick Institute for Archives, in York, (see: www.york.ac.uk/borthwick/) for Prerogative Court of York (PCY) wills. Lower court wills may now be held in local CROs.

For wills dated since 1858 and up to 1966, these can be located on the National Probate Calendar, available through www.ancestry.co.uk, with searching advice on TNA [14] for these and other wills up to the present.

Service Records
Naval Lunatics

Records for mentally ill Royal Navy personnel are kept at TNA in the ADM (Admiralty) series. These cover naval inmates of Hoxton House, near Hackney, London, (1792 – 1818), the Royal Naval Hospital, Haslar, in Gosport, Hampshire, (1787 – 1957), and the Royal Naval Hospital, Great Yarmouth, Norfolk, (1863 – early WW2). Some of Yarmouth's records are in the Norfolk Record Office in Norwich. Additionally, there are records of naval officers admitted to Haslar between 1819 – 1842, which are kept amongst the House of Commons records, in London. Patient records less than 100 years old are not open to view. The 1881 census names all the inmates of these hospitals.

Army Lunatics

The Royal Victoria Hospital at Netley, near Southampton, began to treat soldiers suffering from mental illness from 1870 onwards. During WWI, Netley was used as a clearing station for soldiers with shellshock. However, no patient records survive. It has records dating from 1856 – 1990, now in Hampshire Record Office, but these are of a general, administrative nature.

Some soldiers who were mentally ill may have been court-martialled. These records, dating from 1796 – 1963 are held at TNA in the WO (War Office) series. Patient records less than 100 years old are closed.

RFC / RAF Lunatics

Naturally, very, very few RFC patient records will be relevant, as the RFC was only formed in 1912 and are therefore of short duration. RFC personnel records come under the Army, so you should check the WO series at TNA. There do not appear to be any RAF records available yet to view, detailing personnel suffering from mental illness. The RAF was formed in 1918.

East India Company Lunatics

The archives of the **Oriental and India Office Library** at the **British Library** contain details of employees of the **East India Company** (1600 – 1858) who developed a mental illness, whilst working in India and Asia. Many asylums were set up in India in the 18th and 19th centuries (and Chater's book lists these [15]). If patients did not recover after 6 months, they were shipped back to the UK and treated in British asylums. These and their records in the IOR/K series were for:

    Pembroke House, Hackney, London, (1818 – 1870)
    Royal India Asylum, Ealing, London, (1870 – 1892)

They include admissions, casebooks, discharges, removal and deaths, wills and disputes about wills.

Other Specialist Asylums

There were a number of hospitals set up in the 18th century for naturalised immigrants to this country. The French, German and Italian communities each founded their own hospitals, which treated both the physically and mentally sick patients.

The French Hospital, *La Providence*, was founded in 1718, in Finsbury, London, caring for mentally ill Huguenots until 1791. Lunatics were cared for in *Petites Maisons* and the last admission was in 1785. After 1791, Huguenots and their descendants were admitted to English-speaking asylums. Records of this hospital are kept in the Huguenot Society Library in London.
(See: www.huguenotsociety.org.uk). The hospital itself moved to Rochester, Kent in 1959.

The German Hospital in London, opened in 1845 and closed in 1987. Its patient records, dating from about 1890 – 1950 are housed at the Wellcome Library, in London.
(See: https://wellcomecollection.org/).

The Italian Hospital in London, opened in 1884. Its historic records are housed at the London Metropolitan Archives (LMA). (See: www.cityoflondon.gov.uk/things-to-do/history-and-heritage/london-metropolitan-archives). The hospital closed in 1990.

Other lines of research which may bear fruit in the quest for records of mentally ill ancestors, might include Dr William Perfect's asylum for **Freemasons**, founded in West Malling, Kent, in 1758 and which closed in 1809. Its records are at the Kent History and Library Centre in Maidstone. (See: www.kentarchives.org.uk/).

Friendly Societies records, dating from the late 18th century and housed in various locations, may be of interest in this line of enquiry. Kathy Chater's book gives more details.[16]

Scottish and Irish Records

Scottish mental health records can be checked via this website: www.scottishindexes.com/learninghealth.aspx. The *General Register of Lunatics in Asylums*, dating from 1858 – 1978, (but with admissions dating back to about 1805), can be found in the National Records of Scotland (NRS) website at: www.nrscotland.gov.uk, in the MC series. The HH series holds records of the criminally insane. The Scottish Archive Network

(SCAN) holds records of individual asylums. (See: www.scan.org.uk).

TNA also holds some records dating between 1824-1876, for Perth Asylum's criminally insane. The *British Newspaper Archive* website might be worth checking too.

See: www.britishnewspaperarchive.co.uk, though, because investigations into deaths were held privately, there is likely to be less useful information than in English newspapers into instances of suicide, for example. However, local and national papers are still the best source of information about Scottish suicides. Also, check the newspapers in local libraries and the National Library of Scotland.

The NRS also holds court records from about 1700 – 1897, of 'curators' responsible for looking after the interests of the mentally ill, poor relief and information about investigations into deaths. Records of wills, testaments and probate are also here, but digitised images can be found on www.scotlandspeople.gov.uk. Chater goes into more detail about Scottish lunatics.[17]

Irish lunatic records are very sparse. This is because most records at the Dublin Record Office were destroyed in a fire during the Irish Easter uprising in 1922. Chater [18] goes into more detail.

Workhouses, or Houses of Industry, as they were known in Ireland, began in 1703. In 1708, provision was made for the insane, in sections of these Houses. Private madhouses emerged in the late 1700s. The first dedicated hospital for lunatics was opened in Dublin in 1757 and named St Patrick's Hospital. The first asylum for the mentally ill was opened in Dublin in 1815 and named Richmond Lunatic Asylum. The first public lunatic asylum was opened in Armagh in 1821. The Central Criminal Lunatic Asylum was opened in 1850, outside Dublin. It's records, up to 1900, can be found at www.centralmentalhospital.ie.

After 1923, when Ireland divided into the Irish Free State (Eire) and Northern Ireland, the records divided accordingly. Northern Irish records are held at PRONI (Public Record Office of Northern Ireland) in Belfast. (See: www.proni.gov.uk). Eire records are held in Dublin at the National Archives of Ireland (NAI), (See:

www.nationalarchives.ie), and at the National Library of Ireland (See: www.nli.ie). These hold census records, lunatic asylum records and Poor Law records. Local county heritage centres in Ireland are worth checking.

Irish census records have not survived well. There are some for 1821, 1831, 1841 and 1851, but no more until 1901, followed by 1911 and 1921.

TNA in Kew, West London has some Chancery lunatic records in its C series, for people who held property both in England and Ireland. The previously mentioned Hospital Records Database has details of Northern Irish lunatic asylums.

Having researched your ancestor(s) pasts, it is now time to pray about what you have found.

How to be Set Free of Generational Mental Illness

To start off, I would recommend praying for protection for yourself and your loved ones and for Jesus to lead and guide you in these prayers. Then pray the 'Lordship Prayer.' The declarations and prayers following, are used by several Christian ministries, in various forms, which you can find online and whose address details are included in Appendix F.

Lordship Prayer

"Dear Lord Jesus, I realise my need of You and repent of living my life my own way. I wholeheartedly accept You now as my Saviour, my Redeemer, my Lord and my Deliverer.

I invite You now to be the Lord of every part and moment of my life, from the time of my conception, right up until now:

Lord of my body, my physical health and behaviour.

Lord of my mind and all my attitudes and mental health.

Lord of all my emotions and all my reactions.

Lord of my spirit and my worship of You.

Lord of my family and all my relationships.

Lord of my sexuality and its expression.

Lord of my will and all of my hopes, ambitions, decisions and plans.

Lord of all my work and service for You.

Lord of all my finances.

Lord of all my needs and possessions.

Lord of the manner and time of my death."

Declaration

"Thank you, Jesus, for shedding Your blood and dying on the cross, for the forgiveness of my sins, my ancestors' sins and my descendants' sins. You died and rose again that I might be set free to love and to serve You, in newness of life.

While I thank you, Lord for my ancestors, I do not accept their sinful lifestyles." At this point, it will be important to **confess and repent of one's own sins**, which may have been committed out of rebellion against a mentally ill parent who, out of their own brokenness, inflicted pain on you. They may or may not have realised what they were doing to you. Ask God to forgive you, receive that forgiveness by faith and forgive yourself for whatever you did. Renounce any wrong self-blame for your mental struggles.

Then, **identify** any possible problems caused by generational mental illness found in your family line going further back. If found, **confess the sins in your family line** and the influence it has had in your own life. (Lamentations 5:7). Repent from those found in the family line by identifying with and owning them as one's own. Then forgive them for their sins and any effects these had on you.

We need to also pray for soul ties with our ancestors to be broken:

Breaking of Soul Ties for Inherited Mental Illness

"In the name of Jesus, I place the cross and blood of Jesus

between myself and each of my family members. I break all the ungodly body, soul and spirit ties with:
My parents, if they suffered from a mental illness. (For ancestors who have died, we break the whole soul tie).
With my grandparents, if they suffered from a mental illness.
With my great-grandparents and,
with my great-great-grandparents, (name any relevant ones), *going back 4 generations.*

I also break any ungodly body, soul and spirit ties, particularly with regards mental illnesses, with any other people who suffered from these issues and who had a significant input into my life. I command every ungodly soul and spiritual influence from them to go from me in Jesus' name, and ask that You draw back to me every part of my soul or spirit that rightfully belongs to me.

I ask that you would cleanse me from all the effects of any mental illnesses, passing down to me from every ancestor, through these soul ties."

This prayer will cover the issues mentioned and discernment should be used when waiting upon the Lord for any word of knowledge for a specific revelation. This will be necessary for those ancestral issues which cannot be found in the records.

Breaking Inner Vows & Bitter Root Judgements

Sometimes a person meets an inner psychological brick wall of being unable to form godly friendships and relationships because of previous mental illness issues which have led to mistrust of others. Inner vows can form not to trust again, but the way through them is to ask God to show you what inner vows were made and against whom. Then forgive the person(s) who broke your trust, renounce the inner vow and ask God to break the power of this inner vow over your life. Finally, ask God to help you to trust (wisely) again.

Additionally, a relative with mental health issues may have caused you or an ancestor much pain, resulting in a bitter judgement being made of the person(s). This 'bitter root judgement' may grow to defile your attitudes and relationships with others who may remind you of that relative. When highlighted, this bitter root too needs repenting of, the relative or ancestor forgiven, and Jesus asked to root it out, to replace with His love and grace.

Binding and Loosing – Deliverance

Once the above prayers have been said and worked through, it is then time to conduct self-deliverance from any evil spirits. Pray something like this:

"I put the cross and blood of Jesus between myself and... I bind and cut myself off from the ruling spirits of anxiety, fear, intimidation, control, depression, confusion, insanity, mistrust, anger, hate, isolation, uncleanness etc, coming down my family line. I bind and loose the spirit(s) of……. [use your discernment to name them] from me and tell it / them to go, in the mighty name of Jesus!"

Seek the cleansing blood of Jesus to wash away any stains. *"Lord, I command my body and brain chemistry to come into godly alignment. I speak to the neurotransmitters in my brain and call them into normal functioning. I speak to my nervous system, my endocrine system and my hormonal system and call them into godly order.*

Please fill me now with Your Holy Spirit, to replace and infill all the empty places vacated by these other spirits. Renew my mind and put a right spirit within me, that I may praise and serve You now and forever more."

Deliverance ministry can also be sought from suitably trained lay or ordained ministers.

The Blessing of Jesus

"I ask, Lord, that you turn all these previous curses into blessings, as I rest in Your love and presence and as I find my peace, identity and security in You. If I am carrying any further emotional wounds caused by generational mental illness, I ask, Lord, that You surface them and show me, so that I can give them to You and express them safely, forgive those who need forgiving and be healed.

I ask this in Jesus' name."
Seek to be obedient to His guidance and call on your life.

In Summary

Give thanks for your ancestors. **Identify** any possible mental illness found in your family line. If found, **confess** this brokenness in your family line and the influence it has had in your own life. (Lamentations 5:7). **Repent**, where needed, of sins in the family line, which may have led to mental ill-health, by identifying with and owning them as your own. Ask for and receive God's **forgiveness**. **Cut** soul ties. Seek **deliverance** ministry and / or conduct self-deliverance for any spirits of insanity. Seek the **cleansing blood of Jesus** to wash away any stains.

Ask Jesus to **bless you** and **fill you** afresh with His Holy Spirit. Seek to be **obedient** to His guidance and call on your life.

A Recommendation

As mentioned before, the prayers in this chapter are intended just as openers, to help start you on the journey to freedom. In order to work towards complete freedom, I would recommend working through the material and prayers in the ministry books listed at the end of this chapter. It would also be very worthwhile attending one of the excellent training and ministry courses run by Bethel Sozo, Christian Prayer Ministries, Gilgal House Healing Centre, Ellel Ministries, or Sozo Ministries International, here in the UK. This is not an exhaustive list and the reader may hear of other ministries both in the UK and abroad, which can help in this area.

Further Reading - Select Bibliography

Chater, Kathy. *My Ancestor was a Lunatic*. London: Society of Genealogists Enterprises, (2014).

Hawkey, Ruth. *Freedom from Generational Sin*. Chichester: New Wine Press, (1999).

Horrobin, Peter. *Healing through Deliverance*. (rev). Lancaster: Sovereign World, (2008).

McAll, Kenneth. *Healing the Family Tree*. London: Sheldon Press, (1982).

Prince, Derek. *Blessing or Curse: You Can Choose*. (3rd ed). Grand Rapids, MI: Chosen Books Publishing Co., (2006).

Sandford, John Loren & Paula. *God's Power to Change*. Lake Mary, FL: Charisma House, (2007).

Chapter 10

Genealogical Evidence for Religious Affiliations

> *And God spoke all these words:*
> *"I am the LORD your God, who brought you out of Egypt, out of the land of slavery. You shall have no other gods before me."*
> Exodus 20:1-3, (NIV)

> *"Woe to you, scribes and Pharisees, hypocrites! For you are like whitewashed tombs which indeed appear beautiful outwardly, but inside are full of dead men's bones and all uncleanness. Even so you also outwardly appear righteous to men, but inside you are full of hypocrisy and lawlessness."*
> Matthew 23:27-28, (NKJV)

The whole of Matthew 23 records Jesus' admonitions against the Pharisees. Lest we use this passage as a tool to judge the Pharisees over-harshly, or even modern-day Christian leaders too readily, let us remember that we too are prone to sin and failure. We too need Jesus' forgiveness and restoration.

Definition and Descriptions

By 'religious affiliations' in the title, I mean the mainline Judeo-Christian religions and religious / faith subdivisions or denominations, as can be found in the genealogical records. I have used the word 'religion' reluctantly, because it can convey rather stultifying and divisive ideas about the practice of faith or an expression of belief via certain rituals, to the modern reader. However, because I go on to consider Judaism as well as Christianity and make passing reference to other non-Christian religions, I have decided to use the word, 'religion.' Christianity, after all, is a religion, as well as a living faith. Idolatry is trickier to define, unless one uses the biblical definition, in which case proving it through the records becomes a bit more straightforward.

This being a Christian book, I will cover essentially only

Christianity. This chapter is necessarily brief and so can only describe different expressions of the faith in a broad general overview, rather than being more detailed and specific. It is not meant to be a definitive academic tome *par excellence,* as it is aimed at the lay reader.

Christianity and its records can be divided into the **Roman Catholic** and **Protestant** denominations. The latter are subdivided into the:

>Church of England / Anglican
>Presbyterians / Unitarians / United Reformed Church
>Separatists / Independents / Congregationalists,
>>including Baptists and Quakers
>
>Methodists
>Salvation Army
>Brethren
>
>**Foreign Protestant Churches in Britain**
>French Huguenot and others
>
>**Jews**
>Orthodox, Conservative, Reform
>
>**Other Religions**

As I'm not qualified to speak into researching other religions such as Islam, Hinduism, Sikhism, and the Buddhist faiths, I will not cover them in this book. This also goes for the heretical Christian groups. This chapter focuses on those with Judeo-Christian heritage.

Problems Developing from Faulty Religious Practice

While each Christian denomination has its great strengths, each also has its weaknesses. Faith in Jesus will encourage godly devotion, healing and miracles, right living, care for the unborn, orphans, children, the poor, the family, marginalised groups, the elderly, and the promotion of peace and justice in society. However, where there is an overlap between religion / faith and idolatry, or even evil practices, this is where the existing records can help to pinpoint an area of need for generational prayer. Let me explain.

Where elements of the practice of faith, or denominational faith stray from biblical truth, then that aspect of a later 'tradition' of the church can become idolatrous. Even those aspects of biblical faith practiced in the wrong spirit, instead of true devotion to Christ, can become idolatrous. Some Christians in churches with an emphasis on the sacramental, can sometimes place too much emphasis on the objects of veneration found inside the church buildings. These symbolic objects would have been installed to aid devotion to God, not to inadvertently lead people away from true worship of Jesus. Especially in previous eras, when literacy was not so widespread, such aids to worship would have been very helpful and, I would say, still can be. However, when the focus is misplaced, this can cause a spirit of religion to develop in a church, resulting in individual members being influenced by one or more 'religious' spirits, which are essentially idolatrous in nature. This misfocus can become a convenient religious 'fig leaf' to cover shame caused by a personal sense of inadequacy, rather than taking it to Jesus for His healing.

Peter Horrobin lists in *Healing Through Deliverance*, a whole host of people, practices, denominationalism, things and religious items used in churches which can become more important to the congregation than Jesus himself, leading to idolatry and demonic deception. He and his team have had to deliver people of deceptive religious spirits masquerading as genuine expressions of the true faith, invited in by many of these misplaced emphases.[1]

He writes:

> Once religious practice becomes more important than the foundational principles of living the Christian life, then one is on a potentially very slippery slope indeed, with man (or a denomination) proclaiming principles that are of man, as opposed to God. The dangers of such deception are limitless, giving credence and acceptance to a multitude of "Christian" heresies

that are taught by their proponents as the law of God, as well as to false religions, which make no attempt whatsoever to make Jesus central to their life and doctrine, and to philosophies that owe nothing to the mainstream patterns of Christian belief.[2]

Syncretism, or the introduction of ungodly beliefs and ideologies into church teaching, will cause it to lose its purity and authority with God, and with the people. It can creep in quite unawares. Then, if the problem grows, church leadership can descend into mere formality and ritual. Other denominations can be overly legalistic in their adherence to 'truth' or rules of religious observance. That is also idolatrous. Grace is neglected so that keeping the rules of the denomination in order to be in good standing with the church, becomes a religion of works, not of faith. Of course, *'faith without works is dead'* (James 2:14-26).

The Protestant Reformation restored the centrality of teaching Holy Scripture, which has led millions to find new birth in Christ. The evangelical awakening led to huge numbers of people being brought into the Kingdom of God and to the foundation of mission societies sending out missionaries all over the world. This has had incalculable benefits worldwide. However, at the same time, in their keenness to be true to the Bible, some churches can sometimes over-emphasise the Bible as the written word of God, to the exclusion of the work of the Holy Spirit. This is called 'Bibliolatry.' (*'God the Father, God the Son and God the Holy Bible,'* as has been quipped). Much emphasis is placed on pursuing theological knowledge, while avoiding the emotions of the heart.

At the other end of the spectrum, churches in Britain with liberal theology do not accept the Bible as authoritative, but take their lead from the surrounding culture, rather than God's word, in order to attract people. On the other hand, they are often good at looking after the poor and marginalised and emphasise the social justice aspect of Christ's teaching in the gospels.

The modern Pentecostal / charismatic renewal in the church, which started in about 1901, has restored the practice of the Bible's teaching about the reality, place and work of the Holy Spirit in the lives of believers. Repeated global waves of outpourings of the Holy Spirit over the last 100 years or so, have refreshed and invigorated millions of Christians in a way not seen since New Testament times! People have come to faith, renounced their old destructive lifestyles, been baptised in water and the Holy Spirit, rediscovered the gifts of the Holy Spirit, including speaking in tongues, discernment and prophecy, found refreshment, healing, personal restoration and family reconciliation. Some have even been raised from the dead!

However, with these blessings have also come some misuses. Some individuals in evangelical charismatic churches can soulishly misuse the genuine workings of the Holy Spirit, leading to an excess of emotionalism. The experiences of anointings etc, can end up being sought after more than Jesus Himself (i.e. the gift rather than the giver). Sound biblical teaching, focus on the person of Christ, discernment and structure are needed as counterbalance to excess.

All of these wayward expressions of The Faith could be seen as idolatrous. They can either over-emphasize or under-emphasize the Bible, focus on tradition, liturgy, rules of conduct, the wider culture's needs, or the Holy Spirit's manifestations. Balance, not compromise, is needed. Someone once said half-jokingly that if a Christian has the Word without the Spirit he will dry up. On the other hand, if they have the Spirit without the Word, they will blow up! But, if they have both the Word of God and the Spirit, they will grow up. From this we can conclude how important it is to have both the Word of God and to be filled with the Holy Spirit in order to be an even more productive Christian.

Gordon Dalbey, in his insightful book, *Broken by Religion, Healed by God*, addresses these issues in a balanced way, arguing for a restoration of all four streams into one – the evangelical, sacramental, Pentecostal and social justice aspects of the gospel.[3]

Other problems associated with faulty religious practice can include abuse, coercion, confusion, control, elitism, emotional damage, erroneous teaching, idolatry, judgmentalism, legalism, prejudice, rebellion, rejection, a religious spirit, and unforgiveness.

For example, Peter Horrobin writes in *Healing through Deliverance*:

> Religious spirits can be associated with Christian traditions that are out of the mainstream of Jesus-centered truth. These become controlling factors in the generation line, making descendants potential opponents of Holy Spirit-centered Christian life and worship.[4]

These observations are not to put a dampener on the good work of churches, but to encourage them to greater purity of worship, lifestyle and devotion to Jesus. I need that myself.

What and Where are Church Records Kept?

In terms of how you find out your ancestor's religious or denominational affiliation / membership, this is what you need to do. As it is such a massive topic, this section is necessarily very brief and only includes generalities. For further, more detailed information, see the bibliography at the end of the book and look online.

Church of England / Anglican Records

We start with the Church of England, as historically, most people are either born, baptised, married, or died / buried within the CofE structure, or identify with it. The General Register Office (GRO) **marriage certificates** will give the clearest indication of church preference. If the certificate says the wedding took place in the parish church of St ... (fill in the dots), then you know that your female ancestor at least was nominally Anglican or likely to have been. There are many exceptions, because after Lord Hardwicke's Marriage Act of 1753, all weddings, (including for nonconformists – those not conforming to the CofE), excepting for Quakers and Jews, had to be conducted according to the rites of the Church of England. This state of affairs carried on until civil registration began in 1837.

RELIGIOUS AFFILIATIONS

As mentioned previously, GRO certificates date from 1837 to the present day.

Before civil registration, i.e. before 1837, births / baptisms, marriages and deaths / burials, were recorded in the **parish registers**, kept in each local parish church. It should be noted that parish registers are still kept. The earliest of these date from 1538, with the foundation of the Church of England after the break with Rome under Henry VIII. However, most parish registers were only kept properly from about 1558, the first year of Queen Elizabeth I's reign. Copies were made and these are called 'bishop's transcripts.' Both the originals and the bishop's transcripts (again dating from 1558, where they survive) are now kept in local CROs and can be viewed there, mainly on microfiche or microfilm. The registers vary in quality, information kept and location. The latest parish registers are still in the local parish church.

One unusual set of 'parish' registers are the Fleet Chapel registers, which include over 400,000 weddings and baptisms officiated over by imprisoned clergy, principally in the Fleet Prison in London, between the years 1667 and about 1777. This amounts to a very significant percentage of London's population at the time! These records are kept at The National Archives (TNA). (See: https://discovery.nationalarchives.gov.uk/details/r/C13332)

Of considerable help to those seeking non-conformist ancestors, are the frequent recording by Anglican clergy noting the burial of Protestant dissenters and Roman Catholics. These groups often lacked their own burial grounds centuries ago. The terms, 'Anabaptist' (those baptised again as adult believers), 'Dissenter' (dissenting from the CofE), or 'Papist' (RC), might be noted alongside the burial entry in the register.

Many parish registers have been digitised and are now available on www.ancestry.co.uk and www.findmypast.co.uk. County Record Offices may also have something like Lancashire Archives' 'Online Parish Clerk' for online searching of its Anglican parish registers. (See: www.lan-opc.org.uk)

Apart from parish registers, the other main type of Anglican church records, relevant for researching Church of England ancestors, are the **parish records**. These include the accounts of the churchwardens, constables, the overseers of the poor, the surveyors of highways, and the vestry minutes. There are other records, but these are best dealt with in the chapters on crime and poverty, as are some just listed. Most of these types of records are now stored in local CROs. Anglican clergy ancestors are covered in chapter 4 on education, and chapter 5 on occupations.

Roman Catholic Records

There are basically no surviving Roman Catholic genealogical records of birth/baptism, marriage and death/burial prior to 1538, as these were all destroyed at the time of the Dissolution of the Monasteries. Catholics were persecuted in varying measures from 1559 to 1829 and Catholicism was illegal until 1778, when the Catholic Relief Act was passed. The Catholic Emancipation Act of 1829 allowed Catholics to enjoy the same civil freedoms and privileges as Protestants.

Prior to 1778, there are very few surviving Roman Catholic registers, partly because it was not safe to keep them. There are some survivals in private hands and church collections. Those Roman Catholic countries which had embassies in London, with attached chapels, such as Portugal, Sardinia and Savoy, often allowed English Roman Catholics to baptise and marry there. So, some records survive in these embassies. Other wealthier Catholics went abroad to marry, and thus British entries can be found in registers on the continent.

The earliest post-Reformation register starts in 1657, but not until 1691 do more appear. Most registers are held by County Record Offices (CROs) or local churches. The earliest registers tend to be with local churches. Those records still held by the church, within the Archdiocese of Westminster are held at:

RELIGIOUS AFFILIATIONS

Archbishop's House, Ambrosden Avenue, London, SW1P 1QJ. (See: https://staugustineofcanterbury.org.uk/about/archbishopshouse/)

Unlike the Church of England, baptismal registers usually record the maiden name of the mother, not her married name. If the baptism or confirmation was for an adult, then the person was almost certainly a convert. Between 1753 and 1829, when Hardwicke's Marriage Act was in force, most Catholic marriages took place in the Church of England, as well as in the local Catholic church. It could be dangerous to have the ceremony only in a Catholic church. However, despite this, many Catholics' baptism and burial details were not recorded in Anglican parish registers and Catholic burial grounds were not established by law until 1853.

Michael Gandy has produced the best sources of information on surviving Catholic registers. [5-8] These are produced on a regional basis, covering the period from 1700 to 1880. However, the Catholic Record Society (CRS) has published many registers, including the early ones. (See: www.crs.org.uk/). Where registers are kept by the local church, it will be necessary to write to or email the priest for permission to see them. Catholic registers are usually written in Latin.

Other records of Catholics were kept by the government when it was taking legal action against them for what was termed, 'recusancy,' i.e. for stubbornly refusing to convert to Anglicanism. These records are kept at the Parliamentary Archives, (See: www.parliament.uk/business/publications/parliamentary-archives/), CROs, diocesan record offices (DROs), TNA and Lambeth Palace Library in London. (See: www.lambethpalacelibrary.org/. Again, the CRS has published much of this material. A lot of material is still in the private collections of families, but these can be located via the National Register of Archives.
(See: https://discovery.nationalarchives.gov.uk/). The Catholic Family History Society can be contacted for help in locating Catholic ancestors. (See: https://catholicfhs.online/). Records of Catholic clergy trained on the Continent are described in chapter 4 on

education.

As with the rest of this chapter and indeed book, this outline of Roman Catholic records is necessarily brief. The online and published sources quoted will lead the reader to more detailed information and research.

Other Protestant Denominations

A good general book on nonconformist records is by Stuart Raymond, called *Tracing your Nonconformist Ancestors: a guide for family historians*.[9] Because of the risks of persecution, many nonconformist ministers did not keep a register of names of those baptised, married or died, particularly prior to the late 18th century. Some registers after this time are kept at The National Archives (TNA) at Kew, under RG 4-8, some in local County Record Offices (CROs) and some in major libraries. Digitised versions of these can be found at www.ancestry.co.uk, www.bmdregisters.co.uk and www.familysearch.org. For records after 1837, records will be found in individual churches and CROs. Denominational journals of the 19th century and onwards also have many useful obituaries.

Presbyterians / Unitarians / United Reformed Church Records

Most early dissenters were Presbyterians. They were led by the puritan, Thomas Cartwright, a scholar and fellow of Cambridge University, who was expelled in 1571, fleeing to Holland in 1574, where he began an English church. He wanted to reorganise the Church of England along the lines that John Knox had instigated in Scotland, which lead to the formation of the Scottish Presbyterians. This included less hierarchy and ministers being elected by the congregation. English Presbyterianism was so named from 1604 and adherents generally stayed within the Church of England, agitating for reform of it. Presbyterians were generally better educated and higher socially than other Protestant dissenters and became the established church in 1647, during the Civil War and the Interregnum of Oliver Cromwell. They were horrified at the execution of Charles I as they were loyal to the Crown, and separated from the

RELIGIOUS AFFILIATIONS

Independents as a result.[10] Being more open minded, they tended to appoint more liberal ministers. However, by the 1790s, Presbyterians had lost their way and no longer believed in the Trinity, calling themselves 'Unitarians'. Their meeting houses were still called 'Presbyterian' until 1813, because to be anti-Trinitarian was illegal up until that date.

Presbyterian and Unitarian registers which survive are now with TNA and many entries are in the International Genealogical Index (I.G.I.), compiled by the Mormon Church.
(See: www.familysearch.org/search/collection/igi).

A few early Presbyterian registers are held by the United Reformed Church History Society at Westminster College, Madingley Road, Cambridge, CB3 0AA. (See: https://urchistory.wordpress.com)

Unitarian records are held by some United Reformed churches, and by the United Reformed Church History Society at Westminster College, Madingley Road, Cambridge, CB3 0AA.
(See: https://urchistory.wordpress.com/)

The John Rylands Library at Manchester University also holds such records. (See: www.library.manchester.ac.uk).

Dr William's Library, at 14 Gordon Square, London, WC1H 0AR, is another repository. (See: www.dwlib.co.uk). It dates from 1742/43 has a very good collection of nonconformist marriage and death registers, some dating back to 1716. The births register is held at TNA and online at www.ancestry.co.uk and www.bmdregisters.co.uk

The British Library has a full run of birth, marriage and death notices for Presbyterians and Unitarians. (See: www.bl.uk/#)

The Johnston Index at Harris Manchester College Library, Mansfield Road, Oxford, OX1 3TD, has many records of obituaries dating from 1794 to date. (See: www.hmc.ox.ac.uk/library#/). The Library is not open to the public, so enquiries can only be made by email or post. Further information about researching English Presbyterian and Unitarian ancestors can be found in the book by Alan Ruston.[11]

Separatists / Independents / Congregationalist Records

The United Reformed Church was formed by the merger of the Congregationalists and the Presbyterians in 1972. Congregationalists began to call themselves thus from the early 19th century, as their emphasis was on the autonomy of the local congregation, independent of the Church of England. Prior to this, they had called themselves 'Independents,' a name which had been held since the early 17th century. They had gained strength during the Civil War, because Oliver Cromwell was himself an Independent. Although he was from the minor gentry, most Independents were from the lower classes or the Army. Prior to the early 17th century, Independents had been called 'Separatists'. The first known leader of the Separatists was Robert Browne, in the later 16th century. He was also the founder of Congregationalism.

The Separatists were unhappy with the form of organisation and episcopal church government of the Church of England. They were more radical than the Presbyterians, were persecuted by the established church and state, resulting in them holding illegal assemblies. Many went into exile in Holland, also forming a large contingent of the Pilgrim Fathers, leaving for a better life in the New World.

Registers of births, marriages and deaths for these groups only began in the late 18th or early 19th centuries. The National Archives (TNA) at Kew now hold these records, which can be found in sections RG 4 and 8. Individual chapels hold some old records, as do CROs. Dr William's Library holds a very fine collection on the Congregationalists. Some materials can be found at The United Reformed Church History Society. A useful booklet on Congregational records has been written by D.J.H. Clifford.[12]

Baptist Records

The Baptist Church in England had its origins in the Anabaptists of 16th Century Central Europe and a Separatist group in religiously-free Amsterdam in Holland, who came back over to

RELIGIOUS AFFILIATIONS

England. The essential tenet of Baptists, which distinguished them from the Church of England and from Roman Catholics, was and is their belief and practice of baptising believers only, whether child or adult, by full immersion in water. Babies and infants are not baptised, as they cannot give their consent.

The earliest English Baptists were Calvinistic in flavour, but rejected the doctrine of predestination, believing that salvation was open to all. They rejected completely, the authority of the Church of England over them, with its Episcopal Church governance, preferring a Presbyterian form of leadership. Each congregation was self-governing. This group was formed in Holland as the English Baptist Fellowship, by Thomas Helwys and John Smyth. Thomas Helwys returned to England with his followers in 1611 (the same year as the publication of the King James Bible) and set up a church in London. They became known as the General Baptists and from London, spread outwards. John Bunyan's church in Bedford, was an example of the more open General Baptists. He, of course, is famous as the author of *Pilgrim's Progress,* first published in 1678. General Baptists took an Arminian position, believing that salvation was open to all, as opposed to the Calvinistic position, with its emphasis on predestination and the salvation of a select few, known ultimately only to God.

Another group of London Baptists developed from 1633 onwards, who did hold to the doctrine of predestination, (formulated in the previous century by Jean Calvin). They became known as Particular Baptists. They were more independently minded than the General Baptists.

The Seventh Day Baptists, few in number, as mentioned by Stuart Raymond in his book, *Tracing your Nonconformist Ancestors,*[13] worshipped on Saturdays, rather than Sundays.

Prior to 1688, there are few Baptist records. Some of the earliest records of Baptists would be in the lists known as the **Protestation Oath Returns**, made in 1641/42, during the early stages of the English Civil War. These are now kept in the Parliamentary

Archives in London.
(See: www.parliament.uk/business/publications/parliamentary-archives/)

The **Recusant Rolls**, (1592 - 1691), (kept at The National Archives at Kew), record convictions for Catholic recusancy, but which after 1660, have perhaps an even greater proportion of Protestant nonconformists and therefore some Baptists listed also.

In 1676, the **Compton Religious Census** was compiled. Some of the names in it will include Baptists. These lists are now held in diocesan record offices or CROs.

There are details of individual Baptists in church membership records. Most Baptist birth, baptism, death and burial registers kept prior to 1837 are now housed at TNA. There are few before 1754, but most of them are 18th century. Between 1753 and 1829, Baptist marriages had to be performed in the Anglican church, so records of Baptist marriages must be sought in the parish registers of the period. Baptisms rarely record ages, because only believing adults were baptised. However, ages at burial will help date an ancestor. Baptists commonly gave their sons an additional middle name which was helpfully often the mother's maiden name, making tracing the family line easier. Pre- and post-1837 registers are held by Baptist churches, CROs, Baptist association archives and theological colleges. Geoffrey Breed has written a full national listing of where Baptist registers are kept.[14]

Baptist ministers and churches are listed in the *Baptist Handbook*, which since 1972 has been called the, *Baptist Union Directory*. Nowadays, the denomination is divided into the Baptist Union and the Strict and Particular Baptists. Many histories of Baptist churches are held by the Baptist Historical Society and at Dr William's Library in London. Missionaries' details are kept at the Angus Library in Oxford. See: www.mundus.ac.uk as well as: www.bmsworldmission.org

Names of individual Strict Baptists are recorded on an online database at:

RELIGIOUS AFFILIATIONS

www.strictbaptisthistory.org.uk/pnsearch/searchpn/htm
The addresses of some of these Baptist organisations holding genealogical information, include:

Angus Library, Regent's Park College, Pusey Street, Oxford, OX1 2LB. It has over 5,000 Baptist missionaries recorded on its family history web page, which is at: http://theangus.rpc.ox.ac.uk Oxford University has incorporated the Angus library catalogue into the Bodleian Library catalogue. (See: http://solo.bodleian.ox.ac.uk)

The Baptist Historical Society: Secretary, Revd S.L. Copson B.A., MLitt., 60 Strathmore Avenue, Hitchin, Hertfordshire, SG5 1ST. (See: www.baptisthistory.org.uk)

The Gospel Standard Baptist Library, 5 Hove Park Gardens, Hove, East Sussex, BN3 6HN.
(See: www.gospelstandard.org.uk/Library/Overview)

Northern Baptist College Archive in the John Rylands' Library at Manchester University, 150 Deansgate, Manchester, M3 3EH. (See: www.library.manchester.ac.uk/search-resources/guide-to-special-collections/atoz/northern-baptist-college-archive)

Regent's Park College, Pusey Street, Oxford, OX1 2LB. (See: www.rpc.ox.ac.uk/)

Spurgeon's College Library, 189 South Norwood Hill, London, SE25 6DJ. (See: www.spurgeons.ac.uk/why/library)

The Strict Baptist Historical Society: Secretary, Pauline Johns, 33 Addison Road, Caterham, Surrey, CR3 5LU.
(See: www.strictbaptisthistory.org.uk/index.htm)

Dr William's Library, 14 Gordon Square, Bloomsbury, London, WC1H 0AR, as well as various Baptist Historical Societies, hold many histories of Baptist churches. (See: www.dwl.ac.uk/)

Quaker Records

For those with Quaker ancestors, some background will help. The Quakers were formerly called the 'Religious Society of Friends' and formed by George Fox, (1624-1691), an itinerant Leicestershire preacher, sometime between 1647 and 1652. His message was that *"Christ has come to teach his people himself,"* meaning that we all have the capacity for direct communion with God. He preached that the formal rites of the established church of his day had little to do with true religion. Many people followed him, but the ire of the Church of England was stirred against Fox and his followers, leading to much persecution. Quakers refused to take oaths or to take off their hats to their social superiors, serve in the armed forces, attend Anglican church services or pay the required tithes to their local parish church. For these reasons they were fined and imprisoned with a number dying from the dank prison conditions.

It is said that the name, Quaker, came about as a derogatory term used by opponents to describe the ecstatic and physical shaking that came upon early Friends, as they were overcome by the power of the Holy Spirit. A judge mocked Fox's exhortation to *"tremble at the word of the Lord"*, calling him and his followers, 'Quakers.'

After the respect they gained for helping plague victims during the Great Plague of London in 1665, with the later Act of Toleration in 1689, restrictions on Quakers were relieved and they started to legally build their own Meeting houses, and to keep records without fear of persecution. They were exempted from Hardwicke's Marriage Act of 1753, allowing them to keep their own marriage registers. However, their birth, marriage and death / burial registers start from 1650, and so their members do not generally appear in Anglican parish registers. Baptisms of infants were not performed and so do not appear in Quaker registers. Even after 1837, Quakers kept their own registers.

The structure of Quaker meetings is divided into the Local Meeting, held weekly on a Sunday morning (previously called the Preparative Meeting - PM). Then there is the Monthly Meeting (MM), now called the 'Area Meeting,' (AM). The Area Meeting is the legal entity. Representatives from the Monthly Meetings are sent to the Quarterly and Annual / Year Meetings.

Some modern Quaker registers may be kept in local Meeting

RELIGIOUS AFFILIATIONS

houses, while most old ones are now held at The National Archives (TNA), local CROs, the Guildhall Library in London, the Society of Genealogists Library (www.sog.org.uk/) and Friends House Library in London. Their address is: 173-177 Friends House, Euston Road, London, NW1 2BJ.
(See:www.quaker.org.uk/resources/library/search-library-catalogue)

Friends also kept records of instances of persecution in their *Great Book of Sufferings* from 1650 to 1856. This is indexed and is available to see at Friends House Library. The Library also houses admission books and registers for Quaker schools. Further details about researching Quaker forbears may be found in the book, *My Ancestors were Quakers*, by E.H. Milligan and M.J. Thomas.[15]

Methodist Records

The Methodist movement was founded out of the Church of England, by John and Charles Wesley and George Whitefield in 1740. It remained undivided until 1797 and thereafter spawned a number of splinter groups, including the Methodist New Connexion, the Primitive Methodists, the Bible Christians, the Countess of Huntingdon's Connexion, the United Methodist Free Churches and the Wesleyan Methodists. These finally reunited in 1932.

The basic structure of the Methodist Church, as set up by John Wesley, has remained in place to this day, i.e. Societies (congregations), Circuits, Districts and Conference. The records of the Methodist Church reflect this structure. Few records survive for the 18th century and many Methodists continued to have their baptisms, marriages and burials registered in Church of England churches.

From 1818, the Wesleyan Methodists established a Metropolitan Registry in London, which gathered baptismal entries from all over the country. These date from 1773 to 1838. They are now housed at The National Archives. Burial registers pre-1837 are also housed at TNA and can be seen online at www.bmdregisters.co.uk and www.ancestry.co.uk. Historic records of birth, marriage and death, are also kept in local CRO's, and other

Methodist records such as membership lists are kept in local churches, chapels and CROs.

The Methodist Archives and Research Centre (MARC), holding much useful genealogical information about individual Methodists, is located in the John Rylands Library at Manchester University. (See: www.library.manchester.ac.uk). A very useful digitised list of Methodist ministers may be viewed at: www.methodistheritage.org.uk/research-online-books-ministers-and-circuits.htm.

The most important source of information about individual Methodists amongst donation lists is the Wesleyan Methodist Historic Roll. This roll records the names of over 1 million people throughout the country, who gave a guinea to the Wesleyan Methodist Twentieth Century Fund between 1899 and 1909, in order to build Methodist Central Hall in Westminster.[16] See: www.methodistheritage.org.uk.

Finally, for this section, there are the records of Methodist missionaries sent around the world. These records date from the early 19th century onwards and ended up becoming the archives of the Methodist Missionary Society in 1932. These are now held at the School of Oriental and African Studies (SOAS), part of London University. (See: www.mundus.ac.uk/cats/4/910.htm)

There are many other types of Methodist records, too numerous to mention here.

Salvation Army Records

The Salvation Army, founded by William and Catherine Booth in 1865, grew out of Methodism at their East London Mission. It changed its name to 'The Salvation Army' in 1879. Salvationists appear in the records of the GRO and census returns, but the 'Sally Army' also kept records themselves.

Members are either officers or soldiers and it is necessary to bear this in mind when searching the records. Salvationists record births in a 'Cradle Roll' and do not baptise their children, but dedicate them instead. These dedications are recorded. There are

RELIGIOUS AFFILIATIONS

also registers of marriages and deaths / burials (the latter called 'promotions to glory') and the swearing in of soldiers and officers' commissioning, but these are few in number.

Each Corps (or church) had to keep records from 1907 onwards in their Corps History book. As this is quite recent in date, some of this information will not be available to the public and much of it is not relevant to the genealogist or researcher. Most Corps' records are kept by the Corps officers and few have been deposited in county record offices. So, it will be necessary to contact local Corps to ask about local Salvationists. However, *The War Cry* newspaper (published weekly since 1879) and the *Salvation Army Yearbook* (published annually since 1906), have much useful genealogical information.

The Salvation Army has its main bases in London. **The Salvation Army International Heritage Centre** at 117-121 Judd Street, King's Cross, WC1H 9NN, has a large archive and memorabilia collection about its members. The public are allowed in by appointment to carry out research and the centre also has a research service. (See: www.salvationarmy.org.uk/international-heritage-centre)

Personnel files on officers are kept at **The Salvation Army Territorial Headquarters**, 101 Newington Causeway, London, SE1 6BU. Information from these, if not confidential, may be sent to known relatives if requested. An officer's career progression is listed in these records. However, many of those records predating 1941 have been lost. More recent records of officers, their Corps and Territorial Headquarters posts are published in the *Dispositions of Forces* directory.

The **William Booth Memorial Training College** in Camberwell, London, SE5 8BQ, keeps records of officer cadets and, if not confidential, details on individuals can be released.

Finally, Wiggins has written a useful book on researching Salvation Army ancestors.[17]

Brethren Records

The Brethren or Assemblies of Brethren movement started in Dublin, Ireland in 1820, growing out of Anglicanism. The founders were Anthony Norris Groves, John Nelson Darby, Edward Cronin and John Gifford Bellett. It is a non-conformist church which emphasises the authority of scripture for church doctrine and practice over any other authority.[18] In 1831, the first meeting started in England at Plymouth and so became known as the 'Plymouth Brethren'. It divided into the Open Brethren and Exclusive Brethren branches in 1848.[19] The Open Brethren were founded by George Müller. Subsequent splits followed. Nowadays, the Plymouth Brethren Christian Church is the most hard-line of all the Exclusive Brethren groups.

What unites all Brethren chapels or Gospel Halls, is the rejection of an ordained clergy, an emphasis on the 'priesthood of all believers' (1 Peter 2:4-5) and the independence of its congregations. Like many other non-conformist churches, Brethren congregations observe only two ordinances; that of believers' baptism and communion. Most Brethren have always taught dispensationalism and hold to a cessationist position. This is that the miraculous sign gifts of the Holy Spirit, such as miracles, healing and speaking in tongues were given to the early Church only, and died out at the end of the apostolic age. They are therefore opposed to the charismatic movement.

For a fuller explanation of the Brethren movement, it is best to read the links provided, plus other literature and website links. This text is not intended to be comprehensive.

No Brethren registers were surrendered to the General Register Office, (GRO). Kendal Archive Centre, part of Cumbria Archives, holds collections of Plymouth Brethren records. (See: https://legacy.cumberland.gov.uk/archives/Online_catalogues/defa ult.asp . Their address is: Kendal Archive Centre, Kendal County Offices, Busher Walk, Kendal, Westmorland and Furness, LA9 4RQ.[20] Individual chapels would need to be contacted for further information.

Some Plymouth Brethren registers can be searched online at the Family Search website. (See: www.familysearch.org/wiki/en/England_Nonconformists_Plymouth_Brethren_(National_Institute) [21]

The largest collection of Brethren records in the UK, dating from 1815, is held at the John Rylands Library of the University of Manchester. (See: www.library.manchester.ac.uk/rylands/special-collections/exploring/guide-to-special-collections/christian-brethren-collections/manuscripts/) [22]

It is also possible to find Irish Brethren ancestors on the 1901 and 1911 Census of Ireland, at: www.census.nationarchives.ie [23]

Foreign Protestant Churches in Britain
French Huguenot Records

French Protestant Huguenots were persecuted by the Catholic State for the 40-year period between the years 1680 and 1720. Almost 100,000 Huguenots had migrated to England by the early 1700's. Huguenots, possibly named after Besançon Hugues, followed the teachings of the theologian Jean Calvin (1509-1564). Many Huguenots fled to England, especially to Canterbury, the East End of London, Norwich and Bristol. Most of them were skilled workers, particularly in the weaving trade.

The researcher should start by consulting the records of General Registration (GRO), online via such sites as www.ancestry.co.uk or www.findmypast.co.uk and work backwards, finding the birth, marriage and death certificates back to 1837 and compiling a family tree. This should be supplemented by information from the decennial censuses from 1921, back to 1841. That will get the researcher back almost to within 100 years of the end of the era of Huguenot immigration (1680-1720).

From there, it will be necessary to consult the Anglican parish registers in the relevant local county record offices (CROs), as deduced from the places of birth, marriage, residence or death given in the GRO certificates and censuses. If they were nonconformists, then their birth, (baptism), marriage, marriage licence, death and burial records might also be located in the appropriate CROs. It would be worth consulting the records kept in Dr Williams Library in London (the originals now being housed at The National Archives (TNA) in Kew, Surrey).

One very good source for discovering what records are available to locate Huguenot ancestry, is the book, *Tracing your Huguenot Ancestors: a guide for family historians*, by Dr Kathy Chater.[24] She includes information about researching pedigrees, published family history books, wills, denizations and naturalisations, charities, church registers, nonconformist burial grounds, other parish records, coroner's inquests, censuses and head counts, other local records such as Quarter Sessions and land records, maps, newspapers, periodicals and occupational records. The latter include apprenticeships, freemen and professional bodies.

Chater says that family historians ideally need to trace their ancestry back to at least the middle of the 18th century before they can begin to discover Huguenot ancestry. This can also be the place where it becomes difficult to find records – the proverbial 'brick wall' is run into, and it is precisely this reason which could suggest it is time to research possible Huguenot ancestry. If these 18th century ancestors were living close to known Huguenot settlements, with local French churches, then this could be a good indication of Huguenot ancestry. If those churches had closed, then it is likely that Huguenots had assimilated with the local English or even Scottish community. Ambitious Huguenots would have joined Anglican churches, in order to 'get on' in society and career. Strict Huguenots who did not swear oaths, would have joined the local nonconformist churches, rather than swear the Oath of Allegiance to the Crown, via the Church of England.

Huguenot Names

Some Christian names from the late 17th to mid-18th century might indicate Huguenot roots, especially if the names were derived from the Old Testament, such as Abraham, Benjamin, Elie (Eli), Esther, Daniel, Isaac, Josue (Joshua), Judith, Magdelene, and Rachel.

It is a good idea to check the library of the Society of Genealogists (SoG), as it has an extensive collection of '**One-Name Studies.**' The Guild of One-Name Studies (GOONS) is an association of individuals researching particular names and their website: (www.one-name.org/) is worth checking.

The National Register of Archives website: (https://discovery.nationalarchives.gov.uk/) should be consulted in order to find the location of any family papers, deposited in any number of different county record offices or university college libraries. TNA's ARCHON directory has a list of all 27 locations of different record repositories, and the **A2A – 'Access to Archives'** website produced by TNA has the catalogues of all local archives in England and Wales.

Original documents should be consulted, including such things as Henry Wagner's pedigree lists, held by The Huguenot Society. He was a 19th century genealogist who did much work on the Huguenots, tracing different families and their pedigrees, published by the Huguenot Society.

The journal, *Huguenot Families*, was published between 1999-2009, and is listed on the 'Publications' section of The Huguenot Society website. (See: www.huguenotsociety.org.uk).

The Huguenot Society

Huguenot ancestral records are very good and most of them are held by The Huguenot Society, based on the edge of NW London, at PO Box 444, Ruislip, Middlesex, HA4 4GU. Email enquiries should be addressed to the Hon. Secretary at: secretary@huguenotsociety.org.uk. Its library is based at University College London (UCL).

Immigration Records

The Huguenot Society has a list of the records of **denizations and naturalisations** of Huguenots in Great Britain. Denization was where immigrants were allowed the right to live in the country. Naturalisation was more costly and took longer, being granted by Act of Parliament. By it, immigrants were granted full citizenship.

Another type of record published by the Huguenot Society, are **'Returns of Aliens'** or Strangers. In times of national crisis or threat of invasion particularly, local towns kept records of foreigners. An example of easily identifiable foreigners is found in the 'lay subsidies' or taxes on the movement of goods, lands or wages. The Huguenot Society has published such records, located in the Huguenot Library, the archives of the French Church in Soho Square in London, or, for the Canterbury congregation, in Canterbury Cathedral.

A further type of surviving record are the *reconnaissances*, *abjurations* and *témoignages*, also published by the Huguenot Society. **'Reconnaissances'** meant 'to recognise.' Many French Protestants were forced to convert to Roman Catholicism after the Revocation of the Edict of Nantes in 1685, and to attend Mass, or baptise their infants according to the rites of the RC Church. When they came to Britain and wanted to join a French Huguenot church, they were required to 'recognise' their fault, abjure their former faith and, as it were, re-convert, by choice to Protestantism. This procedure was recorded.

The **'Témoignages'** (testimony or witness) were attestations of Protestant faith, made in front of a church official or vouchsafed by a family member and recorded, once a Huguenot had immigrated to England. These attestations or examinations can pinpoint the date of immigration.

Occupations

Drapers and **weavers** figure prominently amongst Huguenots. The Society of Genealogists has published booklets on several occupations and the most useful for Huguenot ancestry is, *My Ancestors Were Freeman of the City of London*.[25] It also holds a collection of indentures between 1641 - 1888 and apprenticeship records.

RELIGIOUS AFFILIATIONS

The Huguenot Society has published extracts from the Weavers' Company records. Usefully, these records distinguish between British-born members and foreign-born. TNA also holds records of apprenticeships and tax records dated between 1710 – 1811. An index for 1710-1774 can be found on www.findmypast.co.uk A number of Huguenots joined the **Army**, in particular during the period of the 'Glorious Revolution' of 1688-89. An index of Huguenot army officers and related articles, is to be found in the Proceedings of the Huguenot Library in London.

Education

Various **schools** were established to educate Huguenot children, notably, two schools connected to the Threadneedle Street church, but also a school in Spitalfields, in Bethnal Green and in Westminster. These dated from 1719 to 1863. Records survive and are listed in the Proceedings of the Huguenot Society.

Charities

There are a number of Huguenot **charities'** records, all listed and published by the Huguenot Society, which list names of recipients. These come from charities in London, Norwich, and the Kent towns of Sandwich, Rye and Dover.

Records exist for the Huguenot **'Friendly Societies'** which supported the poor. These exist from the late 17th up to the 20th century. Records of these are held at the Huguenot Library, London Metropolitan Archives (LMA) and others at TNA.

The **Royal Bounty** was a regular collection of money, distributed to Huguenot refugees, authorised by King James II in 1686 and endorsed by his daughter, Queen Anne in the early 1700s. It came to an end in 1876. Records of this are kept in the Huguenot Library. Another source of Huguenot records dating from between 1718 and 2006, are those of the **French Protestant Hospital** (almshouse) of **'La Providence'**, in Rochester, Kent. These are held by University College London Archives. Nearby 'La Providence,' in Rochester High Street, stands the Huguenot Museum, the only one in the country.

The Huguenot Library holds copies of **wills**. Original pre-1858 ones are held by the Prerogative Court of Canterbury (PCC), with copies also held at TNA. The Henry Wagner pedigrees and wills date from 1617-1849.

Chater[26] advises when researching **Huguenot ancestry overseas,** to begin searching at the Huguenot Library in London, the Institute of Historical Research at the University of London, the Society of Genealogists and the internet. When language difficulties occur, it is possible to find help online from volunteers, such as on the website called, 'Random Acts of Kindness.' Otherwise it will be necessary to employ a professional genealogist, either from the Huguenot Society or one in France, or go there yourself. Towns with a strong Huguenot past, often have a museum dedicated to such history. Chater lists various books and guides to searching out Huguenot ancestors in France itself.

Other Foreign Churches' Records

There are other foreign churches established in the UK, such as the German Lutheran Church, whose records will be available to those with international heritage. However, these are really outside the scope of this book.

Jewish Records

Traditionally, there are two branches of Jews – the Ashkenazi and Sephardic. The Ashkenazi Jews came from the Rhineland, Eastern Europe and Russia. Sephardic Jews hail from the Iberian Peninsula and north Africa.

Modern Judaism can be divided into the different types of synagogues that Jews attend: Ultra-Orthodox (Haredi), religious Conservative (Dati) and Reform or Liberal, as well as secular Jews, who do not attend synagogue. For most of the history of Judaism, there were no separate strands.

Most synagogues retain their own registers, so family historians will need to contact the synagogue direct. It should be

RELIGIOUS AFFILIATIONS

noted that in Judaism, **babies are circumcised**, not baptised, so Jewish registers record circumcisions (8 days after birth), marriages and deaths. Records, particularly early ones, will be in Hebrew, but after 1870, an English translation is also recorded on the back of the record. Some Jews additionally recorded the births of their children with the local Anglican church, where the incumbent will have recorded, 'Son of a Jew' by the birth entry.

Bar mitzvah's are generally recorded in the *The Jewish Chronicle* and other newspapers. This ceremony marks the entry into adulthood at about age 13. Many Jewish archives and the British Newspaper Library have sets of these.
(See: www.britishnewspaperarchive.co.uk)

Marriages post 1837 appear in the GRO records. Prior to 1837, records of Jewish marriages were recorded by way of the marriage contract, called a *ketubah*, which was kept by the bride, with a copy kept in the congregation's archives. As mentioned under the section on the Church of England, Jews were exempt from Hardwicke's Marriage Act of 1753, so did not have to marry in an Anglican church. Some weddings took place in private homes, particularly the bride's, so this certainly helps in locating the family. Some weddings took place abroad. Wealthy Jewish families often recorded weddings in *The Jewish Chronicle* or *The Gentleman's Magazine*.

Deaths and obituaries (as well as births and marriages) are also recorded in *The Jewish Chronicle* and, as it started in November 1841, will have entries of ancestors who were born in the late 18th century. *The Jewish Year Book*, dating from 1896, gives details of local burial societies. Once the right cemetery and gravestone is found, the researcher will notice that the headstones are usually written in Hebrew, with the date of death written according to the Jewish calendar. This is 3760 years different to the Christian calendar. Additionally, remember that the Jewish New Year begins in the autumn.

Wills can provide an important source of information about

Jewish ancestry. **For English and Welsh** wills dating back to 1858, look for probate records online at: www.gov.uk/search-will-probate and follow the links to order a will. For wills dated earlier than 1858, produced in the South of England, it is necessary to search the online records at: https://discovery.nationalarchives.gov.uk. The indexes to all these wills are held at the National Archives at Kew in West London. For the North of England, wills proved prior to 1858 are held at the Borthwick Institute of Archives in York. (See: www.york.ac.uk/borthwick/) and follow the links.

For **Scottish** wills, the website address to follow up on a will dated between 1926 and 1999 is:
www.nrscotland.gov.uk/research/guides/wills-and-testaments. Prior to 1925, wills may be located via:
www.scotlandspeople.gov.uk/guides/wills-and-testaments.

For Northern Ireland, the website address is:
www.nidirect.gov.uk/information-and-services/search-archives-online/will-calendars. For the **Republic of Ireland**, the following website should be used: www.nationalarchives.ie/.

Wills are explained more fully on pages 51-54 in chapter 3 on rejection and abandonment.

Immigration records are important for tracing Jewish ancestry, as they give the place and country of birth of the person being sought. As for Huguenots, records of denization and naturalization are the most important. However, as the last 100 years of these are closed, it may be helpful to look in associated notices of *The London Gazette* for information about specific immigration. The London Metropolitan Archives (LMA) holds the records of the 'Poor Jews' Temporary Shelter' and the 'Jewish Relief.' These organisations helped over 40,000 Jews fleeing Nazi persecution in the 1930s and give detailed information about these refugees. (See: https://search.lma.gov.uk/)

The Wiener Holocaust Library at 29, Russell Square, London, WC1B 5DP, holds a very large collection of material relating to the Holocaust and also has an International Tracing Service (ITS) for

descendants of Jews massacred under the Nazis.
(See: www.wienerholocaustlibrary.org)

LMA also holds some early registers of synagogues. The London-based Court of the Chief Rabbi keeps records of birth and marriage authorizations from 1845, and burial authorizations dating back to 1896. (See: https://chiefrabbi.org/contact/) The Society of Genealogists (SoG) holds a large collection of these, including the Colyer-Ferguson collection. The latter contains many pedigrees of Jewish families, wills, monumental inscriptions and newspaper cuttings.

Possibly the most important UK centre for Jewish history is the Jewish Studies Library at University College London (UCL). (See: www.ucl.ac.uk/library/special-collections/a-z/jewish-rare). Other organisations important for Jewish genealogy are:

The Jewish Historical Society of England, 33 Seymour Place, London W1H 5AP. (See: www.jhse.org)

The Jewish Museum, 129-131 Albert Street, Camden Town, London NW1 7NB. (See: https://jewishmuseum.org.uk/)

The Jewish Genealogical Society of Great Britain, c/o The Jewish Museum (as above). (See: www.jgsgb.org.uk)

Two other books on tracing Jewish ancestry are, *My Ancestors were Jewish*, by Anthony Joseph [27] and, *Tracing Your Jewish Ancestors*, by Rosemary Wenzerul.[28]

Other Religions

While not covering records of other religions in this book, it is possible to say that marriage certificates going back to 1837 in the GRO records will give an indication as to religious affiliation, for at least one of the marriage partners.

Types of Religious Problems

As well as receiving innumerable blessings, sadly, many Christians, including the author, have experienced a whole host of problems in church or Christian organisations and been hurt by them. It is all too common to hear of such reports in the press these days. We humans are very fallible! That includes leaders. We live in and are saved out of a fallible world and bring our problems with us into church. Typically, we are either victims, perpetrators or both. Issues can include one or more of the following, for example: abortion, abuse, bitterness, competitiveness, confusion, control, deception / erroneous or false teaching, denominational rivalry, discrimination, faithlessness, fear, idolatry, judgmentalism, legalism, liberalism, mistrust, prejudice, presumption, rebellion, rejection, sexual sin, super-spirituality, syncretism, unforgiveness and an unloving spirit.

Abuse. Working through some of these issues alphabetically, abuse comes in various forms, including emotional, financial, physical, sexual, spiritual and verbal. In recent years, exposures of both historic and current sexual scandals have hit a number of denominations, causing much damage and many to leave the church.

Control. The decades of the 1980s and 1990s and into the 2000s, was a period when a number of mainly free churches went overboard in exercising their authority and control over their members, causing much pain, church splits and breakdowns and an unknown number of Christians to leave their churches. This was known as the 'heavy shepherding movement.'

Deception / Erroneous Teaching. Teachers have an especial responsibility for teaching the flock well. Errors can creep in where the Bible is not believed to be the authoritative word of God, leading to the values of the world or liberalism to be taught on the one hand, or some peculiar traditions on the other. Also, sections of God's word can be left out, because of a blind spot or fear in the denomination or preacher.

Denominational Rivalry. In the past, there was more rivalry, disagreement and strife between different denominations, particularly between Protestants and Catholics.

Faithlessness. We are all on the journey of faith, but some struggle with faith much more than others. If they have been let down by church, by a church leader or parents, or had no perceived experience of God's faithfulness or miracle-working power, then a life of faithlessness and mediocrity can be the result.

Idolatry. Following on from erroneous teaching, where certain practices or teachings over-emphasize an aspect of the faith or secular life, then idolatry can be present in the life of a church or member. This topic is covered more extensively in the next chapter. However, it is worth noting that Otto Bixler writes [29] that these problems will manifest in both physical and spiritual ways.

Legalism. Where a church is overly strict in the outworking of its faith, teaching, life and discipline, then legalism can take hold. Observance of rules and right behaviour becomes more important than knowing Jesus, who enables the keeping of His commandments. The loving fatherhood of God is unknown. He is seen as severe and one who will punish the sinner without mercy, rather than being a forgiving and restoring God. There is a wrong fear of Him, traceable to a poor or missing relationship with the natural father. Christianity becomes a religion of fear, not of love.

Liberalism. This can be seen as the polar opposite of legalism, where anything goes and where God and the church does not hold its members accountable for sin. As a pastor friend has written, 'Conservatives condemn sin, Liberals 'baptise' sin, Jesus overcomes sin.'

Mistrust. Do you struggle with mistrust of God, your church leaders or others? Did some disaster happen in the family line that caused your ancestors to abandon the faith? Was there any abuse or poor fathering in the family, that made it difficult or impossible to trust Father God? Did your ancestors just drift away from God, pulled by the attractions of the world, the flesh and the devil?

Prejudice. Churches can be quite cliquey sometimes, attracting only people of one type. When this happens, it is more likely to take on the prejudices of the culture around it, simultaneously being blind to these. Those outside will see!

Rejection. Interpersonal fallouts in churches are common, hence the need to take communion or the eucharist seriously and attempt reconciliation with those who have hurt you. All too often this doesn't happen and people carry around unresolved hurts and a sense of rejection, ultimately sometimes leaving that church.

Super-spirituality. We may have met some Christians who to us, seem overly spiritual somehow, or unreal, and seem to interpret too many ordinary things in a 'spiritual' way. Such people may initially seem very godly, but after a while, we may notice that they can also display some odd personality traits or be emotionally unstable. This super-spirituality can be a way to compensate for emotional or psychological deficiencies and actually be rooted in some kind of self-deception to make themselves feel better. It's another kind of religious fig leaf.

Syncretism. The term 'syncretism' can be applied to any mixture of beliefs with orthodox Christianity, which waters down the faith and weakens the individual Christian. This can happen where an accommodation with 'the world' is sought. One example is where the pure faith of the early church was added to by a mixture of pagan philosophies such as Platonism and Stoicism, as well as antisemitic beliefs current in the Roman world, which led to the Jewishness of the faith being squeezed out.

Unforgiveness. Unforgiveness ultimately hurts the person who won't or can't forgive the offender more than the offender themselves. It can lead to bitterness and torment, even finally losing one's faith. It is essential to seek God and ask Him to help us forgive those who have hurt us, as, in our own strength, we are often powerless to do so. Careful teaching on what and how to forgive should be basic and essential for all churches. If we want God to forgive us, then we must find a way to forgive others. Matthew 6:15 and 1 John 1:9 are clear about this:

> ...but if you do not forgive men their trespasses, neither will your Father forgive your trespasses.   Matthew 6:15 (RSV)

> If we confess our sins, he is faithful and just, and will forgive our sins and cleanse us from all unrighteousness.   1 John 1:9, (RSV)

Remember, that forgiveness is not the same as trust. Forgiveness is a decision, that takes time to work out in the emotions. It can be necessary to choose to forgive many times before forgiveness is achieved at the heart level, and then maintained by the occasional need to keep forgiving. However, trust, once broken, can be very difficult to restore. It is possible to forgive, yet be unwise to trust the offender again, especially if there has been gross, unrepented of sin involved. An abuser may be so damaged themselves that they should not be trusted in certain situations again. For example, childcare.

Evidence of Religious Problems in your Family Line

Where there has been wrongful control or abuse of any kind, deep hurt and eventual rebellion is usually the result. But where will the evidence of this be found? Your ancestors may have changed denominations because of this, as evidenced by generational changes on their birth, marriage and burial records. Have any letters they wrote or other documents been handed down to you?

The marriage certificates of ancestors may give some indication of the religious denomination they belonged to, though will not guarantee it. The wedding nuptials were required to be held in churches, even if the participants were not adherents. Before 1829, most people, excepting Quakers and Jews, were required to marry in the Church of England, even if they belonged to a different denomination. Maybe your ancestors married someone from a different denomination to their own, which, in previous ages, was more frowned upon and caused tension in the family.

However, if proof of your ancestors' denominational loyalties can be found, then with some knowledge of that church denomination's history and practice, it may be possible to discern whether any of the problems listed above were experienced by them. If you have any surviving photographs of your forebears, close scrutiny of their faces may indicate to you the type of characters they were and of any problems they carried, etched into their faces. You may have been told some family legends by your elders when you were growing up.

Indeed, do you struggle with church, denomination or spiritual difficulties? Have you inherited something similar from your forebears? Is there some unexplained prejudice against a certain church or denomination?

How to be Set Free of Generational Religious Problems

To start off, I would recommend praying for protection for yourself and your loved ones and for Jesus to lead and guide you in these prayers. Then pray the 'Lordship Prayer.' The declarations and prayers following, are used by several Christian ministries, in various forms, which you can find online and which are listed at the end of this chapter.

Lordship Prayer

"Dear Lord Jesus, I realise my need of You and repent of living my life my own way. I wholeheartedly accept You now as my Saviour, my Redeemer, my Lord and my Deliverer.

I invite You now to be the Lord of every part and moment of my life, from the time of my conception, right up until now:

Lord of my body, my physical health and behaviour.

Lord of my mind and all my attitudes and mental health.

Lord of all my emotions and all my reactions.

Lord of my spirit and my worship of You.

Lord of my family and all my relationships.

Lord of my sexuality and its expression.

Lord of my will and all of my hopes, ambitions, decisions and plans.

Lord of all my work and service for You.

Lord of all my finances.

Lord of all my needs and possessions.

Lord of the manner and time of my death."

A Recommendation:

Those unhelpful church or denominational activities and attitudes which may have become habitual in your life, or those in any of your ancestors' lives, may have given permission for a religious spirit or legalism to develop, instead of the freedom of the Holy Spirit and proper self-discipline. These will need to be recognised, confessed and repented of. Any pleasure, false comfort, wrong identity or sense of superiority over others, gained from them need also to be repented of, and taken to the cross for God to slay and forgive.

Declaration

"Thank you, Jesus, for shedding Your blood and dying on the cross, for the forgiveness of my sins, my ancestors' sins and my descendants' sins. You died and rose again that I might be set free to love and to serve You, in newness of life.

*While I thank you, Lord, for my ancestors, especially my father and mother who brought me into this world and whom I honour, I do not stand in agreement with them on sinful matters. In these cases, in your presence, Lord, I **confess** and **repent** on behalf of all my parents,' grandparents' and forefathers' unwittingly allowing any religious spirit or legalism to develop in their lives. I confess that these are not of you, and I **renounce** them off my life and off the life of my family. Thank you for dying in my place, so that I might go* free. I ask that You would **forgive** my ancestors' religious or legalistic spirituality, as I forgive them also. I claim Your **blood cleansing** from all the effects of this on my life."

Breaking of Soul Ties

"In the name of Jesus, I break all the ungodly body, soul and spirit ties with:

my parents,

other family members, (name them),

my grandparents, (For ancestors who have died, we break the whole soul tie),

great-grandparents and,

any other ancestors who I know were devout churchgoers.

I ask that you cleanse me from all spiritual defilement passing down to me, through these soul ties.

I ask Lord, that you would cleanse my blood line and my spirit, soul and body with your precious blood and fill me afresh with your love and your Holy Spirit, in Jesus' name."

Wait upon the Lord for any word of knowledge for a specific revelation. This will be necessary for those ancestral sins which cannot be found in the records.

Inner Vows & Bitter Root Judgements

When people have been let down by organised, lifeless religion, judged unfairly and rejected, they may have made what is called, a 'bitter root judgement' out of the bitterness of their hearts. This same attitude can be passed down to their children. Or they may make inner vows never to let their children suffer in the same way and cause their children to seek a life outside of church influence. Some atheists are formed in this way.

But these self-protective pronouncements and decisions, rather than helping, actually work to enslave the person who made them in ways they could not foresee at the time. Only later will the person find that negative issues recur again and again. A life without God has no eternal value and ultimately leads to permanent separation from Him.

When the person meets these sorts of brick walls, the way through them is to repent of and renounce these bitter root judgements and to ask God to help them to live wisely. They need to renounce the inner vows that they made and ask God to break the power of these vows over their lives. They may need to forgive several people from the past and ask God to show them who they can trust.

Binding and Loosing - Deliverance

"I bind and cut myself off from the ruling spirits of the church denomination that enslaved my forebear(s) and from the religious spirit that bound my ancestor. I bind and loose the spirit(s) of....... [use your discernment to name them] *from me and tell it / them to go, in the mighty name of Jesus!"*

Identity in Christ

As Christians, we have a new identity. We are no longer enemies of God, alienated from Him, from others and from ourselves. While some of our ancestors may have been enslaved and broken by religion, this inheritance need not define us. Similarly, if some of our ancestors rejected God because of their negative church experiences, their attitudes and behaviour need not be repeated in us. We are now accepted as beloved sons and daughters of the King of Kings! We have worth and value and therefore a new, godly reason and purpose for living. As Christians, ALL are set free and adopted into God's family and need to learn a new identity: our identity in Christ! John 1:12-13 says this clearly:

> Yet to all who did receive Him, to those who believed in His name, He gave the right to become children of God – children born not of natural descent, nor of human decision or a husband's will, but born of God. John 1:12-13, (NIV)

We are loved by God more than we can possibly know. We can discover this through the scriptures and personally through prayer, receive His love and hear His words of affirmation and delight in us. As we rest in His presence, we can soak in his warmth, approval, and love. His *rhema* voice and words, heard in our spirits, back up His written, *logos* words in the Bible. As we dwell on these, they will gradually counteract the lies we have been taught to believe about ourselves. God truly is LOVE! He loves us unconditionally! He is truth and His truth-telling will change us as we believe what He says about us; that we are loved and valued.

The Blessing of Jesus

"I ask, Lord, that you turn all these curses into blessings, as I rest in Your love and presence and as I find my true identity in You. If I am carrying any emotional wounds caused by the influence of inherited religious spirits and legalistic self-righteousness, I ask, Lord, that You surface them and show me, so that I can give them to You and express them safely, forgive and be healed of them. Help me to live and work for You in the power of Your Spirit. I ask this in Jesus' name."

In Summary

Give thanks for your ancestors. **Identify** any possible problems caused by misplaced religious practices found in your family line. If found, **confess** the sins in your family line and the influence they have had in your own life. (Lamentations 5:7). **Repent** from personal issues caused by the harm of wrongful church or religious practices and repent from those found in the family line by identifying with and owning them as one's own. Ask for and receive God's **forgiveness**. **Cut** soul ties. Seek **deliverance** ministry and / or conduct self-deliverance for any spirits taking advantage of these problems. Seek the cleansing **blood of Jesus** to wash away any stains. **Soak** in God's presence and **find** your **true identity** in Him.

Ask Jesus to **bless** you and **fill** you afresh with His Holy Spirit. Seek to be **obedient** to His guidance and call on your life.

A Recommendation

As mentioned before, the prayers in this chapter are intended just as openers, to help start you on the journey to freedom. In order to work towards complete freedom, I would recommend working through the material and prayers in the ministry books listed at the end of this chapter. It would also be very worthwhile attending one of the excellent training and ministry courses run by Bethel Sozo, Christian Prayer Ministries, Gilgal House Healing Centre, Ellel Ministries, or Sozo Ministries International, here in the UK. This is not an exhaustive list and the reader may hear of other ministries both in the UK and abroad, which can help in this area.

Further Reading - Select Bibliography

Bixler, Otto. *It isn't Free and it isn't Masonry*. UK: Zaccmedia, (2016).

Dalbey, Gordon. *Broken by Religion, Healed by God: Restoring the Evangelical, Sacramental, Pentecostal, Social Justice Church*. Folsom, CA: Civitas Press, (2011).

Hawkey, Ruth. *Freedom from Generational Sin*. Chichester: New Wine Press, (1999).

Horrobin, Peter. *Healing through Deliverance*. (rev). Lancaster: Sovereign World, (2008).

Prince, Derek. *Blessing or Curse: You Can Choose*. (3rd ed). Grand Rapids, MI: Chosen Books Publishing Co., (2006).

Sandford, John Loren & Paula. *God's Power to Change*. Lake Mary, FL: Charisma House, (2007).

Chapter 11

Genealogical Evidence for Generational Idolatry

> *You must not make for yourself an idol of any kind or an image of anything in the heavens or on the earth or in the sea. You must not bow down to them or worship them, for I, the LORD your God, am a jealous God who will not tolerate your affection for any other gods.*   Exodus 20:4-5, (NLT)

Idolatry is more widespread than most people realise. You probably right think of carved images of other gods or religious symbols, when you think of idolatry, but it is far more than this.

In order to gain freedom from the negative power and influence of idolatry, we need to understand what it is and to be able to recognise it in our own lives. To help in focusing our thoughts on what idolatry means biblically, here are the relevant Commandments from Exodus 20 and also the New Testament which speak of it: -

Idolatry in the 10 Commandments
1st Commandment

> You shall have no other gods before Me.
>   Exodus 20:3, (NIV)

> You shall worship the Lord your God, and Him alone shall you serve.   Luke 4:8, 1 Corinthians 8:4 – 6, (NKJV)

2nd Commandment

> You shall not make for yourself a carved image - any likeness of anything that is in heaven above, or that is in the earth beneath, or that is in the water under the earth; you shall not bow down to them nor serve them . . .   Exodus 20:4 – 5, (ESV)

> Little children, keep yourselves from idols
>   1 John 5:21, Acts 17:29, (ESV)

> But the cowardly, and unbelieving . . . and idolaters . . . shall have their part in the lake that burns with fire and brimstone . . .
> Revelation 21:8, (NKJV)

Isaiah 44:9 says:

> All who make idols are nothing, and the things they delight in do not profit; their witnesses neither see nor know. And so, they will be put to shame.

Later, in Isaiah 65:6-7, the prophet warns against the sin of idolatry because:

> See, it is written before me: I will not keep silent, but I will repay; I will indeed repay into their laps their iniquities and their ancestors' iniquities together, says the LORD;...

Definition of Idolatry

So, idolatry has to do with seeking guidance, protection, power and blessing from or through a god or spiritual power, other than Jesus and Father God. As we shall see in the next chapter, the main sin issue in **Freemasonry** is idolatry. It can also involve any interest which takes a place of overarching importance in our lives. Idolatry is deceptive and can involve a subtle mockery of God.

It can even invade **the church,** whatever the denomination. Peter Horrobin writes about and lists a whole host of idolatrous practices and misplaced focus on people, practices and things found in church, and how his team have had to pray deliverance for Christians caught up in them.[1]

Sexual sin is a form of idolatry. In our modern age, sex is seen as all important and the pursuit of it and the pleasure it brings is regarded as being the primary goal in life, irrespective of the damage done to others or self. We can make an idol of another person, or indeed an animal. Think of Britons' love of cats, dogs and other animals.

Those driven to **work excessively**, whose primary motivation in life is their career, are also guilty of the sin of idolatry. 'Thou shall have no other gods before me,' as the 1st Commandment states.'

Sabbath breaking (the 4th Commandment) or not resting properly, can also be a consequence of overwork.

The worship of **money** and the obsessive acquiring of possessions that money enables, is also a primary form of idolatry, especially in the rich West, or in the lives of anyone from any other country. These sins can affect several generations and may even be dismissed as part of the 'culture' of the region or country, and even justified as part of its tradition. However, such practices may not be morally neutral, but actually sinful, according to the biblical definition. In such cases, they need to go out of the life of a Christian! Culture needs to be redeemed!

What all of these three classic forms of sin (money, sex and power) have in common, apart from idolatry, is the elevation of self, to the exclusion of God and others. Self-idolatry can be added to the list to make it up to four.

Idolatry can also be detected in activities or in the use of substances which try to bring **comfort** and peace to our otherwise stressed or pain-filled lives. Did your ancestors have particular hobbies, sports or pastimes that occupied their time excessively? Did they smoke, misuse alcohol, use drugs, over-indulge in food, engage in ritualistic practices or the occult, have extra-marital affairs or even be on every church council or activity going? Of course, it is only God who can bring real peace to our troubled hearts.

The prophet Ezekiel reminded the backslidden Israelites what God had previously said:

> And I said to their children in the wilderness, "Do not walk in the statutes of your fathers, nor keep their rules, nor defile yourselves with their idols." Ezekiel 20:18, (ESV)

Idolatry and rebellion are grouped together with and likened to **witchcraft** in 1 Samuel 15:23, where the prophet Samuel, admonishes King Saul:

> For rebellion *is* as the sin of witchcraft, and stubbornness *is* as iniquity and idolatry. Because you have rejected the word of the LORD, He also has rejected you from *being* king.
> 1 Samuel 15:23, (NKJV)

Witchcraft is also warned against in numerous other Old Testament scriptures. It is also grouped together with idolatry in the New Testament. See: Galatians 5:19-21, Acts 8:9-13 & Acts 19:18-20.

> The acts of the flesh are obvious: sexual immorality, impurity and debauchery; idolatry and witchcraft; hatred, discord, jealousy, fits of rage, selfish ambition, dissensions, factions and envy; drunkenness, orgies, and the like. I warn you, as I did before, that those who live like this will not inherit the kingdom of God.
> Galatians 5:19-21, (NIV)

Otto Bixler writes [2] that the effects of the sin of idolatry can come down three or four generations. But what are the consequential effects of idolatry on those caught up in it and how do you detect it in the genealogical records?

Effects of Idolatry

Peter Horrobin, commentating on 1 Corinthians 10, in his textbook on the healing ministry, *Healing Through Deliverance*, writes that:

> Idolatry, therefore, is a serious sin with enormous potential consequences, which can lead to many ordinary Christians being in bondage to the demonic.[3]

He quotes Paul, who wrote:

> So then...keep away from the worship of idols.
> (1 Corinthians 10:14)

Later, he writes that:

> What happens is that a demon takes up residence over the idol, assumes the characteristics that have been imposed upon it by man, and then rewards and punishes the worshipers according to how they appease the demonic demands of the idol, which has become their god. The individual worshipers then become demonised with a spirit that is under the control of the ruling spirit of the idol.[4]

Explaining further, Peter Horrobin shows that:

> So idolatry (and most sin is ultimately a form of idolatry) gives the demonic a right of entry. And once the demon is in, it is only through repentance and deliverance that the person can be set free. Furthermore, it is not just restricted to the person who has sinned, but it will seek to transfer down the generation lines to future generations. The sin of one generation "uncovers" the next generation, leaving the children unprotected in the area of that particular sin. This whole area of transference down the generation line is therefore a major topic in deliverance ministry.[5]

The Bible gives us clues as to the possible negative consequences and effects on those who have practiced idolatry, either knowingly or in ignorance. Psalm 135:15-18 reveals them:

> The idols of the nations are silver and gold, made by human hands.
> They have mouths, but cannot speak, eyes, but cannot see.
> They have ears, but cannot hear, nor is there breath in their mouths.
> Those who make them will be like them, and so will all who trust in them.   Psalms 135:15-18, (NIV)

The last line of the quotation indicates that those who practice idolatry will display similar characteristics to the lifeless idols they have bowed down to. Such people may develop **mobility** issues, **speech** difficulties, **eyesight** problems, **hearing** issues and **breathing** difficulties.

Otto Bixler writes [6] that these problems will manifest in both physical and spiritual ways. Statues cannot move their limbs. Those who practice idolatry may develop an inability to move their hands, legs or feet properly and therefore be unable to walk in the ways of God fully. Apart from natural speaking difficulties, it may be difficult to speak in tongues (one of the charismatic gifts listed in Acts 2:4, amongst other places). Idolatry could be the cause of sight defects, requiring corrective glasses, as well as affecting spiritual discernment and vision.

It may be difficult to hear, thus requiring the use of hearing aids. But perhaps more importantly, it may be difficult to hear from God and be guided by the Holy Spirit, resulting in confusion as to the will of God and therefore an over-reliance on human reason and / or the (faulty) advice of others.

Finally, breathing could be affected. This might be caused by allergies, asthma, emphysema or even lung cancer. You might say that the latter two are obvious signs of smoking, rather than idolatry, but then smoking is so often resorted to as a false comfort, (instead of turning to Jesus for comfort), i.e. it is an idol, according to the above definition. These illnesses all cause distress and a lack of peace. A sign of not being able to 'breath' in the comfort and strength of Jesus?

Now that the reader is (hopefully) convinced of the dangers associated with idolatry, how do you go about finding evidence of idolatry in your family line?

Evidence of Idolatry in Your Family Line

In your family archives (if you have any), there may be letters, magazines, photos, paintings, artifacts or other paperwork which give hints as to your ancestors' lifestyles or membership affiliations. Are there any clues in an old address book? Where were they born? Were they born in a country whose main religious practice is non-Christian? What religious or denominational affiliation is shown on their marriage certificates? Is there evidence of a non-Christian religion, such as Buddhism, Hinduism, Islam, Mormonism, a cult, the occult, or even atheism? If you cleared out their house or flat after they died, were empty cigarette packets or many drinks bottles found? What does the death certificate show? Is a cause of death given which would indicate a substance-use related death?

It may be very difficult finding evidence of idolatry in the usual records useful in genealogical research. It is highly unlikely that anything will be noticed in birth, marriage and death certificates. One thought is that if an ancestor was found to have had multiple marriages, or divorces, that would indicate a problem in relationships, with a possible root caused by idolatry of some kind. Census records will show standard information, but from 100 years ago plus, they will be unlikely to show the sort of instability in relationships that we have today. The British Newspaper Archive may possibly contain digitised articles about any peculiarities in your ancestors' lives. (See: www.britishnewspaperarchive.co.uk/). Perhaps wills might give some clues as to idolatrous family practices. See the section on wills and probate in chapter 7 on poverty and wealth, for more details.

While finding proof of generational occultic activity in the family line in official records might be impossible, near ancestors may have left occultic items or books around after they died. In which case, it is possible to pray into this.

How to be Set Free of Generational Idolatry

We can begin with a promise given by God himself:

> I will sprinkle clean water on you, and you shall be clean from all your uncleannesses, and from all your idols I will cleanse you. And I will give you a new heart, and a new spirit I will put within you.
> Ezekiel 36:25-26a, (ESV)

To start off, I would recommend praying for protection for yourself and your loved ones and for Jesus to lead and guide you in these prayers. Then pray the 'Lordship Prayer.' The declarations and prayers following, are used by several Christian ministries, in various forms, which you can find online and which are listed at the end of this chapter.

Lordship Prayer

"Dear Lord Jesus, I realise my need of You and repent of living my life my own way. I wholeheartedly accept You now as my Saviour, my Redeemer, my Lord and my Deliverer.

I invite You now to be the Lord of every part and moment of my life, from the time of my conception, right up until now:

Lord of my body, my physical health and behaviour.

Lord of my mind and all my attitudes and mental health.

Lord of all my emotions and all my reactions.

Lord of my spirit and my worship of You.

Lord of my family and all my relationships.

Lord of my sexuality and its expression.

Lord of my will and all of my hopes, ambitions, decisions and plans.

Lord of all my work and service for You.

Lord of all my finances.

Lord of all my needs and possessions.

Lord of the manner and time of my death."

A Recommendation:

Those unhelpful activities and passions which may have become all-engrossing in your life, or those of any of your ancestors' lives, may have given permission for a spirit of idolatry, or self-idolatry to take hold in you. Jesus is no longer No.1 in your life. These will need to be recognised, confessed and repented of. The pleasure, false comfort, wrong identity and priority gained from them need also to be repented of and taken to the cross for God to slay and forgive. Ask Him to order your priorities.

Declaration

"*Thank you, Jesus, for shedding Your blood and dying on the cross, for the forgiveness of my sins, my ancestors' sins and my descendants' sins. You died and rose again that I might be set free to love and to serve You, in newness of life.*

While I thank you, Lord, for my ancestors, especially my father and mother who brought me into this world and whom I *honour, I do not stand in agreement with them on sinful matters. In these cases, in your presence, Lord, I **confess** and **repent** on behalf of all my parents,' grandparents' and forefathers' unwittingly allowing idolatry and / or self-idolatry to develop in their lives. I confess that these are not of you, and I **renounce** them off my life and off the life of my family.*

I reject and renounce any occult, pagan, New Age or satanic practices that I or any of my ancestors were involved in." A list of some of these is provided by Dr David Wells and is included here in a re-ordered, alphabetical layout: Amulets, astrology, automatic writing, black magic, channelling, clairvoyance, contacting the dead, crystals, crystal gazing, demonology, divination, dungeons and dragons games, extra-sensory perception, Feng Shui, fetishes, fortune telling, freemasonry, incantations, mediums, mesmerizing, Ouija boards, pagan religions, palm reading, pantheism, pendulums, pornography, psychic phenomena, pyramids, reincarnation or rebirthing, reiki, Rosicrucianism, runes or occult writing, satanic worship, spiritualism, talismans, tarot cards, telepathy, thought transfer, transcendental meditation, voodoo practices or worship, white magic, witchcraft, worship of the dead.[7]

*"Thank you for dying in my place, so that I might go free. I ask that You would **forgive** my ancestors' idolatry, self-idolatry, and any evil occult practices, as I forgive them also. I claim Your **blood cleansing** from all the effects of this on my life."*

Breaking of Soul Ties

"In the name of Jesus, I break all the ungodly body, soul and spirit ties with:
my parents,
other family members, (name them),
my grandparents, (For ancestors who have died, we break the whole soul tie),
great-grandparents and,
any other ancestors who I know or suspected were guilty of idolatry or self-idolatry.

I ask that you cleanse me from all self-focus and idolatry passing down to me, through these soul ties.

"I ask Lord, that you would cleanse my blood line and my spirit, soul and body with your precious blood and fill me afresh with your love and your Holy Spirit, in Jesus' name."

Wait upon the Lord for any word of knowledge for a specific revelation. This will be necessary for those ancestral sins which cannot be found in the records.

Inner Vows & Bitter Root Judgements

When people have been let down by those who were primarily focused on themselves, they may have made what is called, a 'bitter root judgement' out of the bitterness of their hearts. This same attitude can be passed down to their children. Or they may make inner vows never to let their children suffer in the same way and cause their children to seek a life outside of church influence. Some atheists are formed in this way.

But these self-protective pronouncements and decisions, rather than helping, actually work to enslave the person who made them in ways they could not foresee at the time. Only later will the person find that negative issues recur again and again. A life without God has no eternal value and ultimately leads to permanent separation from Him.

When the person meets these sorts of brick walls, the way through them is to repent of and renounce these bitter root judgements and to ask God to help them to live wisely. They need to renounce the inner vows that they made and ask God to break the power of these vows over their lives. They may need to forgive several people from the past and ask God to show them who they can trust.

Binding and Loosing - Deliverance

"I bind and cut myself off from the spirit and effects of idolatry and self-idolatry coming down my family line. I bind and *loose the spirit(s) of....... [use your discernment to name them] from me and tell it / them to go, in the mighty name of Jesus!"*

Identity in Christ

As Christians, we have a new identity. We have died and are dying to self! We are no longer enemies of God, alienated from Him, from others and from ourselves. While some of our ancestors may have been imprisoned by self-absorption and idolatry, this inheritance need not define us. Their attitudes and behaviour need not be repeated in us. We are now accepted as beloved sons and daughters of the King of Kings! We have worth and value and therefore a new, godly reason and purpose for living, beyond our own personal needs and interests. As Christians, ALL are set free from ourselves and adopted into God's family. We need to learn a new identity: our identity in Christ! John 1:12-13 says this clearly:

> *Yet to all who did receive Him, to those who believed in His name, He gave the right to become children of God – children born not of natural descent, nor of human decision or a husband's will, but born of God.* John 1:12-13, (NIV)

We are loved by God more than we can possibly know. We can discover this through the scriptures and personally through prayer, receive His love and hear His words of affirmation and delight in us. As we rest in His presence, we can soak in his warmth, approval, and love. His *rhema* voice and words, heard in our spirits, back up His written, *logos* words in the Bible. As we dwell on these, they will gradually counteract the lies we have been taught to believe about ourselves and help to 'dethrone' us. God truly is LOVE!

The Blessing of Jesus

"I ask, Lord, that you turn this curse of idolatry into blessing, as I rest in Your love and presence and find my true identity in You. If I am carrying any emotional wounds caused by the influence of inherited idolatry or self-idolatry, I ask, Lord, that You surface them

and show me, so that I can give them to You and express them safely, forgive and be healed of them. Help me to live and work for You in the power of Your Spirit. I ask this in Jesus' name."

In Summary

Give thanks for your ancestors. **Identify** any possible idolatry or idolatrous practices found in your family line. If found, **confess** the sin of idolatry in your family line and the influence it has had in your own life. (Lamentations 5:7). **Repent** from personal idolatry and any idolatry or witchcraft in the family line, by identifying with and owning it as your own. Ask for and receive God's **forgiveness**. **Cut** soul ties. Seek **deliverance** ministry and / or conduct self-deliverance for any spirits of idolatry. Seek the **cleansing blood of Jesus** to wash away any stains.

Ask Jesus to **bless you** and **fill you** afresh with His Holy Spirit. Seek to be **obedient** to His guidance and call on your life.

A Recommendation

As mentioned before, the prayers in this chapter are intended just as openers, to help start you on the journey to freedom. In order to work towards complete freedom, I would recommend working through the material and prayers in the ministry books listed at the end of this chapter. It would also be very worthwhile attending one of the excellent training and ministry courses run by Bethel Sozo, Christian Prayer Ministries, Gilgal House Healing Centre, Ellel Ministries, or Sozo Ministries International, here in the UK. This is not an exhaustive list and the reader may hear of other ministries both in the UK and abroad, which can help in this area.

Further Reading - Select Bibliography

Bixler, Otto. *It isn't Free and it isn't Masonry*. UK: Zaccmedia, (2016).

Hawkey, Ruth. *Freedom from Generational Sin*. Chichester: New Wine Press, (1999).

Horrobin, Peter. *Healing through Deliverance*. (rev). Lancaster: Sovereign World, (2008).

Prince, Derek. *Blessing or Curse: You Can Choose*. (3rd ed). Grand Rapids, MI: Chosen Books Publishing Co., (2006).

Sandford, John Loren & Paula. *God's Power to Change*. Lake Mary, FL: Charisma House, (2007).

Chapter 12

Genealogical Evidence for Generational Freemasonry

> *"I am the LORD your God, who brought you out of the land of Egypt, out of the house of slavery. You shall have no other gods before Me."*
> Exodus 20:2-3, (BSB)

Although the reader of this book is probably not a Freemason, and may not know of any Freemasonry running in their family line, it would be a mistake to think this chapter is of no relevance. I made that mistake years ago in thinking that I had no Freemasonry ancestors, until I started finding items and references in the house sorting and clearing, after my parents had died. That started my researches.

It would also be a mistake to think that only men are, or were Freemasons. There are and have been women Freemasons, especially in Canada and the USA. There are also Lodges connected to the military, to prisoners of war, schools, universities, other organisations and to alms-houses. It has often been used as a means of gaining success in the business world and other careers, such as the police and legal profession, and to gain power and influence in society. There have been and are some very notable people involved in Freemasonry. Even some ministers of churches and leaders of denominations are members of Lodges. However, many church leaders in both the protestant and catholic church denominations have spoken out against Freemasonry, including General Booth and nine popes. It is estimated there are currently over 200,000 Freemasons in the UK and about 6 million worldwide. Adherents are made up of Buddhists, Christians, Hindus, Jews, Muslims and anyone else who believes in 'God.'

What is Freemasonry and Why is it Harmful?

Freemasonry is a semi-secret society which is fundamentally a spiritually-focused organisation and a successor of the ancient mystery religions, with secret worship rites of pagan gods. These pagan gods include a mixture of the names, Jahbulon, Gaotu, Ahura-Mazda, Allah, Aum and Lucifer and stem from the Middle East, including ancient Egypt, Judaea, Arabia, Persia, and as far as India. So, this includes Baal worship, Hinduism, Islam, Judaism, Zoroastrianism, the occult and Christianity! It's a syncretistic hotch-potch and effectively, a false religion. It is therefore idolatry and breaks the 1st of the 10 Commandments, 'You shall have no other gods before me' (Exodus 20: 3). Freemasons call their god, 'the Great Architect of the Universe.'

Gilgal House minister into Freemasonry, and quote Albert Pike, a 33rd degree Freemason in the 19th century, who wrote in his book, *Morals and Dogma* (1871), (and now in modern reprints),

> Freemasonry is not only a religion, but it is above all religions and that, it is a universal, eternal, immutable religion.[1]

Hidden behind a public-spirited front of charitable works, are secret handshakes, initiation rites, Christ-less prayers and hymns, oaths and curses, conducted within Masonic 'temples' all over the world. Initiates are unaware of the increasingly darker aspects of Freemasonry that take place the higher up members progress in the organization. More is gradually revealed, but members are blind to its destructive power. At the top, is the 'pure' worship of Lucifer, but this aspect is kept secret, even from most Freemasons. The god of Freemasonry is not revealed until the 13th degree. Albert Pike, who reshaped Freemasonry into the form it is today, wrote,

> The blue degrees (or symbolic degrees) are but the outer court or portico of the Temple. Part of the symbols are displayed there to the initiate, but he is intentionally misled by false interpretations. It is not intended that he should understand them; it is intended that he imagines that he understands them. Their true explication is reserved for the Adept, the Princes of Freemasonry, this comes in the high degrees.[2]

It is only through books on Freemasonry, written by top Freemasons, by those who have come out of it, and by those with ministry experience of helping ex-Masons, that the truth about this dark, occult organisation has come to light. For instance, Derek Prince (1915-2003), the renowned Bible scholar and teacher, wrote in his book *Blessing or Curse*,

> For my part, I had no interest at all in Freemasonry until I began to discover the harmful effects it had produced in the lives of people who came for prayer. Some of the most frightening examples that I have encountered of curses at work in people's lives were associated with Freemasonry. The effects were manifested in the second and third generations of those who had a Mason in their family background.[3]

Catherine and Frank Fabiano write in their book, *Healing Your Past Releasing Your Future*, about a Christian named Erika who sought prayer from them for the bizarre and frightening nightmares she was suffering from. It was revealed that her grandfather had dedicated her to serve false spirituality and Freemasonry before she was born. After she became a Christian in her teens, the generational curse of Freemasonry kicked in and she started having the nightmares. She was set completely free after she forgave her grandfather and her forebears, broke the dedication to Freemasonry and the curse of death associated with it.[4] As the authors put it so aptly, *'What the Lord reveals, He heals.'*

There are spiritual and medical consequences for involvement in Freemasonry and for several generations later. Otto Bixler writes,

> Freemasonry, which by its nature and function opposes God's plan for families, turns the hearts of men towards its own gods and principles.[5]

Freemasonry is structured into 33 levels or degrees, with members rising potentially, from the 1st to the 33rd degree, via a series of initiation rites accompanied by oaths of loyalty, sworn over a masonic bible, using the words, *"So mote it be."* Upon this bible is placed a set square and compass, two symbols of Freemasonry.

Other symbols of Freemasonry, include the occultic pentagram and black and white squares, depicted on the floors of its Lodges, the 'eye of Horus' (an Egyptian god), and the obelisk, often seen in city centres and cemeteries.

Most Freemasons only progress through the 'blue degrees' to the 3rd degree, that of Master Mason. Beyond that, there are basically two strands to follow, that of the Scottish rite or the York rite. They meet in halls called 'Lodges' and these start with the local 'Craft Lodge,' which is under the county Provincial Grand Lodge, which is itself under the jurisdiction of the United Grand Lodge of Great Britain. This HQ is based in London at, 60 Great Queen Street, Holborn.

Diseases and Problems Stemming from Freemasonry

It has been repeatedly found that the negative effects of the oaths and curses made by Freemasons during their initiations, only really kick in if they leave the organisation and / or start to follow Jesus. These oaths and curses have been described as forming 'a blasphemous covenant' with Satan, by Ken Symington of CRi-Ireland. They also begin to operate in the children, grandchildren, great-grandchildren and possibly other descendants of Freemasons. Peter Horrobin writes from his team's experience in praying release for the descendants of Freemasons:

> ...we have had to free many children (both men and women) from spirits of Freemasonry, when they themselves have never had any involvement, but have been descended from Freemasons.[6]

Physical Diseases

There are numerous physical diseases which can be traced back to involvement in the Craft. Although there will be other causative factors, those which can be caused by Freemasonry involvement include allergies, bowel problems such as Crohn's disease and colitis, cancer, dyslexia, gall bladder problems, glandular fever, M.E, gynaecological problems, headaches and migraines, heart disease, problems with the hips (especially the right one), kidneys and knees, mouth, teeth and gum disease, tinnitus, psoriasis, respiratory issues such as bronchitis and pneumonia and those causing problems with the sinus, throat, neck and thyroid. Being accident prone and having work and money problems may also have a causal link to Freemasonry.

Mental / Emotional Problems

There are several emotional problems which may have a root cause in Freemasonry. These can include confusion, suppression of true emotions, scepticism and cynicism, delusion, depression, disdain, a sense of superiority, pride and false strength, fear, a sense of humiliation or wretchedness, and panic attacks.

Spiritual Problems

Even for Christians there can or will be spiritual problems which are caused by actual and generational influences of Freemasonry. These can include attraction to false religions, blasphemous thoughts and actual spoken blasphemy, rebellion, mockery, deception, heresy, idolatry, difficulty reading the Bible, doubting one's salvation, a dumb spirit on the tongue, hypnotism, mind control, secrecy, spiritual blindness, unbelief and a general sense of being under a yoke of bondage.

To gain further understanding of the influence of Freemasonry on your family, it is helpful to know something of its history and how to research its historic records, as a prelude to praying into the issues and receiving prayer ministry.

Additionally, Freemasonry also negatively impacts churches and church buildings. Peter Horrobin writes:

> ...there are many churches that were partially financed in their construction with money from Freemasons. Some even have special Masonic foundation stones or symbols built into their designs. Freemasonry is a form of idolatry, which always gives access to demonic spirits. Spirits of Freemasonry over a church will be directly opposed to the renewing power of the Holy Spirit,

and these must be dealt with if the people are to be free to move forward under the anointing of the Holy Spirit.[7]

History of Freemasonry

Freemasonry originated centuries ago when the stonemasons who built the cathedrals, were required to be Christians. The 'Old York Constitution' of AD 926 specified this.[8] This requirement carried on in the craft guilds of the mediaeval period, in the 14th to 16th centuries. As less and less stone was used in buildings by the 18th century, the guilds opened membership to non-stonemasons in 1703. In 1717, four independent masons' lodges came together to form the United Grand Lodge in London. Records of the Lodge start at this date. The standards and practices of this Lodge were codified in 1723, but at the same time, stepped away from Christianity and allowed a plurality of pagan and philosophical beliefs. This caught the attention of the authorities.

The Seditious Societies Act of 1799, required a certificate of membership to be handed over to the Clerk of the Peace. This recorded the names of Freemasons, their age, address, occupation, and the name of the Freemasonry lodge and number to which they belonged, to be recorded once a year. If Lodges had existed from earlier times, their identifying numbers changed in 1863. Masons, such as Albert Pike, (erroneously) wrote in 1871, that Freemasonry began in ancient Egypt and King Solomon's Temple in Jerusalem. Many countries now have Freemasons.

Researching Freemasonry Ancestors

If you want to try to find out if any of your ancestors were Freemasons, then you have several options. First, you could try looking for online records, held by the United Grand Lodge in **Freemasons' Hall**, Holborn, London. (See: www.ugle.org.uk/). This headquarters kept (and still keeps) records of members' names and their lodges. A few years ago, a change in the law required the release of this information to the public. These are also available online at www.ancestry.co.uk and cover the period 1751-1921. At

the time of writing, records since 1921 are not publicly available, because the Data Protection Act keeps living Mason's identities confidential. It is also possible to search for ancestors through the Museum of Freemasonry, which is at the same address in London. (See: https://museumfreemasonry.org.uk/family-history).
The postal address is:

Freemasons' Hall
60 Great Queen Street
Holborn
LONDON
WC2B 5AZ

Tel: 020 7395 9257

There are large collections of both published and manuscript material, including annual year books produced after 1908. The *Masonic Year Book Historical Supplement* lists approximately 35,000 senior masons alive between 1717 and 1968. It is probable that there have been millions of people, mostly men, who were Freemasons. However, do remember that the records since 1921 are covered by the Data Protection Act and so it is not possible, using online methods to find Freemasons who are still actively involved.

Freemasons' Hall also has records of individuals connected with schools specifically set up for the education of the children of Freemasons. These began in 1788 and in some cases, still operate. Also operated or operating, are hospitals, homes for elderly Freemasons and a Masonic Samaritan Fund.

County Record Offices

You can also look online to see if your local **County Record Office** (CRO) has any Freemasonry records for the county you are interested in. As mentioned, certificates of membership of Freemasonry lodges were made by the Clerk of the Peace and these records were housed in the Quarter Sessions records (the forerunner of today's magistrates' courts). These records are now kept in local CRO's. The years covered by the Quarter Sessions records will be from 1799-1967, the latter date being when under the Criminal Law Act, 1967, registers of Lodges and annual certificates were no longer necessary.

Registers of the Lodges and their own membership books might therefore be found in the Quarter Sessions records in local archives and CROs. A visit to the archives might well be necessary, but check the online catalogue of each CRO first.

Freemasonry Regalia

For those who have inherited what they believe to be Freemasonry regalia – apron, collars, sashes and gauntlets, hats, jewels and medals, or photographs of ancestors wearing these items, there are several possible ways to identify them. Contact can be made by writing to or visiting the museum at Freemasons' Hall, a local Craft Lodge or Provincial Grand Lodge. It would be advisable to pray for spiritual protection if a visit to Freemasons' Hall, or any other Freemasonry building is planned. Alternatively, photos of these items can be taken and posted with a covering letter to Freemasons' Hall, asking their museum staff to identify the items. Certificates of membership, items of China pottery, glassware and metal artifacts may also be found amongst family ephemera and these can also be photographed and sent to Freemasons' Hall for identification.

Additionally, publications such as *Freemasons' Hall* by Stubbs and Haunch (1983), current editions of *The Constitutions* of The United Grand Lodge, and the reprinted version of *The Medals of the Masonic fraternity, described and illustrated*, (1880) by W.T.R. Marvin, can be consulted either at the above museum or perhaps secured via the inter-library loan system through your local library. These publications have descriptions and photographs of many items of Masonic regalia.

It should be possible to identify the name of a Freemasonry ancestor, his age on joining a Craft Lodge, residence, occupation and possibly details of any transfers to other Lodges and date of death.

When stepping away from the influence of Freemasonry, it will be important to completely destroy all inherited regalia from the Craft.

Further Reading

You should also read up about tracing Freemasonry forebears, through the book, *My Ancestor was a Freemason*, by Pat Lewis.[9] This gives further details of background information, useful addresses and a select bibliography. Five books covering the topic of ministering into Freemasonry are given at the end of this chapter and also at the end of the book.

How to be Set Free of Generational Freemasonry

The prayers following give only a very brief introduction or taster, to the 'how to' part of really being set free from all the negative consequences of Freemasonry. It is recommended that you follow up these prayers by reading and praying through one or more of the books or workbooks on the subject, listed at the end of this chapter, and also attend a ministry course or website teaching on Freemasonry. These are available through such Christian organisations as CRi-Ireland, Gilgal House Healing Centre, Ellel Ministries, Sozo Ministries International or Fruitful Vine Ministries International. Contact details are given in Appendix F.

As with all sins, the process of removing the enemy's rights of access into our lives involves the following with Freemasonry:

    Confession
    Repentance
    Asking for and receiving God's forgiveness and forgiving ourselves
    Cutting soul ties
    Renouncing Curses
    Deliverance
    Blessing

All these stages presuppose a commitment to Jesus and Christianity. Indeed, it is essential that the reader be a born-again Christian, ideally baptised in water and the Holy Spirit, who has a living relationship with Jesus. Only in this way can ministry into Freemasonry begin and be worked through.

To start off, I would recommend praying for protection for yourself and your loved ones and for Jesus to lead and guide you in these prayers. Then pray the 'Lordship Prayer.' The 'Lordship Prayer' and the declarations and prayers following, are used by several Christian ministries, in various forms, whose details you can find online and which are listed in Appendix F.

Lordship Prayer

"Dear Lord Jesus, I realise my need of You and repent of living my life my own way. I wholeheartedly accept You now as my Saviour, my Redeemer, my Lord and my Deliverer.

I invite You now to be the Lord of every part and moment of my life, from the time of my conception, right up until now:

Lord of my body, my physical health and behaviour.

Lord of my mind and all my attitudes and mental health.

Lord of all my emotions and all my reactions.

Lord of my spirit and my worship of You.

Lord of my family and all my relationships.

Lord of my sexuality and its expression.

Lord of my will and all of my hopes, ambitions, decisions and plans.

Lord of all my work and service for You.

Lord of all my finances.

Lord of all my needs and possessions.

Lord of the manner and time of my death."

Declaration

"Thank you, Jesus, for shedding Your blood and dying on the cross, for the forgiveness of my sins, my ancestors' sins and my descendants' sins. You died and rose again that I might be set free to love and to serve You, in newness of life.

While I thank you, Lord, for my ancestors, especially my father and mother who brought me into this world and whom I honour, I do not stand in agreement with them on sinful matters. In these cases, in your presence, Lord, I **confess** and **repent** on behalf of all my parents,' grandparents' and forefathers' willing involvement in and submission to Freemasonry, and the oaths and curses which they unwittingly put themselves and their descendants under. I confess that Freemasonry is a sin against you, which I **renounce** off my life and off the lives of my family, including all the inherited oaths and curses. Thank you for becoming a curse for me on the cross, so that I might go free. I ask that You would **forgive** my ancestors' involvement in Freemasonry as I forgive them also. I claim Your **blood cleansing** from all the effects of generational Freemasonry on my life."

Breaking of Soul Ties

"In the name of Jesus, I break all the ungodly body, soul and spirit ties with:
my parents,
other family members, (name them)
my grandparents, (For ancestors who have died, we break the whole soul tie),
great-grandparents and,
any ancestors who I know were Freemasons and,
with any Lodge members.

I ask that you cleanse me from all defilement passing down to me, through these soul ties."

Renouncing of Curses

"*I renounce all the curses flowing from the oaths, rituals and mind and emotional control of the Freemasonry ceremonies. I renounce the curse spoken by the initiate over himself in the 1st Degree ceremony of:*

"*...having my throat cut across from ear to ear, my tongue torn out by the root and buried in the sand of the sea at low water or a cable's length from the shore where the tide regularly ebbs and flows twice in 24 hours*", finishing with the declaration, "*So mote it be.*"

Etc

As a <u>minimum</u>, it will be necessary to pray through all the curses invoked in the **first three degrees** of Freemasonry, that of 'Entered Apprentice,' 'Fellow Craft' and 'Master Mason.' Details of these curses and degrees can be found in the books listed at the end of this chapter and on courses specialising in freedom from Freemasonry. For some people, it may be necessary to pray through the vows and curses spoken by their ancestors right up to the highest degrees. However, before any of that, do pray:

"*In the name of Jesus, I close the spiritual 'Eye of Horus' over my forehead.*"

Binding and Loosing - Deliverance

"*I bind and cut myself off from the ruling spirits of the Craft Lodge(s), Provincial Lodge(s) and Grand Lodge. I bind and loose the spirit(s) of.......* [use your discernment to name them] *from me and tell it / them to go, in the mighty name of Jesus!*"

The Blessing of Jesus

"*I ask, Lord, that you turn all these curses into blessings, as I rest in Your love and presence and as I find my true identity in You. If I am carrying any emotional wounds caused by this generational Freemasonry, I ask, Lord, that You surface them and show me, so that I can give them to You and express them safely, forgive and be healed of them. I ask this in Jesus' name."*

In Summary

Give thanks for your ancestors. **Identify** any possible Freemasonry involvement found in your family line. If found, **confess** this sin and the influence it has had in your own life. (Lamentations 5:7). **Repent** on behalf of your ancestors of their involvement in Freemasonry, by identifying with and owning it as one's own sin. Ask for and receive God's **forgiveness**. **Cut** soul ties. Work through specific prayers for Freemasonry. Seek **deliverance** ministry and / or conduct self-deliverance for all evil spirits. Seek the **cleansing blood of Jesus** to wash away any stains.

Ask Jesus to **bless you** and **fill you** afresh with His Holy Spirit. Seek to be **obedient** to His guidance and call on your life.

A Cautionary Word

As mentioned before, the prayers in this chapter are intended just as openers, to help start you on the journey to freedom. With known Freemasonry in your family line, in order to work towards complete freedom, I would recommend working through the material and prayers on the CRi-Ireland website listed below and /or in Otto Bixler's, Derek Robert's and Yvonne Kitchen's books, also listed at the end of this chapter. It would also be very worthwhile attending one of the excellent training and ministry courses run by Gilgal House Healing Centre, Ellel Ministries, or Sozo Ministries International, here in the UK, or for the more adventurous, Fruitful Vine Ministries in Australia. This is not an exhaustive list and the reader may hear of other ministries both here in the UK and abroad, which can help in this area.

Further Reading - Select Bibliography

Bixler, Otto. *It isn't Free and it isn't Masonry*. UK: Zaccmedia, (2016).

Fabiano, Catherine and Frank. *Healing Your Past Releasing Your Future*. Grand Rapids, MI: Chosen Books, (2014).

Horrobin, Peter. *Healing through Deliverance*. (rev). Lancaster: Sovereign World, (2008).

Kitchen, Yvonne. *Freemasonry: Death in the Family*. (5th ed). Mountain Gate, VIC, Australia: Fruitful Vine Ministries, (2002).

Lewis, Pat. *My Ancestor was a Freemason.* (3rd ed, rev). London: Society of Genealogists Enterprises, (2012).

Prince, Derek. *Blessing or Curse: You Can Choose*. (3rd ed). Grand Rapids, MI: Chosen Books Publishing Co., (2006).

Robert, Derek. *Christian Set Yourself Free from Freemasonry*. (2nd rev ed). Freedom Ministries International, (2002).

Conclusion

In the preface I sought to explain the background as to why God gave me this book to write. My personal testimony of recovering from generational wounding has been fundamental to understanding the necessity of being willing to cooperate with God in the process of restoration. Years ago, He put the desire to follow Him in my heart, an interest in my family's history and a desperation to find healing. Having grown up the child of divorced parents, with limited contact with them for several years, and knowing very little of my ancestry, led me to want to fill the inner void, to know and to research. There was a big hole in my heart and a sense of incompleteness, that needed to be filled.

Each chapter of this book has been written describing the main genealogical themes that researchers follow, but with reference to the 10 Commandments and how the breaking of these relate to family history, with the resulting effects on descendants. The topics of sexual sin, rejection and abandonment, education and occupations, war trauma, poverty and wealth, crime, mental illness, religious background, idolatry and freemasonry have been outlined to help in understanding what sources of generational sin and iniquity can include.

The main sources of information and different record repositories have been described, whether they be in manuscript form in Britain's archives and record offices, in book form, or in digitally recorded material available on websites. I've listed the main genealogical organisations, books and websites which can help with such research.

The aim of this research is to find out the clues as to the sins and iniquities of our ancestors, with a view to confessing them and praying for release from their effects. From there, I have included descriptions of the primary Christian inner healing and deliverance ministry approaches that deal with inner brokenness, and include specific prayers at the end of each chapter to help the reader work through his or her issues. A list of some UK-based Christian healing ministries is included in Appendix F, should the reader wish to contact them for further help. There are a further two specialist ministries added at the end, which deal with freemasonry; one in Ireland, one in Australia.

As stated in chapter 1, with so much focus on the sins and iniquities of our ancestors, it is important to remember the countless ways they blessed us and how all our ancestors had many good qualities. We also need to discover what they were, and keep their good points in mind, for scripture commands us to:

> Honour your father and your mother, so that you may live long in the land the LORD your God is giving you.
> Exodus 20:12, (NIV)

We are not to worship or idolise our parents, grandparents, or more distant ancestors, as some Asian cultures do. The Lord forbids this, because we are to worship Him alone. However, in Britain the reverse seems to be the case – where our culture seems to encourage individuals to complain, criticise and remember the worst points in others and in events. This makes it even more important to remember and give thanks for the good in our parents, grandparents and beyond. Rightfully honouring them will give us a sense of well-being, of healthy identity and where they, and therefore we come from. This will help us take the long view, to know where we are going, what God put us on this earth for, and with a deeper sense of our God-given skills and purpose.

A future project might be to further simplify the material described in this book and produce a real beginners guide to generational exploration and healing.

It is my hope and prayer that you have been blessed by this book and will be motivated to conduct your own family tree research and follow up prayers, leading to long-sought after and permanent healing.

Appendices

Appendix A

The 10 Commandments in Exodus 20: 1-17, and Deuteronomy 5:6-21

Beneath are God's 10 Commandments from Exodus, chapter 20, which can also be found in Deuteronomy 5:6-21. Along with each one is where they are repeated, either exactly or in principle, in the New Testament.

No.1   Idolatry
You shall have no other gods before Me. (Exodus 20:3).
You shall worship the Lord your God, and Him alone shall you serve. (Matthew 4:10, see also 1 Corinthians 8:4-6).

No.2   Idolatry
You shall not make for yourself a carved image - any likeness of anything that is in heaven above, or that is in the earth beneath, or that is in the water under the earth; you shall not bow down to them nor   serve them . . (Exodus 20:4-5).
Little children, keep yourselves from idols. (1 John 5:21, also Acts 17:29). But the cowardly, and unbelieving . . . and idolaters . . . shall have their part in the lake that burns with fire and brimstone . . .   (Revelation 21:8).

No.3   Idolatry
You shall not take the name of the Lord your God in vain, for the Lord will not hold him guiltless who takes His name in vain. (Exodus 20:7).
Our Father Who is in heaven, hallowed be Your name . . . (Matthew 6:9, see also 1 Timothy 6:1).

No.4   Sabbath Day Rest
Remember the Sabbath day, to keep it holy . . . (Exodus 20:8-11).

The Sabbath was made for man, and not man for the Sabbath; Therefore, the Son of man is Lord even of the Sabbath. (Mark 2:27 - 28, Hebrews 4:4, 10, Acts 17:2).

No.5 Sexual Sin
Honour your father and your mother . . . (Exodus 20:12).
Honour your father and your mother. (Matthew 19:19, also Ephesians 6:1).

No.6 Crime
You shall not murder. (Exodus 20:13).
You shall not murder. (Matthew 19:18, also Romans 13:9, Revelation 21:8).

No.7 Sexual Sin
You shall not commit adultery. (Exodus 20:14).
You shall not commit adultery. (Matthew 19:18, see also Romans 13:9, Revelation 21:8).

No.8 Crime
You shall not steal. (Exodus 20:15).
You shall not steal. (Matthew 19:18, see also Romans 13:9).

No.9 Crime
You shall not bear false witness against your neighbour. (Exodus 20:16).
You shall not bear false witness. (Matthew 19:18, see also Romans 13:9, Revelation 21:8).

No.10 Crime
You shall not covet your neighbour's house . . . your neighbour's wife . . . nor anything that is your neighbour's. (Exodus 20:17).
You shall not covet. (Romans 13:9, see also Romans 7:7).

Appendix B

Baptism in the Holy Spirit

Scriptures to support baptism in the Holy Spirit:

"I baptize you with water for repentance. But after me comes one who is more powerful than I, whose sandals I am not worthy to carry. He will baptize you with the Holy Spirit and fire." (Matthew 3:11, NIV)

"I baptize you with water, but he will baptize you with the Holy Spirit." (Mark 1:8, NIV)

"And I myself did not know him, but the one who sent me to baptize with water told me, "The man on whom you see the Spirit come down and remain is the one who will baptize with the Holy Spirit." (John 1:33, NIV)

Jesus answered, "Very truly I tell you, no one can enter the kingdom of God unless they are born of water and the Spirit." (John 3:5, NIV)

As soon as Jesus was baptized, he went up out of the water. At that moment heaven was opened, and he saw the Spirit of God descending like a dove and alighting on him. (Matthew 3:16, NIV)

When all the people were being baptized, Jesus was baptized too. And as he was praying, heaven was opened and the Holy Spirit descended on him in bodily form like a dove. And a voice came from heaven: "You are my Son, whom I love; with you I am well pleased." (Luke 3:21-22, NIV)

By this he meant the Spirit, whom those who believed in him were later to receive. Up to that time the Spirit had not been given, since Jesus had not yet been glorified. (John 7:39, NIV)

"Therefore, go and make disciples of all nations, baptizing them in the name of the Father and of the Son and of the Holy Spirit, and teaching them to obey everything I have commanded you. And surely, I am with you always, to the very end of the age." (Matthew 28:19-20, NIV)

"I am going to send you what my Father has promised; but stay in the city until you have been clothed with power from on high." (Luke 24:49, NIV)

Again, Jesus said, "Peace be with you! As the Father has sent me, I am sending you." And with that he breathed on them and said, "Receive the Holy Spirit." (John 20:21-22, NIV)

He said to them, "Go into all the world and preach the gospel to all creation. Whoever believes and is baptized will be saved, but whoever does not believe will be condemned. And these signs will accompany those who believe: In my name they will drive out demons; they will speak in new tongues; they will pick up snakes with their hands; and when they drink deadly poison, it will not hurt them at all; they will place their hands on sick people, and they will get well."
After the Lord Jesus had spoken to them, he was taken up into heaven and he sat at the right hand of God. Then the disciples went out and preached everywhere, and the Lord worked with them and confirmed his word by the signs that accompanied it. (Mark 16:15-20, NIV)

On one occasion, while he was eating with them, he gave them this command: "Do not leave Jerusalem, but wait for the gift my Father promised, which you have heard me speak about. For John baptized with water, but in a few days, you will be baptized with the Holy Spirit." (Acts 1:4-5, NIV)

"But you will receive power when the Holy Spirit comes on you; and you will be my witnesses in Jerusalem, and in all Judea and Samaria, and to the ends of the earth." (Acts 1:8, NIV)

When the day of Pentecost came, they were all together in one place. Suddenly a sound like the blowing of a violent wind came from heaven and filled the whole house where they were sitting. They saw what seemed to be tongues of fire that separated and came to rest on each of them. All of them were filled with the Holy Spirit and began to speak in other tongues as the Spirit enabled them.
Now there were staying in Jerusalem God-fearing Jews from every nation under heaven. When they heard this sound, a crowd came together in bewilderment, because each one heard their own language being spoken. (Acts 2:1-4, NIV)

There are different kinds of gifts, but the same Spirit distributes them. There are different kinds of service, but the same Lord. There are different kinds of working, but in all of them and in everyone it is the same

APPENDICES

God at work. Now to each one the manifestation of the Spirit is given for the common good. To one there is given through the Spirit a message of wisdom, to another a message of knowledge by means of the same Spirit, to another faith by the same Spirit, to another gifts of healing by that one Spirit, to another miraculous powers, to another prophecy, to another distinguishing between spirits, to another speaking in different kinds of tongues, and to still another the interpretation of tongues. All these are the work of one and the same Spirit, and he distributes them to each one, just as he determines. (1 Corinthians 12:4-11, NIV)

Peter replied, "Repent and be baptized, every one of you, in the name of Jesus Christ for the forgiveness of your sins. And you will receive the gift of the Holy Spirit.
The promise is for you and your children and for all who are far off—for all whom the Lord our God will call." (Acts 2:38-39, NIV)

'As I began to speak, the Holy Spirit came on them as he had come on us at the beginning. Then I remembered what the Lord had said: "John baptized with water, but you will be baptized with the Holy Spirit." (Acts 11:15-16, NIV)

While Apollos was at Corinth, Paul took the road through the interior and arrived at Ephesus. There he found some disciples and asked them, "Did you receive the Holy Spirit when you believed?" They answered, "No, we have not even heard that there is a Holy Spirit."
So, Paul asked, "Then what baptism did you receive?"
"John's baptism," they replied.
Paul said, "John's baptism was a baptism of repentance. He told the people to believe in the one coming after him, that is, in Jesus." On hearing this, they were baptized in the name of the Lord Jesus. When Paul placed his hands on them, the Holy Spirit came on them, and they spoke in tongues and prophesied. (Acts 19:1-6, NIV)

Appendix C

Seize Quartiers

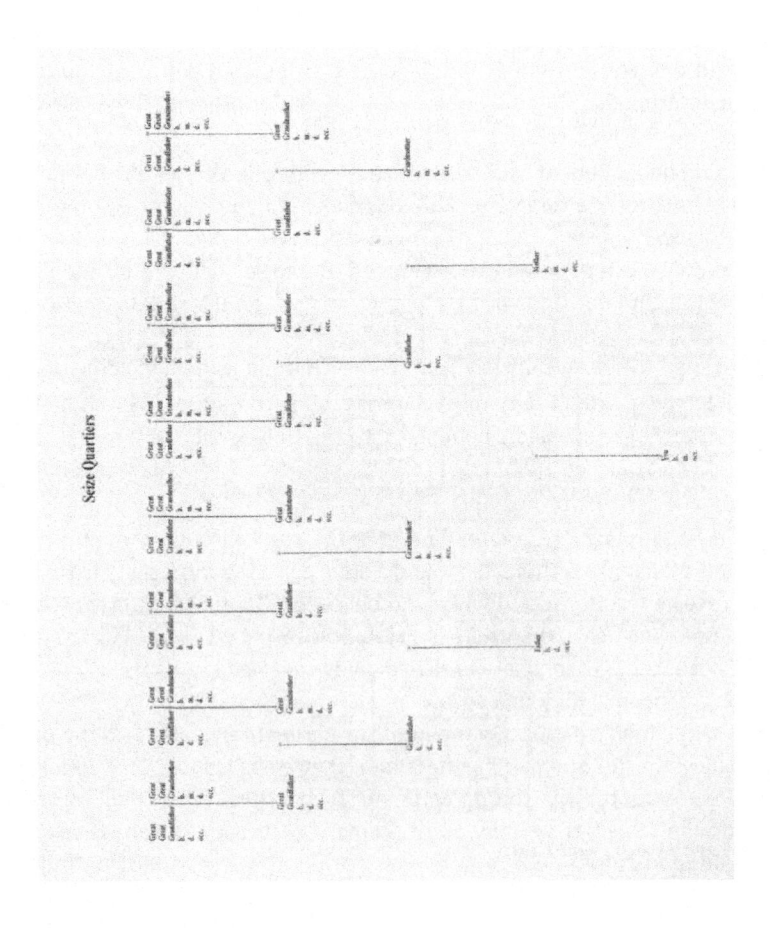

Appendix D

Renunciation of Generational Curses

(Based on prayers by Quinn Schipper in his book, *'Trading Faces,'* pp.239-240, and used with his permission)

"*I confess that Jesus is the Christ, the Son of the Living God. He has saved me by His precious blood, shed on the Cross at Calvary. By virtue of my relationship with Him, I take authority over the enemy, Satan, and his evil works against me, through my ancestry and via others.*

In the name of Jesus Christ of Nazareth and by the power of His blood, I confess, renounce and reject all the sins, word curses, ungodly soul ties, involuntary and unwanted inheritances and demonic influences that have affected me from my ancestors and any other person whatsoever, from working in or through me. In the name of Jesus, I ask that all the generational sins and iniquities of my forebears, from both my father's and mother's bloodlines be forgiven and revoked. I choose to forgive everyone, whether living or dead, of their sins and of those sins which have affected me. I ask that all ancestral sins and iniquities and their effects be stopped and wiped away. I take authority over all generational influences and effects of the demonic and tell them to go in the mighty name of Jesus and by His blood. I declare that they will not be visited upon my children, my children's children or subsequent generations.

In Him I have complete forgiveness and full redemption for all my sins. I surrender myself completely to Jesus' love and mercy and dedicate my life to Him as my Lord and Master. I ask, Jesus, that you be Lord over every part of my life, so that I may praise and serve you for evermore. I pray these things in the name of Jesus and thank you Lord for what you have done, what you are doing and what you will do in my life. Amen."

(Some of the scriptures Quinn Schipper refers his readers to are Psalm 103, Galatians 2:20, Ephesians 1:7, 2:4-7 and Colossians 1:13).

See also: Appendix A, **Generational Curses,** in *Healing Your Past, Releasing Your Future*, by Catherine and Frank Fabiano. pp.209-213.

Appendix E

Abbreviations

AGRA   Association of Genealogists and Record Agents

BL   British Library

BRO   Borough Record Office

BRS   British Record Society

CAP   Christians Against Poverty

CCC   Central Criminal Court

CRO   County Record Office

CRS   Catholic Record Society

CWGC   Commonwealth War Graves Commission

DRO   Diocesan Record Office

GOONS   Guild of One-Name Studies

GRO   General Registration Office

IHGS   Institute of Heraldic and Genealogical Studies

LMA   London Metropolitan Archives

MDR   Manorial Documents Register

NAM   National Army Museum

NLS   National Library of Scotland

NRS   National Records of Scotland

NMRN   National Museum of the Royal Navy

RCP   Royal College of Physicians

RCS Royal College of Surgeons

RQG Register of Qualified Genealogists

SoG Society of Genealogists

TNA The National Archives

UCL University College London

Appendix F

Further help

Christian organisations

Bethel Sozo UK (Various UK venues)
Registered address: Miller's Barn, Church Farm Mews, Stalham, Norfolk, NR12 9RU
Web: www.bethelsozo.org.uk/

Christian Prayer Ministries / CPM (Various UK regional locations)
113 Tinkers Green Road, Wilnecote, Tamworth, Staffordshire, B77 5LJ
Email: web_admin@christianprayerministries.uk

Gilgal House Healing Centre
16 Pigott Drive, Shenley Church End, Milton Keynes, MK5 6BY
Tel: 01908 749526
Email: info@gilgalhouse.com
Web: www.gilgalhouse.com
The courses and events are held at:
Stony Stratford Community Church,
Horsefair Green, Stony Stratford, Milton Keynes, MK11 1JW

Ellel Ministries (Several UK and various international centres)
Headquarters:
Ellel Grange, Bay Horse, Lancaster, LA2 0HN
Tel: 01524 751651
Email: info@ellel.org
Web: www.ellel.org/uk/

Premier Lifeline (a national Christian confidential helpline, part of Premier Christian Radio)
Registered Office: Unit 6 April Court, Sybron Way, Crowborough, TN6 3DZ
Tel: 0300 111 0101
Web: www.premierlifeline.org.uk

Sozo Ministries International
Dunwood Oaks, Danes Road, Awbridge, Romsey, Hampshire, SO51 0GF
Tel: 01794 344920
Email: info@sozo.org
Web: www.sozo.org

UCB Prayerline (Part of United Christian Broadcasters)
UCB Operations Centre: Westport Road, Burslem, Stoke-on-Trent, ST6 4JF
UK: Tel: 01782 36 3000
Ireland: Tel: 1890 940 300
Email: prayerline@ucb.co.uk
Web: www.ucb.co.uk/pray

Christian Restoration in Ireland – CRi-Ireland
Founded by Ken Symington. Website with information and prayer ministry guidelines about Freemasonry.
Web: www.christian-restoration.com/

APPENDICES

Fruitful Vine Ministries International
Specializes in ministering into freemasonry
500 Kelletts Road, Lysterfield, VIC 3156, AUSTRALIA.
Tel: +61 3 9752 7767
Web: www.fruitfulvine.org

Genealogical Organisations

Association of Genealogists and Record Agents (AGRA)
PO Box, Unit 2, 40 Wharf Road, London, N1 7GS
Email: info@agra.org.uk
Web: www.agra.org.uk

Institute of Heraldic and Genealogical Studies (IHGS)
(Short courses, Correspondence Course, Higher Certificate & Diploma)   79-82 Northgate, Canterbury, Kent, CT1 1BA
Tel: +44 (0)1227 768664
Email: enquiries@ihgs.ac.uk
Web: www.ihgs.ac.uk

Register of Qualified Genealogists (RQG)
Email: admin@qualifiedgenealogists.org
Web: www.qualifiedgenealogists.org

Society of Genealogists (SoG)
Unit 2, 40 Wharf Road, London, N1 7GS
Tel: +44 (0)20 7251 8799
General email: hello@sog.org.uk
Members Email: genealogy@sog.org.uk
Non-members Email: eventsoffice@sog.org.uk
Email Librarian: librarian@sog.org.uk
Web: www.sog.org.uk

University of Dundee
(Various short and postgraduate courses)
Centre for Archive and Information Studies, University of Dundee, Nethergate, Dundee, DD1 4HN, Scotland, UK
Tel: +44 (0)1382 386472
Email: SHSL-cais@dundee.ac.uk
Web: www.dundee.ac.uk/cais/

University of Limerick
(MA in Family History)
Department of History, University of Limerick, Limerick, V94 T9PX, Ireland
Tel: +353 061 213166
Email: Ciara.breathnach@ul.ie
Web: www.ul.ie/gps/course/history-family-ma

University of Strathclyde
(Postgraduate Certificate, Diploma, or MSc in Genealogical Studies, PhD)
Strathclyde Institute for Genealogical Studies,
Centre for Lifelong Learning,
Graham Hills Building,
50 George Street,
Glasgow, G1 1QE
Tel: +44 (0)141 548 2116
Email: cll-sigs@strath.ac.uk
Web: www.strath.ac.uk/genealogy/

Select Bibliography, Organisations & Websites

Christian Healing Books:

Baker, Stephen. *Healing Present Hurts Rooted in the Past*. France, Saint-Benoit-du-Sault: Editions Benedictines, (2007). (On behalf of the Generational Healing Trust).

Bixler, Otto. *It isn't Free and it isn't Masonry*. Lancaster: Zaccmedia, (2016).

Dalbey, Gordon. *Broken by Religion, Healed by God: Restoring the Evangelical, Sacramental, Pentecostal, Social Justice Church*. Folsom, CA: Civitas Press, (2011).

Dalbey, Gordon. *Healing the Masculine Soul*. Nashville: W Publishing Group, (2003).

Dalbey, Gordon. *Sons of the Father*. Eastbourne: Kingsway Communications Ltd, (2002).

Fabiano, Catherine & Frank. *Healing Your Past, Releasing Your Future*. Bloomington, MN, USA: Chosen Books, (2012).

Hawkey, Ruth. *Freedom from Generational Sin*. Chichester: New Wine Press, (1999).

Hawkey, Ruth. *Generational and Family Blessings*. Chichester: New Wine Press, (2008).

Hickey, Marilyn. *Break the Generation Curse*. Denver: Marilyn Hickey Ministries, (1988).

Hintze, Rebecca Linder. *Healing Your Family History*. London: Hay House UK, (2006).

Horrobin, Peter. *Healing from the Consequences of Accident, Shock & Trauma*. Lancaster: Sovereign World, (2016).

Horrobin, Peter. *Healing through Deliverance*. (rev). Lancaster: Sovereign World, (2008).

Kitchen, Yvonne. *Freemasonry: Death in the Family*. (5th ed). Mountain Gate, VIC, Australia: Fruitful Vine Ministries, (2002).

McAll, Kenneth. *Healing the Family Tree*. London: Sheldon Press, (1982).

Milligan, E.H. & Thomas, M.J. *My Ancestors were Quakers*. London: Society of Genealogists, (2005).

Parker, Russ. *Healing Wounded History*. London: Darton, Longman & Todd, (2001).

Prince, Derek. *Blessing or Curse: You Can Choose*. (3rd ed). Grand Rapids, MI: Chosen Books Publishing Co., (2006).

Robert, Derek. *Christian Set Yourself Free from Freemasonry*. (2nd rev ed). Freedom Ministries International, (2002).

Sandford, John Loren & Paula. *God's Power to Change*. Lake Mary, FL: Charisma House, (2007).

Sandford, John Loren & Paula. *Growing Pains*. Lake Mary, FL: Charisma House, (2008).

Sandford, John Loren & Paula. *Letting Go of the Past*. Lake Mary, FL: Charisma House, (2008).

Schipper, Quinn. *Trading Faces. Dissociation: A Common Solution to Avoiding Life's Pain*. (2nd ed). OK, Stillwater: New Forums Press, (2005).

Schipper, Quinn. *Trading Faces. Dissociation: A Common Solution to Avoiding Life's Pain*. (3rd ed). Stillwater, OK: Quinn Schipper, (2020).

Schlink, Basilea. *Praying Our Way Through Life*. Basingstoke: Lakeland, (1970, 1980, 1984).

SELECT BIBLIOGRAPHY, ORGANISATIONS & WEBSITES

Smith, Patricia A. *From Generation to Generation: A Manual for Healing.* Jacksonville, FL: Jehovah Rapha Press, (1996).

Tauke, Beverly T. *Healing Your Family Tree.* Carol Stream, IL: SaltRiver, (2004).

Wells, David. *Praying for the Family Tree.* France, Saint-Benoit-du-Sault: Editions Benedictines, (2006). (On behalf of the Generational Healing Trust).

Wright, Andrew. *Kingdom Think.* Warboys: Impression Publishing, (2012).

Wright, Henry W. *A More Excellent Way.* (Commemorative ed). New Kensington, PA: Whitaker House, (2009).

Christian Healing Ministries:

Bethel Sozo UK
Various locations throughout UK.
Kingdom Ministries, PO Box 1393, Bradford, Yorkshire, BD5 5FT
Email: enquiries@kingdom-ministries.org.uk
Web: https://www.bethelsozo.org.uk/

Christian Prayer Ministries / CPM (Various UK regional locations)
113 Tinkers Green Road, Wilnecote, Tamworth, Staffordshire, B77 5LJ
Email: web_admin@christianprayerministries.uk

Christian Restoration in Ireland – Cri-Ireland
Founded by Ken Symington. Website with information and prayer ministry guidelines about Freemasonry.
Web: https://www.christian-restoration.com/

HEALING ANCESTRAL WOUNDS

Ellel Ministries (Several UK and various international centres)
Headquarters:
Ellel Grange, Bay Horse, Lancaster, LA2 0HN
Tel: 01524 751651
Email: info@ellel.org
Web: https://ellel.org/uk/

Gilgal House Healing Centre

16 Pigott Drive, Shenley Church End, Milton Keynes, MK5 6BY

Tel: 01908 749526

Email: info@gilgalhouse.com

Web: http://www.gilgalhouse.com

The courses and events are held at:

Stony Stratford Community Church,

Horsefair Green, Stony Stratford, Milton Keynes, MK11 1JW

Harnhill Centre of Christian Healing

Harnhill, Cirencester, Gloucestershire, GL7 5PX

Tel: 01285 850283

Web: https://www.harnhillcentre.org.uk/

Sozo Ministries International
Dunwood Oaks, Danes Road, Awbridge, Romsey, Hampshire, SO51 0GF
Tel: 01794 344920
Email: info@sozo.org
Web: www.sozo.org

Fruitful Vine Ministries International
500 Kelletts Road, Lysterfield, VIC 3156, AUSTRALIA
Tel: +61 3 9752 7767
Web: https://fruitfulvine.org

SELECT BIBLIOGRAPHY, ORGANISATIONS & WEBSITES

Genealogical Books:

Adolph, Anthony. *Tracing Your Aristocratic Ancestors: a guide for family historians.* Barnsley: Pen & Sword Family History, (2013).

Aldous, Vivienne. *My Ancestors were Freemen of the City of London.* London: Society of Genealogists, (1999).

Bali, Karen. *Researching Adoption: an essential guide to tracing birth relatives and ancestors.* Bury: The Family History Partnership, (2015).

Barratt, Nick. *Tracing the History of Your House.* (2nd ed). Kew: The National Archives, (2006).

Blanchard, Gill. *Tracing Your House History: A guide for family historians.* Barnsley: Pen & Sword, (2013).

Breed, Geoffrey. *My Ancestors were Baptists: how can I find out more about them?* (4th rev. ed). London: Society of Genealogists, (2007).

Brooks, Brian C.G. & Herber, Mark D. *My Ancestor was a Lawyer.* London: Society of Genealogists Ltd, (2006).

Burlison, Robert. *Tracing Your Pauper Ancestors.* Barnsley: Pen & Sword, (2009).

Chater, Kathy. *My Ancestor was a Lunatic.* London: Society of Genealogists Enterprises, (2014).

Chater, Kathy. *Tracing Your Huguenot Ancestors: A Guide for Family Historians.* Barnsley: Pen & Sword, (2012).

Clifford, D.J.H. *My Ancestors were Congregationalists in England and Wales.* London: Society of Genealogists, (1997).

Crail, Mark. *Tracing Your Labour Movement Ancestors.* Barnsley: Pen & Sword Books, (2009).

Drummond, Di. *Tracing Your Railway Ancestors.* Barnsley: Pen & Sword Books Ltd, (2010).

Fowler, Simon. *Tracing Your Army Ancestors.* (2nd ed). Barnsley, Pen & Sword, (2013).

Gandy, Michael. *Catholic Family History: A Bibliography of General Sources*, (1996).

Gandy, Michael. *Catholic Family History: A Bibliography of Local Sources*, (1996).

Gandy, Michael. *Catholic Missions and Registers, 1700 – 1881:* 6 Volumes.

Gandy, Michael. *Catholic Parishes in England, Wales and Scotland: An Atlas,* (1993).

Gibson, Jeremy. *Quarter Sessions for Family Historians.* (5th ed). Bury: Family History Partnership, (2008).

Gibson, Jeremy & Raymond, Stuart. *Probate Jurisdictions: where to look for wills.* 6th ed. Bury: The Family History Partnership, (2016).

Gibson, Jeremy & Paskett, Pamela. *Record Offices: How to find them.* FFHS, (2002).

Herber, Mark. *Ancestral Trails.* (2nd ed). Stroud: Sutton Publishing, (2005).

Humphery-Smith, Cecil R. *The Phillimore Atlas & Index of Parish Registers.* 3rd ed. Chichester: Phillimore & Co., (2003).

Joseph, Anthony. *My Ancestors were Jewish.* London: Society of Genealogists, (2008).

Lewis, Pat. *My Ancestor was a Freemason.* (3rd ed, rev). London: Society of Genealogists Enterprises, (2012).

Milligan, E.H. & Thomas, M.J. *My Ancestors were Quakers*. London: Society of Genealogists, (2005).

Paley, Ruth. *My Ancestor was a Bastard*. (rev). London: Society of Genealogists Enterprises, (2011).

Pappalardo, Bruno. *Tracing Your Naval Ancestors*. Kew: Public Record Office, (2003).

Probert, Rebecca. *Divorced, Bigamist, Bereaved?* Kenilworth: Takeaway (Publishing), (2015).

Ratcliffe, Richard. *The Wesleyan Methodist historic roll*. Basic facts about...series. Federation of Family History Societies, (2007).

Raymond, Stuart. *Birth and Baptism Records for Family Historians*. Family History Partnership, (2010).

Raymond, Stuart. *Death and Burial Records for Family Historians*. Family History Partnership, (2011).

Raymond, Stuart. *Marriage Records for Family Historians*. Family History Partnership, (2010).

Raymond, Stuart. *My Ancestor was an Apprentice*. London: Society of Genealogists Enterprises Limited, (2010).

Raymond, Stuart A. *My Ancestor was a Gentleman*. London: Society of Genealogists Enterprises Ltd, (2012).

Raymond, Stuart. *Parish Registers: a History and Guide*. Family History Partnership, (2009).

Raymond, Stuart. *Tracing your Nonconformist Ancestors: a guide for family historians*. Barnsley: Pen & Sword Family History, (2017).

Reaney, P.H. & Wilson, R.M. (eds), *Oxford Dictionary of English Surnames*. Oxford: OUP, (2005).

Ruston, Alan. *My Ancestors were English Presbyterians / Unitarians – How can I find out more about them?* London: Society of Genealogists, (1993).

Shearman, Anthony. *My Ancestor was a Policeman.* London: Society of Genealogists Enterprises Ltd, (2000).

Spencer, William. *Air Force Records.* (2nd ed). Kew: The National Archives, (2008).

Tate, W.E. *The Parish Chest.* Chichester: Phillimore & Co., (1983).

Towey, Peter. *My Ancestor was an Anglican Clergyman.* London: Society of Genealogists Enerprises Ltd, (2015).

Wade, Stephen. *Tracing Your Criminal Ancestors.* Barnsley: Pen & Sword Family History, (2009).

Waller, Ian. *My Ancestor was an Agricultural Labourer.* 2nd ed. London, Society of Genealogists Enterprises Ltd, (2019).

Wenzerul, Rosemary. *Tracing Your Jewish Ancestors.* Barnsley: Pen & Sword Family History, (2014).

Wiggins, R. *My Ancestor was in the Salvation Army.* (3rd ed). London: Society of Genealogists, (2007).

Genealogical Websites:

www.ancestry.co.uk : Very good online subscription service for researching family records.

www.findmypast.co.uk : Very good online subscription service for researching family tree.

www.familysearch.org : The International genealogical Index (IGI) is very helpful for finding baptisms and marriages, census returns, other parish registers and school registers.

www.freebmd.org.uk : Free searching of transcribed records of birth, marriage and death, 1837-1983.

www.genuki.org.uk : Good for parish registers.

www.gro.gov.uk : For ordering birth, marriage and death certificates, 1837-2017.

https://one-name.org/ : Guild of One-Name Studies.

www.scotlandspeople.gov.uk : For ordering Scottish birth, marriage and death certificates.

http://www.nationalarchives.gov.uk/ : The National Archives, Kew, Surrey.

Genealogical Organisations:

Institute of Heraldic and Genealogical Studies (IHGS)
79-82 Northgate, Canterbury, Kent, CT1 1BA
Tel: (01227) 768664
Web: www.ihgs.ac.uk

Society of Genealogists
Unit 2, 40 Wharf Road, London, N1 7GS
Tel: (020) 7251 8799
Web: www.sog.org.uk

County Record Offices

Local Libraries

Other Books:

Friedman, Dennis. *Inheritance: A Psychological History of the Royal Family*. London: Sidgwick & Jackson, (1993).

Wolynn, Mark. *It Didn't Start With You: How Inherited Family Trauma Shapes Who We Are and How to End the Cycle*. New York: Penguin Books, (2017).

Endnotes

Preface

1. Friedman, Dennis. *Inheritance: A Psychological History of the Royal Family*. London: Sidgwick & Jackson, (1993).
2. Ibid, p.194.

Chapter 1: Definitions

1. Hawkey, Ruth. *Freedom from Generational Sin*. Chichester: New Wine Press, (1999).
2. Fabiano, Catherine & Frank. *Healing Your Past, Releasing Your Future*. Bloomington, MN: Chosen Books, (2012), p.209.
3. Smith, Patricia A. *From Generation to Generation: A Manual for Healing*. Jacksonville, FL: Jehovah Rapha Press, (1996), p.57.
4. Ibid., p.95.
5. Wells, David. *Praying for the Family Tree*. Saint-Benoit-du-Sault: Editions Benedictines, (2006) (On behalf of the Generational Healing Trust), p.5.
6. Wolynn, Mark. *It Didn't Start With You: How Inherited Family Trauma Shapes Who We Are and How to End the Cycle*. New York: Penguin Books, (2017), p.1.
7. Ibid, p.11.
8. Wright, Henry W. *A More Excellent Way*. (Commemorative ed). New Kensington, PA: Whitaker House, (2009). p.307.
9. Morrissette, Robert John. *Generational Restoration*. Coeur d'Alene, ID: Big Blue Skies of Idaho LLC, (2016), pp.20-26.
10. Ibid, p.26.
11. Ibid, p.29.
12. Ibid. p.74.
13. Ibid, p.66.

ENDNOTES

14. Wright, Henry W. *A More Excellent Way.* (Commemorative ed). New Kensington, PA: Whitaker House, (2009). p.317.
15. Morrissette, Robert John. *Generational Restoration.* Coeur d'Alene, ID: Big Blue Skies of Idaho LLC, (2016), p.32.
16. Hickey, Marilyn. *Break the Generation Curse.* Denver, CO: Marilyn Hickey Ministries, (1988), p.41.
17. Ibid, p.77.
18. Bixler, Otto. *It isn't Free and it isn't Masonry.* Preston: Zaccmedia, (2016), p.64.
19. *The ESV Archaeology Study Bible.* Wheaton, IL: Crossway, (2017), p.1789.
20. Wells, David. *Praying for the Family Tree.* Saint-Benoit-du-Sault: Editions Benedictines, (2006) (On behalf of the Generational Healing Trust). p.10.
21. Morrissette, Robert John. *Generational Restoration.* Coeur d'Alene, ID: Big Blue Skies of Idaho LLC, (2016), p.17.
22. Wells, David. *Praying for the Family Tree.* Saint-Benoit-du-Sault: Editions Benedictines, (2006) (On behalf of the Generational Healing Trust). pp.6-7.
23. Morrissette, Robert John. *Generational Restoration.* Coeur d'Alene, ID: Big Blue Skies of Idaho LLC, (2016), pp.81-82.
24. Wells, David. *Praying for the Family Tree.* Saint-Benoit-du-Sault: Editions Benedictines, (2006) (On behalf of the Generational Healing Trust). p.18.
25. Morrissette, Robert John. *Generational Restoration.* Coeur d'Alene, ID: Big Blue Skies of Idaho LLC, (2016), p.83.
26. Dalbey, Gordon. *Do Pirates Wear Pajamas?* San Jose, CA: Civitas Press, LLC, (2013).
27. Barratt, Nick. *Tracing the History of Your House.* (2nd ed). Kew: The National Archives, (2006).
28. Blanchard, Gill. *Tracing Your House History: A guide for family historians.* Barnsley: Pen & Sword, (2013).
29. Symington, Ken. See: *Christian Restoration in Ireland.* At: www.christian-restoration.com/. Accessed on 2 April, 2023.

Chapter 2: Sexual Sin

1. Schlink, Basilea. *Praying Our Way Through Life.* Basingstoke: Lakeland, (1970, 1980, 1984), p.13.
2. See: www.openbible.info/topics/sexual_sin. Accessed on 28 July, 2021.
3. See: *Centers for Disease Control and Prevention.* At: www.cdc.gov/std/general/default.htm. Accessed on 26 July, 2021.
4. See: www.gov.uk/government/statistics/abortion-statistics-for-england-and-wales-2021/abortion-statistics-england-and-wales-2021. Accessed on 4 April 2023.
5. See: www.statista.com/statistics/294571/live-births-in-england-wales-uk-by-age-and-marital-status-of-mother/. Accessed on 4 April; 2023.
6. Schipper, Quinn. *Trading Faces. Dissociation: A Common Solution to Avoiding Life's Pain.* (2nd ed). Stillwater, OK: New Forums Press, (2005), p.109.
7. Prince, Derek. *Blessing or Curse: You Can Choose.* (3rd ed). Grand Rapids, MI: Chosen Books Publishing Co., (2006).
8. Bali, Karen. *Researching Adoption: An essential guide to tracing birth relatives and ancestors.* Bury: The Family History Partnership, (2015).
9. McAll, Kenneth. *Healing the Family Tree.* London: Sheldon Press, (1982), pp.22-23.
10. Ibid. p.49.
11. Ibid. pp.50-55.
12. Wells, David. *Praying for the Family Tree.* Saint-Benoit-du-Sault: Editions Benedictines, (2006) (On behalf of the Generational Healing Trust), p.6.
13. Sandford, John Loren & Paula. *Growing Pains.* Lake Mary, FL: Charisma House, (2008).

ENDNOTES

Chapter 3: Rejection & Abandonment

1. Parker, Russ. *Healing Wounded History*. London: Darton, Longman & Todd Ltd, (2001). pp.125.
2. Ibid. pp.122-123.
3. Bali, Karen. *Researching Adoption: an essential guide to tracing birth relatives and ancestors.* Bury: The Family History Partnership, (2015).
4. See:www.todayswillsandprobate.co.uk/main-news/less-half-uk-adults-will/#:~:text=The%20key%20points%20are%20summarised,Will%20than%20their%20older%20counterparts. Accessed mid, 2022.
5. Herber, Mark. *Ancestral Trails*. (2nd ed.) (Rev). Stroud: Sutton Publishing, (2005). p.221.
6. Gibson, Jeremy & Raymond, Stuart. *Probate Jurisdictions: where to look for wills.* 6th ed. Bury: The Family History Partnership, (2016).
7. Parker, Russ. *Healing Wounded History*. London: Darton, Longman & Todd Ltd, (2001). pp.123-124.

Chapter 4: Education

1. See: *This Be the Verse.* At: *www.poetryfoundation.org/poems/48419/this-be-the-verse*. Accessed on 2 January, 2023.
2. See: *Sati or Suttee.* At: https://en.wikipedia.org/wiki/Sati_(practice). Accessed on 14 April, 2023.
3. See: *Dame Schools.* At: https://en.wikipedia.org/wiki/Dame_school. Accessed on 3 March, 2023.

4. See: *SPCK archives*. At: www.lib.cam.ac.uk/collections/departments/rare-books/collections/society-promoting-christian-knowledge-spck. Accessed on 22 March, 2023.
5. See: *National Schools*. At: https://en.wikipedia.org/wiki/National_school_(England_and_Wales)#:~:text=A%20National%20school%20was%20a,the%20children%20of%20the%20poor. Accessed on 3 March, 2023.
6. See: *Jewish school records UK*. At: www.jewishgen.org/databases/uk/schools.htm. Accessed on 3 March, 2023.
7. See: *Jewish school records UK*. At: www.familysearch.org/en/wiki/England_Jewish_Records Accessed on 3 March, 2023.
8. See: *Jewish school records UK*. At: www.manchester.gov.uk/info/324/family_history_searches/7375/jewish_records/4. Accessed on 3 March, 2023.
9. See: *National Museum of the Royal Navy*. At: www.nmrn.org.uk/collections. Accessed on 3 March, 2023.
10. Raymond, Stuart. *My Ancestor was a Gentleman*. London: Society of Genealogists Enterprises Limited, (2012). pp.112-114.

Chapter 5: Occupations

1. See: *Guild*. At: https://en.wikipedia.org/wiki/Guild. Accessed on 8 March, 2023.

ENDNOTES

2. See: *List of Guilds in the United Kingdom.* At: https://en.wikipedia.org/wiki/List_of_guilds_in_the_United_Kingdom. Accessed on 8 March, 2023.
3. See: *City of London livery companies.* At: www.cityoflondon.gov.uk/about-us/law-historic-governance/livery-companies. Accessed on 8 March, 2023.
4. See: *London, England, Freedom of the City Admission Papers, 1681-1930.* At: https://search.ancestry.co.uk/search/dbextra.aspx?dbid=2052. Accessed on 10 April, 2023.
5. Waller, Ian. *My Ancestor was an Agricultural Labourer.* 2nd ed. London, Society of Genealogists Enterprises Ltd, (2019).
6. See: *First railway in Britain.* At: https://en.wikipedia.org/wiki/History_of_rail_transport_in_Great_Britain. Accessed on 9 March, 2023.
7. Drummond, Di. *Tracing Your Railway Ancestors.* Barnsley: Pen & Sword Books Ltd, (2010).
8. Shearman, Anthony. *My Ancestor was a Policeman.* London: Society of Genealogists Enterprises Ltd, (2000).
9. Raymond, Stuart A. *My Ancestor was a Gentleman.* London: Society of Genealogists Enterprises Ltd, (2012), pp.117-122.
10. See: *List of British royal residences.* At: https://en.wikipedia.org/wiki/List_of_British_royal_residences. Accessed on 13 March, 2023.
11. See: *Sir John Sainty.* At: https://en.wikipedia.org/wiki/John_Sainty_(parliamentary_official). Accessed on 15 March, 2023.
12. Raymond, Stuart A. *My Ancestor was a Gentleman.* London: Society of Genealogists Enterprises Ltd, (2012), p.122.
13. Ibid.
14. See: *Inns of Court.* At: https://en.wikipedia.org/wiki/Inns_of_Court. Accessed on 15 March, 2023.

15. See: *Inner Temple calendars*. At: www.innertemple.org.uk/who-we-are/history/calendars-of-inner-temple-records-1505-1845/. Accessed on 15 March, 2023.
16. See: *Inns of Chancery*. At: https://en.wikipedia.org/wiki/Inns_of_Chancery. Accessed on 15 March, 2023.
17. See: *Notary public*. At: https://en.wikipedia.org/wiki/Notary_public. Accessed on 28 June, 2023.
18. Raymond, Stuart A. *My Ancestor was a Gentleman*. London: Society of Genealogists Enterprises Ltd, (2012), p.132-136.
19. See: *Five Mile Act*. At: https://en.wikipedia.org/wiki/Five_Mile_Act_1665. Accessed on 21 March, 2023.
20. See: *Test Acts*. At: https://en.wikipedia.org/wiki/Test_Acts. Accessed on 21 March, 2023.
21. Dalbey, Gordon. *Healing the Masculine Soul*. London: Word Publishing, (1988), pp.130-144.
22. Dalbey, Gordon. *Sons of the Father*. Eastbourne: Kingsway Publications, (2002), pp.119-141.

Chapter 6: War Trauma

1. See: *War trauma in the Bible*. At: www.ncbi.nlm.nih.gov/pmc/articles/PMC6322145/. Accessed on 11 April, 2023.
2. See: *What is war trauma?* At: www.google.com/search?q=war+trauma+definition&sxsrf=APq-WBuulqSmGoPrdnGJv1AFkHgITVveaA%3A1643741169751&ei=8X_5YfetLdaX8gKuobLIAQ&oq=war+trauma&gs_lcp=Cgdnd3Mtd2l6EAMYAjIFCAAQgAQyBQgAEIAEMgUIABCABDIFCA

ENDNOTES

AQgAQyBQgAEIAEMgUIABCABDIFCAAQgAQyBQgAEIAEMgUI
ABCABDIFCAAQgAQ6BwgAEEcQsAM6BwgAELADEEM6CggAE
OQCELADGAA6DAguEMgDELADEEMYAToECCMQJzoHCCMQ
6glQJzoNCC4QxwEQrwEQ6glQJzoECAAQQzoECC4QQzoHCAA
QsQMQQzoHCC4QsQMQQzoFCAAQkQI6CgguEMcBEK8BEE
M6CggAELEDEIMBEEM6CAgAELEDEIMBOgslABCABBCxAxCD
AToKCAAQgAQQhwIQFDoFCC4QgARKBAhBGABKBAhGGAFQ
3QRYoiRgVoAnACeASAAa0BiAHyGJIBBDAuMjaYAQCgAQGw
AQrIARHAAQHaAQYIABABGAnaAQYIARABGAg&sclient=gws-
wiz. Accessed on 1 February, 2022.

3. See: *Post-Traumatic Stress Disorder*. At: www.nhs.uk/mental-health/conditions/post-traumatic-stress-disorder-ptsd/overview/. Accessed on 1 February, 2022.
4. See: *Post-Traumatic Stress Disorder*. At: www.mind.org.uk/information-support/types-of-mental-health-problems/post-traumatic-stress-disorder-ptsd-and-complex-ptsd/about-ptsd/. Accessed on 1 February, 2022.
5. See: *Number of British orphans after WWI*. At: www.ons.gov.uk/peoplepopulationandcommunity/populationandmigration/populationestimates/articles/censusunearthedpopulationwidowsandorphansin1921/2022-04-12. Accessed on 11 April, 2023.
6. See: *The National Archives research guides*. At: www.nationalarchives.gov.uk/help-with-your-research/research-guides/?research-category=military-and-maritime. Accessed on 2 February, 2022.
7. See: *Royal Navy rating's service records, 1853-1928*. At: www.nationalarchives.gov.uk/help-with-your-research/research-guides/royal-navy-ratings-service-records-1853-1928/. Accessed on 5 February, 2022.
8. Pappalardo, Bruno. *Tracing Your Naval Ancestors*. Kew: Public Record Office, (2003).

9. See: *Merchant Navy WW2 losses.* At: www.bbc.co.uk/history/ww2peopleswar/timeline/factfiles/nonflash/a6652091.shtml#:~:text=30%2C248%20merchant%20seamen%20lost%20their,any%20of%20the%20armed%20forces. Accessed on 8 February, 2022.
10. See: *Merchant Navy WW1 losses*: At: https://www.iwm.org.uk/history/a-short-history-of-the-merchant-navy#:~:text=By%20the%20end%20of%20the,than%2029%2C000%20merchant%20seamen%20died. Accessed on 8 February, 2022.
11. Horrobin, Peter. *Healing from the Consequences of Accident, Shock & Trauma.* Lancaster: Sovereign World, (2016).
12. Ibid. pp.145-148.
13. Ibid.
14. McAll, Kenneth. *Healing the Family Tree.* London: Sheldon Press, (1982), pp.74-75.
15. Baker, Stephen. *Healing Present Hurts Rooted in the Past.* Saint-Benoit-du-Sault: Editions Benedictines, (2007) (On behalf of the Generational Healing Trust). pp.41-42.
16. Smith, Patricia A. *From Generation to Generation: A Manual for Healing.* Jacksonville, FL: Jehovah Rapha Press, (1996), p.131.
17. Wells, David. *Praying for the Family Tree.* Saint-Benoit-du-Sault: Editions Benedictines, (2006) (On behalf of the Generational Healing Trust), p.6.
18. Ibid. p.5.

Chapter 7: Poverty & Wealth

1. See: *Settlement and removal orders.* At: www.genguide.co.uk/source/settlement-certificates-

ENDNOTES

examinations-and-removal-orders-parish-poor-law/. Accessed on 11 December, 2022.
2. See: *Ragged schools*. At: https://en.wikipedia.org/wiki/Ragged_school. Accessed on 16 December, 2022.
3. Burlison, Robert. *Tracing your Pauper Ancestors: a guide for family historians.* Barnsley: Pen & Sword, (2009), pp.159-160.
4. Ibid, p.161.
5. See: *Friendly societies*. At: https://en.wikipedia.org/wiki/Friendly_society. Accessed on 16 December, 2022.
6. See: *Abbots Hospital, Guildford*. At: www.abbotshospital.org/. Accessed on 14 December, 2022.
7. See: *Burial clubs*. At: https://historyhouse.co.uk/articles/burial_clubs.html. Accessed on 15 December, 2022.
8. Burlison, Robert. *Tracing your Pauper Ancestors: a guide for family historians.* Barnsley: Pen & Sword, (2009).
9. Reaney, P.H. & Wilson, R.M. (eds), *Oxford Dictionary of English Surnames*. Oxford: OUP, (2005).
10. Adolph, Anthony. *Tracing Your Aristocratic Ancestors: a guide for family historians.* Barnsley: Pen & Sword Family History, (2013), pp.32-34.
11. Raymond, Stuart A. *My Ancestor was a Gentleman.* London: Society of Genealogists Enterprises Ltd, (2012), pp.19-25.
12. Ibid, pp.25-28.
13. Adolph, Anthony. *Tracing Your Aristocratic Ancestors: a guide for family historians.* Barnsley: Pen & Sword Family History, (2013), pp.70-74.
14. Raymond, Stuart A. *My Ancestor was a Gentleman.* London: Society of Genealogists Enterprises Ltd, (2012), pp.33-35.

15. Adolph, Anthony. *Tracing Your Aristocratic Ancestors: a guide for family historians*. Barnsley: Pen & Sword Family History, (2013), pp.76-77, 79.
16. See: *Welsh visitation records at The National Library of Wales*. At: https://archifau.llyfrgell.cymru/index.php/visitation-records-5. Accessed on 6 February, 2023.
17. See: *National Library of Ireland*. At: www.nli.ie/en/genealogy-advisory-service.aspx. Accessed on 6 February, 2023.
18. See: *Scottish Record Society*. At: www.scottishrecordsociety.org.uk/. Accessed on 6 February, 2023.
19. Adolph, Anthony. *Tracing Your Aristocratic Ancestors: a guide for family historians*. Barnsley: Pen & Sword Family History, (2013), pp.82-94.
20. Raymond, Stuart A. *My Ancestor was a Gentleman*. London: Society of Genealogists Enterprises Ltd, (2012), pp.57-76.
21. Ibid, pp.63-65.
22. Adolph, Anthony. *Tracing Your Aristocratic Ancestors: a guide for family historians*. Barnsley: Pen & Sword Family History, (2013), pp.99-100.
23. Raymond, Stuart A. *My Ancestor was a Gentleman*. London: Society of Genealogists Enterprises Ltd, (2012), pp.69-75.
24. Adolph, Anthony. *Tracing Your Aristocratic Ancestors: a guide for family historians*. Barnsley: Pen & Sword Family History, (2013).
25. Raymond, Stuart A. *My Ancestor was a Gentleman*. London: Society of Genealogists Enterprises Ltd, (2012), pp.113.
26. Ibid, pp.117-122.
27. See: *Inner Temple Archives*. At: https://archives.innertemple.org.uk/records/ADM. Accessed on 15 February, 2023.

28. Raymond, Stuart A. *My Ancestor was a Gentleman*. London: Society of Genealogists Enterprises Ltd, (2012), pp.128-132.
29. Ibid, pp.122-124.
30. Adolph, Anthony. *Tracing Your Aristocratic Ancestors: a guide for family historians*. Barnsley: Pen & Sword Family History, (2013), p.104.
31. Raymond, Stuart A. *My Ancestor was a Gentleman*. London: Society of Genealogists Enterprises Ltd, (2012), pp.132-136.
32. Ibid, pp.136-140.
33. Adolph, Anthony. *Tracing Your Aristocratic Ancestors: a guide for family historians*. Barnsley: Pen & Sword Family History, (2013), pp.116-126.
34. Hickey, Marilyn. *Break the Generation Curse*. Denver, CO: Marilyn Hickey Ministries, (1988). p.47.

Chapter 8: Crime

1. See: *Capital punishment in the United Kingdom*. At:https://en.wikipedia.org/wiki/Capital_punishment_in_the_United_Kingdom. Accessed on 29 June, 2022.
2. See: *Most common crimes in 19th century*. At:www.bbc.co.uk/history/british/victorians/crime_01.shtml. By Emsley, Clive, (2011). Accessed on 29 June, 2022.
3. See: *Capital punishment in the United Kingdom*. At:https://en.wikipedia.org/wiki/Capital_punishment_in_the_United_Kingdom. Accessed on 29 June, 2022.
4. Schipper, Quinn. *Trading Faces. Dissociation: A Common Solution to Avoiding Life's Pain*. (3rd ed). Stillwater, OK: Quinn Schipper, (2020), pp.238-240.
5. Dalbey, Gordon. *Sons of the Father*. Folsom, CA: Civitas Press, (2012), p.30.
6. Dalbey, Gordon. *Sons of the Father*. Eastbourne: Kingsway, (2002), p.9.

7. Gibson, Jeremy. *Quarter Sessions for Family Historians*. (5th ed). Bury: Family History Partnership, (2008).
8. Ibid.
9. McAll, Kenneth. *Healing the Family Tree*. London: Sheldon Press, (1982), pp.13-15.

Chapter 9: Mental Illness

1. Chater, Kathy. *My Ancestor was a Lunatic*. London: Society of Genealogists Enterprises, (2014), pp.3-4.
2. McAll, Kenneth. *Healing the Family Tree*. London: Sheldon Press, (1982), pp.5-21.
3. Chater, Kathy. *My Ancestor was a Lunatic*. London: Society of Genealogists Enterprises, (2014), p.72.
4. Gibson, Jeremy & Rogers, Colin. *Coroner's Records in England and Wales*. (3rd ed.) Bury: The Family History Partnership, (2009).
5. Chater, Kathy. *My Ancestor was a Lunatic*. London: Society of Genealogists Enterprises, (2014), pp.77-78.
6. Ibid. p.75.
7. See: *Workhouse records*. At: www.workhouses.org.uk/records/. Accessed on 9 March, 2022.
8. Chater, Kathy. *My Ancestor was a Lunatic*. London: Society of Genealogists Enterprises, (2014), pp.8-10, 11, 19, 26-27.
9. See: *Bethlem Hospital Admissions Registers*. At: https://search.findmypast.co.uk/search-world-records/london-bethlem-hospital-patient-admission-registers-and-casebooks-1683-1932. Accessed on 7 March, 2022.
10. See: *Bethlem Hospital The National Archives*. At: www.nationalarchives.gov.uk/hospitalrecords/details.asp?id=149&page=6. Accessed on 7 March, 2022.

ENDNOTES

11. See: *Index of English and Welsh asylums*. At: http://studymore.org.uk/4_13_TA.HTM. Accessed on 10 March, 2022.
12. See: *Old Manor Hospital, Salisbury*. At: https://en.wikipedia.org/wiki/Old_Manor_Hospital,_Salisbury Accessed on 12 March, 2022.
13. See: *Ashworth Hospital*. At: https://en.wikipedia.org/wiki/Ashworth_Hospital. Accessed on 3 March, 2022.
14. See: *Wills and Administrations after 1858*. At: www.nationalarchives.gov.uk/help-with-your-research/research-guides/wills-or-administrations-after-1858/. Accessed on 8 March, 2022.
15. Chater, Kathy. *My Ancestor was a Lunatic*. London: Society of Genealogists Enterprises, (2014), pp.55-56, 59-60.
16. Ibid. pp.58, 61.
17. Ibid. pp.93-100.
18. Ibid. pp.101-105.

Chapter 10: Religion

1. Horrobin, Peter. *Healing through Deliverance*. (rev). Lancaster: Sovereign World, (2008), pp.360-361.
2. Ibid., pp.264-265.
3. Dalbey, Gordon. *Broken by Religion, Healed by God: Restoring the Evangelical, Sacramental, Pentecostal, Social Justice Church*. Folsom, CA: Civitas Press, (2011).
4. Horrobin, Peter. *Healing through Deliverance*. (rev). Lancaster: Sovereign World, (2008), p.252-253.
5. Gandy, Michael. *Catholic Family History: A Bibliography of General Sources*. UK: Gandy, (1996).
6. Gandy, Michael. *Catholic Family History: A Bibliography of Local Sources*. UK: Gandy, (1996).

7. Gandy, Michael. *Catholic Missions and Registers, 1700 – 1881.* 6 Volumes. UK: Gandy, (1993).
8. Gandy, Michael. *Catholic Parishes in England, Wales and Scotland: An Atlas.* UK: Gandy, (1993).
9. Raymond, Stuart. *Tracing your Nonconformist Ancestors: a guide for family historians.* Barnsley: Pen & Sword Family History, (2017).
10. See: *English Presbyterianism.* At: https://en.wikipedia.org/wiki/English_Presbyterianism. Accessed 21 June, 2023.
11. Ruston, Alan. *My Ancestors were English Presbyterians / Unitarians – How can I find out more about them?* London: Society of Genealogists, (1993).
12. Clifford, D.J.H. *My Ancestors were Congregationalists in England and Wales.* London: Society of Genealogists, (1997).
13. Raymond, Stuart. *Tracing your Nonconformist Ancestors: a guide for family historians.* Barnsley: Pen & Sword Family History, (2017).
14. Breed, Geoffrey. *My Ancestors were Baptists: how can I find out more about them?* (4th rev. ed). London: Society of Genealogists, (2007).
15. Milligan, E.H. & Thomas, M.J. *My Ancestors were Quakers.* London: Society of Genealogists, (2005).
16. Ratcliffe, Richard. *The Wesleyan Methodist historic roll.* Basic facts about...series. Federation of Family History Societies, (2007).
17. Wiggins, R. *My Ancestor was in the Salvation Army.* (3rd ed). London: Society of Genealogists, (2007).
18. See: *Plymouth Brethren.* At: https://en.wikipedia.org/wiki/Plymouth_Brethren. Accessed 5 November, 2021.
19. See: *Open Brethren.* At: https://en.wikipedia.org/wiki/Open_Brethren. Accessed 5 November, 2021.

ENDNOTES

20. See: *Plymouth Brethren records at Kendal Archives Centre.* At: https://legacy.cumberland.gov.uk/archives/Online_catalogues/default.asp. Accessed 13 July, 2023.
21. See: *Plymouth Brethren registers at Family Search website.* At: www.familysearch.org/wiki/en/England_Nonconformists_Plymouth_Brethren_(National_Institute). Accessed 6 November, 2021.
22. See: *Brethren records at John Rylands Library.* At: www.library.manchester.ac.uk/rylands/special-collections/exploring/guide-to-special-collections/christian-brethren-collections/manuscripts/. Accessed 6 November, 2021.
23. See: *1901 & 1911 Census of Ireland.* At: www.census.nationarchives.ie . Accessed 6 November, 2021.
24. Chater, Kathy. *Tracing Your Huguenot Ancestors: A Guide for Family Historians.* Barnsley: Pen & Sword, (2012).
25. Aldous, Vivienne. *My Ancestors were Freemen of the City of London.* London: Society of Genealogists, (1999).
26. Chater, Kathy. *Tracing Your Huguenot Ancestors: A Guide for Family Historians.* Barnsley: Pen & Sword, (2012), pp.89-90.
27. Joseph, Anthony. *My Ancestors were Jewish.* London: Society of Genealogists, (2008).
28. Wenzerul, Rosemary. *Tracing Your Jewish Ancestors.* Barnsley: Pen & Sword Family History, (2014).
29. Bixler, Otto. *It isn't Free and it isn't Masonry.* Preston: Zaccmedia, (2016), pp.350-351.

Chapter 11: Idolatry

1. Horrobin, Peter. *Healing through Deliverance.* (rev). Lancaster: Sovereign World, (2008), pp.360-361.

2. Bixler, Otto. *It isn't Free and it isn't Masonry*. Preston: Zaccmedia, (2016), p.72.
3. Horrobin, Peter. *Healing through Deliverance*. (rev). Lancaster: Sovereign World, (2008), p.253.
4. Ibid., p.303.
5. Ibid., p.345.
6. Bixler, Otto. *It isn't Free and it isn't Masonry*. Preston: Zaccmedia, (2016), pp.350-351.
7. Wells, David. *Praying for the Family Tree*. Saint-Benoit-du-Sault: Editions Benedictines, (2006) (On behalf of the Generational Healing Trust), pp.37-40.

Chapter 12: Freemasonry

1. Pike, Albert. *Morals and Dogma of the Ancient and Accepted Scottish Rite of Freemasonry*. Andesite Press, (2015), p.185.
2. Ibid., p.819.
3. Prince, Derek. *Blessing or Curse, you can choose*. Grand Rapids, MI: Chosen Books, (2006), p.147.
4. Fabiano, Catherine and Frank. *Healing Your Past Releasing Your Future*. Grand Rapids, MI: Chosen Books, (2014), pp.42-43.
5. Bixler, Otto. *It isn't Free and it isn't Masonry*. Preston: Zaccmedia, (2016), p.99.
6. Horrobin, Peter. *Healing through Deliverance*. (rev). Lancaster: Sovereign World, (2008), p.252.
7. Ibid., p.268.
8. Bixler, Otto. *It isn't Free and it isn't Masonry*. Preston: Zaccmedia, (2016), pp.8-9
9. Lewis, Pat. *My Ancestor was a Freemason*. (3rd ed, rev). London: Society of Genealogists Enterprises, (2012).

About the Author

A practicing genealogist, *Christopher Eve* is also a student member of the Institute of Heraldic and Genealogical Studies, and a member of the Society of Genealogists, London. His passion for his work comes from his interest in his own family tree which he has been researching since the late 1980s. Prior to that, Chris qualified in the social sciences (BSc (Hons) Psychology and Sociology from Surrey University, via the Roehampton Institute of Higher Education, London), and Librarianship, specialising in English Local History, (MA Librarianship, Loughborough University). He worked in a number of different specialist libraries. Chris became a born-again Christian, following a profound conversion experience in June 1986, having had a Christian education and (some) Christian family roots going back much further. From then on he was led to find more of God's healing power for himself and much later, this journey continued with Ellel Ministries, (a non-denominational Christian healing ministry), with whom he also trained as a prayer minister, working for them in various capacities for seven and half years. Chris takes an active interest in amateur archaeology, history, fell walking, swimming, sailing, aviation, travel and model making. He lives in Lancaster, England, worships locally, and is involved in prayer for revival.

Christopher R.T. Eve

Lancaster, UK

Printed in Great Britain
by Amazon